Psychosocial Criminology

Psychosocial Criminology

David Gadd and Tony Jefferson

SAGE Publications
Los Angeles ▪ London ▪ New Delhi ▪ Singapore

First published 2007

SAGE Publications Ltd
1 Oliver's Yard
55 City Road
London EC1Y 1SP

SAGE Publications Inc.
2455 Teller Road
Thousand Oaks, California 91320

SAGE Publications India Pvt Ltd
B 1/I 1 Mohan Cooperative Industrial Area
Mathura Road, New Delhi 110 044
India

SAGE Publications Asia-Pacific Pte Ltd
33 Pekin Street #02-01
Far East Square
Singapore 048763

Library of Congress control number available

British Library Cataloguing in Publication data

A catalogue record for this book is available
from the British Library

ISBN 978-1-4129-0078-2
ISBN 978-1-4129-0079-9 (pbk)

Typeset by C&M Digitals (P) Ltd., Chennai, India
Printed in Great Britain by TJ International, Padstow, Cornwall
Printed on paper from sustainable resources

CONTENTS

PREFACE AND ACKNOWLEDGEMENTS

Tracing the gestation of any particular project is always somewhat artificial since behind every 'beginning' there is always another potential starting point. But, in the case of this book, one that has as strong a claim as any other was the invitation (to TJ), warmly extended by Russell Hogg and Kerry Carrington, to present a paper at the 'Whither Critical Criminology?' Conference held at the University of Western Sydney in February 2001. The resulting paper, 'For a Psychosocial Criminology' (subsequently published in K. Carrington and R. Hogg (eds) *The Future of Critical Criminology*, Willan, 2002) provided both a justification and a template for a longer, more developed project. Around the same time, DG inaugurated a new course for final year undergraduates and Masters students called 'Psychosocial Controversies in Criminology'. This course provided both a theoretical justification for a psychosocial turn in criminology and, using a variety of criminological topics, showed how a psychosocial approach could offer deeper, more incisive understandings. Since then the course has been taught by one or other of us, with slightly different emphases and topics, every semester. The enthusiasm with which our students greeted this course sustained our belief that a book of this kind was a necessary addition to the ever-expanding criminological literature. This, then, constituted another important starting point as it provided the book's central argument and structure.

This dual starting point, as conference paper and teaching course, is important to stress since it assists in understanding what kind of book this is, namely, a research-based text book. Though few academic books these days are purely research monograph or textbook, most tend to concentrate either on reporting research findings for the benefit of academic scholars or synthesising the field for the benefit of students. Our objective has been to attempt both. So, whatever the particular substantive topic, we offer both critical (albeit truncated) overviews of relevant literatures and a research-based argument why a psychoanalytically informed, psychosocial transformation of the field is imperative. Thus, this is not a book that overviews, textbook fashion, everything psychosocial in the criminological domain. Rather, this is a research-based intervention into the battleground of criminological ideas – making the case for a particular kind of psychosocial turn – that we hope will engage both academic novices and accomplished scholars in equal measure.

Much of the research upon which this book is based would not have been possible without the generous support of the Economic and Social Research Council. The ESRC funded study (RES-000-23-0171) 'Context and Motive in the Perpetration of Racially Motivated Violence and Harassment' contributed directly to the research reported in chapter 8; the data discussed in chapters 5 and 11 was generated in the course of the ESRC funded study (L210252018) 'Gender Difference, Anxiety and the Fear of Crime'; and (DG's) ESRC funded doctorate, *Deconstructing Male Violence* (supervised by TJ and defended in January 2001) provided essential materials for Chapter 10.

If starting points are difficult because there are never pure beginnings, acknowledging debts, intellectual and practical, is a potentially endless task: behind every acknowledged debt is an unpaid one (as anyone who has taken time to return to classic texts will have discovered). However (and with apologies to those inadvertently omitted), we wish to thank: Steve Farrall, for introducing us to the field of criminal careers and desistance over a number of years, as well as feedback on Chapter 5; Shadd Maruna, Amanda Matravers, Mechthild Bereswill, Ankie Neuber, Almut Koesling, Alison Brown, and Loraine Gelsthorpe who all contributed to a session at the BSC Leeds conference in 2005 devoted to rereading the Jack Roller; Eugene McLaughlin and Lynn Chancer for agreeing to devote a whole issue of *Theoretical Criminology* to publishing the Leeds papers; Lynn Chancer (again) for her thoughtful comments on TJ's article 'Subordinating hegemonic masculinity' (published in TC 6(1) 2002) that underpins some of the ideas in chapter 4; The Lifelong Learning Centre at Roskilde University Centre and the International Research Group for Psycho-Societal Analysis for providing interested, thoughtful, informed audiences and hospitable venues, over many years; those who attended the ESRC Methods in Dialogue IV Seminar held at the University of East London in December 2004 where the case material presented in chapter 8 was presented; Phil Cohen, Ben Bowling, Mark Israel and Pnina Werbner who also offered useful comments on our work on racially motivated crime; former and current Keele colleagues for their theoretical curiosity and receptiveness to many of the ideas contained herein; Abby Stein for her enthusiastic reception of TJ's presentation of the book's themes at John Jay College in October 2006; Marian Fitzgerald for her careful comments on an earlier version of chapter 11; Mike Nellis for his knowledgeable responses at several conferences where parts of the book have been presented; Paul Gray and Claire Fox, PhD students with whom DG has worked through an understanding of psychoanalytic texts over several years; Stephen Frosh, Mike Rustin, Kerry Carrington, Russell Hogg and Lynn Froggett for their general enthusiasm, support and encouragement for a psychosocial approach; Bill Dixon, whose involvement in the research on racial violence has continuously proved an invaluable check on our psychoanalytic imaginations; and Wendy Hollway, whose own work, earlier collaborations with TJ, and eagle-eyed comments on practically everything written by us, both independently and together, has been consistently inspirational and incisive. We e would also like to thank the many people we have interviewed in the course of various research projects whose raw data we have drawn upon so extensively to make our psychosocial argument. Without our research subjects' willingness to share their sometimes painful, often touching, stories, the case for a psychosocial criminology would be much less compelling than the one set out on the pages that follow. Finally, we need to acknowledge that we alone are responsible for any errors, be they of judgement, interpretation or fact.

1

WHY PSYCHOSOCIAL CRIMINOLOGY?

Our starting point is a concern, developed over many years of teaching criminology, that the individual criminal offender has long ceased to be of much interest to criminologists, especially to those of a radical persuasion. The result is that the subject (the conception of what it is to be a person) presupposed in existing theories of crime – whether psychological, sociological, psychosocial or integrated – is woefully inadequate, unrecognizable as the complex and contradictory human being operating in often difficult and cross-pressured social circumstances we know to be the reality of all our lives. In place of messily complex human subjects shot through with anxiety and self-doubt, conflictual feelings and unruly desires, we are offered depleted caricatures: individuals shorn of their social context, or who act – we are told – purely on the basis of reason or 'choice', interested only in the maximization of utility. Or, we are presented with individuals who are nothing but the products of their social circumstances who are not beset by any conflicts either in their inner or their outer worlds: pure social constructions, to use the fashionable jargon.

We think this matters for several reasons. At the level of theory, these inadequate conceptualizations of the subject are a contributory factor in criminology's persistent failure to explain, convincingly, very much about the causes of crime. (There are other obvious reasons, such as the slightly absurd attempt by some to produce a general theory about something as diverse and context-bound as crime, but this only strengthens our general point.) This failure presents us with our primary objective, namely, to begin to rectify this situation. By replacing the caricatured subjects of criminological theorizing with recognizably 'real' (internally complex, socially situated) subjects and then examining particular cases in some detail, we hope to contribute to understanding the causes of particular crimes. Additionally, we believe that a more adequately theorized psychosocial subject can help us think more productively about other concerns within criminology: debates about victimization (in Chapter 5) and about particular kinds of punishments (in Chapters 10 and 11).

The failure to say something convincing about the causes of crime matters also at the level of student interest. What often intrigues many criminology students, especially those who are also studying psychology, is the question of motive: 'why did he/she/they "do" it?', especially if the crime is particularly unusual, extreme or bizarre. Indeed, the widespread popular interest in 'true crime' stories tells us that the fascination with unusual crimes extends far beyond the academy. One response to this interest is to see it as somehow unhealthily voyeuristic (which it may be, of course) and to redirect students to the 'real' concerns of criminology, which tends to mean matters to do with control and criminalization. It is certainly part of our job as criminologists to show students that criminology embraces questions of control and criminalization as well as crime, and that crime routinely involves the mundane and the petty rather than the serious and the extraordinary. But, it must surely also be part of our job to address what might colloquially be called 'questions of criminality': why it is that particular individuals commit particular crimes, including the very serious and relatively rare sort – *especially* as it is perennially fascinating. Isn't part of our job to convert voyeurism into a proper understanding?

Part of criminology's reluctance to stray too far from the routine and the mundane has to do, we think, with an approach to theorizing dominated by the 'rule', rather than any exceptions to it. Thus, if most delinquency is commonplace and short-lived – teenage fighting, vandalism, shoplifting and drunkenness, for example – then a theory that seems to account for much of this – the rule – tends to be seen as serviceable enough for all practical purposes (the serviceability of theory being an endemic concern of a discipline rooted in an eclectic pragmatism and with strong links to practice). Thus, theories of delinquency do not seem to feel the need also to embrace the less common delinquent activities such as teenage paedophilia, serial rape and extreme violence, for example. These can be sidelined as 'exceptions' – which, in practice, tends to mean largely left to the discourses of pathology (psychopath, sociopath, antisocial personality disorder) to 'explain'. So, part of our interest in some of the more extreme crimes has to do with our feeling that theory must be able to encompass the exception as well as the rule, an approach to theorizing that relates to our commitment to the case study.

Ontologically speaking, our interest in explaining exceptional crimes stems from a view that all crime, including the most apparently bizarre, is normal in the sense that it can be understood in relation to the same psychosocial processes that affect us all – much in the way that Freud saw mental illness. We are all more or less neurotic and life, given certain psychosocial exigencies, can make psychotics of any one of us. This does not obviate the need for understanding, but it does require that we do so using understandings of psychic life and of the social world – and their interrelationship – that are applicable to all: pacifist church-goer as well as multiple murderer. This should humanize the criminal, however awful his or her deeds, and rescue him or her from the uncomprehending condescension of pathologizing discourses and the exclusionary practices these tend to promote. Which brings us to a further, political, reason why criminology's failure to produce recognizable subjects plausibly committing particular crimes matters: those we do not understand we can more readily demonize, thus enabling 'folk devils and moral panics' to continue to figure prominently in the contemporary politics of law and order. The current demonization of the 'asylum seeker' and 'terrorist' may make some feel better, but, in moving away from a better understanding of those whom they scapegoat, demonizing discourses make the world a more fearful place than it is already. Since such scapegoating tends to be directed at the least powerful groups in society these demonizing discourses also make the world a less just place than it is already, demonstrating that tackling questions of criminality and motivation is not unrelated to questions of control and criminalization.

Finally, our failure as criminologists to take seriously questions of individual subjects, as offenders or victims, will allow psychology – the long-time, disciplinary 'poor relation' in the criminological project – to reclaim some territory. The renewed interest shown by psychologists in criminology, evidenced by the emergence of textbooks (McGuire, 2004) and articles (Hollin, 2002) dedicated to psychological criminology, and the growth of university courses in forensic psychology, suggests this is already happening. Although it would no longer be fair to characterize all of this work as having a traditional 'over-emphasis on the individual' (McGuire, 2004: 1), it is still the case that the conception of the offender remains, in our terms, inadequate. When both criminologists and psychologists fail to explain particular crimes adequately, only the writer/journalists are left to plug the gap. Given that they are usually untrained in the social sciences, however interesting and thoughtful their work – and much good work on particular crimes, especially on murder, has stemmed from writer/journalists (e.g. Burn, 1984, 1998; Gilmore, 1994; Mailer, 1979; Masters, 1985, 1993; Morrison, 1998; Sereny, 1995, 1999; Smith, D. J., 1995; Smith, J., 1993) – this is hardly a satisfactory state of affairs (a point we return to below, in the section 'Why case studies?').

So, this is a book that demonstrates the inadequacies of the presumed subject within some of the main theoretical approaches to explaining crime within criminology; then shows, through a series of case studies, how particular, relevant approaches fail to make adequate sense of a crime, victimization or particular punishment and how the use of an appropriately theorized psychosocial subject can better illuminate matters. This procedure makes two things crucial: the nature of our psychosocial subject and our reliance on case studies. We need, therefore, to say something here briefly in justification of both.

What is a psychosocial subject?

As any cursory literature search shows, 'Quite often ... the term "psychosocial" is used to refer to relatively conventional articles dealing with social adjustment or interpersonal relations, for example' (Frosh, 2003: 1547). In the specific case of criminology, it tends to be used to describe an atheoretical combination of psychological and social measures – understood as 'variables' or 'risk' and 'protective factors' – to differentiate delinquents from non-delinquents, for example. Sir Cyril Burt's *The Young Delinquent*, published in 1925 and often regarded as 'the first major work of modern British criminology' (Garland, 2002: 37), explained delinquency as the outcome of a plethora of psychosocial factors: 'typically as many as nine or ten – operating at once upon a single individual' (ibid: 38). Nearly 60 years later, Rutter and Giller

(1983: 219), after a comprehensive review of empirical research on juvenile delinquency originally undertaken for the Home Office and the DHSS, concluded that 'a wide range of psycho-social variables are associated with delinquency'. These variables ('family characteristics', 'films and television', 'the judicial response', 'school influences', 'area', 'the physical environment' and 'social change') were each then briefly discussed in terms of what was then known (usually not much, it seemed) about the impact of each and their relative strengths as causative factors.

This is not our meaning of the term psychosocial. Rather, our understanding is in line with Stephen Frosh's: 'a brand of "psychosocial studies" that adopts a critical attitude towards psychology as a whole, yet remains rooted in an attempt to theorise the "psychological subject"' (Frosh, 2003: 1545). Most of the initiatives have emerged, Frosh notes, 'primarily from disciplines that lie in a critical relationship with mainstream academic psychology – sociology and psychoanalysis, with applications such as social work and cultural studies' (ibid: 1549). Although these initiatives differ in precisely how they understand the psychosocial, they share several features that distinguish their approaches from conventional attempts interested only in identifying a range of unproblematically conceptualized psychosocial factors. The first is the need to understand human subjects as, simultaneously, the products of their own unique psychic worlds *and* a shared social world. This is not an easy notion to conceptualize. At one point Frosh talks of the psychosocial as being 'a seamless entity … a space in which notions that are conventionally distinguished – "individual" and "society" being the main ones – are instead thought of together, as intimately connected or possibly even the same thing' (ibid: 1547). Elsewhere, Frosh spells this out more specifically when he talks of the subject being 'both a centre of agency and action (a language-user, for example) and the subject *of* (or subjected *to*) forces operating from elsewhere – whether that be the "crown", the state, gender, "race" and class, or the unconscious … it is … a site, in which there are criss-crossing lines of force, and out of which that precious feature of human existence, subjectivity, emerges' (ibid: 1549, emphasis in original). The important point is how to hang on to both the psychic and the social, but without collapsing the one into the other.

Conceptualizing this psychosocial subject non-reductively implies that the complexities of both the inner and the outer world are taken seriously. Taking the social world seriously means thinking about questions to do with structure, power and discourse in such a way that 'the socially constructed subject can be theorized as more than just a "dupe" of ideology; that is, … [as] more than the social conditions which give rise to them' (ibid: 1552). Taking the inner world seriously involves an engagement with contemporary psychoanalytic theorizing because only there, in our view, are unconscious as well as conscious processes, and the resulting conflicts and contradictions among reason, anxiety and desire, subjected to any sustained, critical attention. Crucial to linking the psychoanalytic subject to the social domain of structured power and discourse is 'the psychoanalytic concept of 'fantasy' because 'fantasy is not "just" something that occupies an internal space as a kind of mediation of reality, but … it also has material effects' (ibid: 1554). Here Frosh's use of the term 'fantasy' incorporates not only the wildly outlandish – our more bizarre sexual fantasies, for example – but also ordinary people's everyday imaginings and ruminations. To illustrate, think of how we sometimes imagine quarrels with those who have upset us in our heads (in internal space) without actually verbalizing our disquiet, and then how this fantasy quarrel can influence how we later relate to that same person when we next speak to them (in external space), even though we think we have forgotten all about it (Segal, 2000). What psychoanalysis teaches us is that people's feelings about and investments in particular experiences and everyday activities are directed by this kind of fantasizing. In other words,

> the social is [always] psychically invested and the psychological is socially formed, neither has an essence apart from the other. Just as we need a theory of how 'otherness' enters what is usually taken as the 'self', so we need concepts which will address the ways in which what is 'subjective' is also found out there.

> (Frosh, 2003: 1555)

One final point about how our notion of the psychosocial differs from that of the conventional: if we take the psychosocial seriously in the way just suggested, this necessarily reduces the utility of cross-sectional studies, where factors abstracted from context and person are analysed statistically to assess their correlative impact (which is so easily assumed to be causative). This reduction in the usefulness of cross-sectional studies is because the psychosocial in our sense is *always social* (ibid: 1551; emphasis in original) and *always biographical*. Therefore, to abstract psychosocial factors from particular biographies in order to conduct a cross-sectional analysis is to denude the factors of any real meaning since such factors only operate in the way that they do in the context of a particular life; within another life with its own peculiar psychosocial contingencies, their meanings inevitably differ somewhat. It is this feature of the psychosocial that makes our attention to individual case studies not simply an idiosyncratic preference but, as we argue in the next section, theoretically important too.

Why case studies?

As with the recent emergence of interest in psychosocial studies, so, too, there would appear to be a burgeoning interest in case study methodology, as the annotated bibliography at the end of the excellent anthology *Case Study Method* edited by Gomm, Hammersley and Foster attests. Although there is a sense in which all research can be called case-study work because 'there is always some unit, or set of units, in relation to which data are collected and/or analysed' (Gomm et al., 2000: 2), usually the term has a more restricted meaning. In contrast to the experiment or the social survey (two influential forms of modern social research) Hammersley and Gomm (2000: 4) suggest several defining characteristics of case study research. Broadly, a lot of information is collected about only a few 'naturally occurring cases', 'sometimes just one', which is usually analysed qualitatively. Given our interest in the complex processes involved in thinking about the psychosocial subject, a commitment to the case study as a method of demonstration/explication seems not only appropriate but probably unavoidable. Despite their own rather different methods, Rutter and Giller endorse this. In their psychosocial overview of the 'causes and correlates' of delinquency referred to earlier, they spell out 'the family characteristics most strongly associated with delinquency', namely, 'parental criminality, ineffective supervision and discipline, familial discord and disharmony, weak parent–child relationships, large family size, and psycho-social disadvantage' (Rutter and Giller, 1983: 219). They go on to say:

> Less is known about the precise mechanisms by which these family variables have their effects, but recent observational studies of interaction in the home offer promise of progress on this question. More research of that type [i.e. case studies] is required.
>
> (ibid)

If we *need* detailed observational case studies of everyday interactions of real families to make sense of family factors in delinquency, why has so much criminological time and money been spent reproducing lists of factors that seem to have altered little from the time of Burt's psychosocial enquiries?

Those wedded to the notion that there is a 'normal' or 'rational' subject that can best be grasped through decontextualized aggregation often answer this question defensively, asserting that nothing, aside from conjecture, can be gleaned from the analysis of single cases. Yet, for advocates of the case study approach, it is the working through of the entirety and complexity of the data, as it applies in very particular contexts, that enables 'how?' and 'why?' questions to be adequately broached. Inevitably, views on what case studies can contribute differ even amongst those who advocate case-study methods. Stake (2000: 22), for example, advocates the case-study approach as a means of ascertaining 'a full and thorough knowledge of the particular'. Such knowledge can provide the basis for what Stake calls 'naturalistic generalization', by which he means that, armed with such knowledge, the reader is in a position to make generalizations based on their own experiences. Is this a good enough answer? Is an experientially based recognition of the applicability of a particular case study 'in new and foreign contexts' (ibid) what we find valuable in single cases and therefore what we hope to achieve with our chosen examples? Although we are not against the thoughtful use of experience as a basis for generalization, we are mindful of the fact that, given our notion of a conflicted psychosocial subject whose self-knowledge is always less than complete – indeed who is often motivated to defend against painful self-knowledge – experience can deceive as well as inform. In other words, experience is never transparent (or natural) but always subject to interpretative work. For us, then, Stake's idea that the purpose of the case study method is to facilitate naturalistic generalization is insufficient.

An alternative account of the use of case studies can be found in Lincoln and Guba (2000). From a similar epistemological starting point to Stake, Lincoln and Guba argue that generalization is intrinsically reductive. However, they would prefer 'a new formulation proposed by Cronbach (1975): *the working hypothesis*' (p. 38, emphasis in original) to the idea of generalization. Does the change in terminology alter matters much? Lincoln and Guba go on to suggest that the basis of '*transferability*' across contexts 'is a direct function of the *similarity* between the two contexts, what we shall call *fittingness*' (ibid: 40, emphases in original), a concept they go on to define as 'the degree of congruence between sending and receiving contexts' (ibid). How is such 'fittingness' to be judged? To make an informed judgement about this we will need an 'appropriate base of information' (ibid) about both contexts. By this they mean, following Geertz (1973), a 'thick description' of both. Whilst such an approach is more systematic than a reliance on 'naturalistic' experience alone, it remains wedded to the empirical since the similarity between contexts is said to be an empirical issue. Given our focus on interpretation, it is hard to see how 'fittingness' can be arrived at entirely empirically.

Lincoln and Guba also follow up Schwartz and Ogilvy's (1979) suggestion that, as Lincoln and Guba (2000: 41) put it, 'the metaphor for the world is changing from the machine to the hologram'. This enables them to suggest that it matters little where we start or what we sample because 'full information about a whole is stored in its parts' (ibid: 43), a notion not dissimilar to the psychological idea of Gestalt (Hollway and Jefferson, 2000: 68). It also brings to mind the psychoanalytic idea, with which we have much sympathy, that symptoms, 'free associations', slips of the tongue, dreams, etc. reveal more about the 'whole' (person) than is apparent at first blush. But, and here is the crucial point, the information contained in the part is not self-revelatory: we have to know how to interpret it (ibid: 43). And, just as the psychoanalytic interpretation of dreams, etc. is reliant on an elaborate theoretical edifice, so too will any 'part' need theoretical assistance, an interpretative schema, before it can be used to illuminate the 'whole'.

Now we are in a position to offer our answer to the question: what is it we can learn from a single case study? The nub of the answer is that cases assist theory-building. Indeed, they are essential to it. All theories need testing to see how well they explain particular cases. When applied to a new case, the theory may be confirmed, or only partially, in which situation the unexplained parts of the case act as a stimulus to refining or developing the theory. Mitchell (2000: 170) makes the point very strongly: 'A case study is essentially heuristic; it reflects in the events portrayed features which may be construed as a manifestation of some general, abstract theoretical principle.' However, it is important to distinguish this idea from that of typicality. For, when people ask, 'what is it we can learn from a single case?', what they often mean is 'how typical is it?'. This implies that 'atypical' cases can reveal nothing of value. Mitchell's response to this is to argue that to ask such a question of a case study is to be guilty of confusing two different inferential processes: the statistical one, which is aimed at answering the question of how representative, or typical, is the phenomenon under study, and the very different theoretical one, which is aimed at uncovering logical or causal connections. What this means in terms of generalization is that a case is generalizable to the extent that the new case confirms the theoretical framework informing the analysis; the empirical question of how often this will happen is simply not something case studies are designed to answer.

Several things follow from this. First, the atypical case is as useful as any other providing that 'the theoretical base is sufficiently well-developed to enable the analyst to identify within these events the operation of the general principles incorporated in the theory' (ibid: 180). This relates back to our earlier point about our intended use of 'exceptional' cases and is, hopefully, now properly justified. Second, the theoretical purpose of the case studies will inform the interpretation, which will mean, inevitably, some loss of the case's complexity. In particular, this leads to some simplification of the case's context. However, Mitchell (ibid: 182) draws on the earlier work of Gluckman (1964) to make the point that this 'is perfectly justified ... provided that the impact of the features of that context on the events being considered in the analysis is incorporated rigorously into the analysis'. Third, and following on from this, whatever contextual features are suppressed in the interests of the theoretical analysis (and brevity), it is vital 'to provide readers with a minimal account of the context to enable them to judge for themselves the validity of treating other things as equal in that instance' (ibid).

We started this section with Stake's idea that the purpose of a case study is to provide 'a full and thorough knowledge of the particular' (2000: 22). In the light of our journey through this section, we can now be more specific about our relationship to this notion. Basically, we see such particularistic versions of case studies, which for us mean detailed, *descriptive* accounts ('thick descriptions') of particular events, as our starting point. Thus, for example, we often use journalistic accounts of particular crimes, which may indeed be book-length accounts, as the basis, or part of the bases, of our own case studies. But what we will be interested in is how such particular cases, each in their different ways, manifest, to use Mitchell's phrase again, the 'general, abstract theoretical principle', of, in our case, psychosocial subjectivity and how without such a principle the cases cannot be fully understood. In presenting our cases we hope to abide by the strictures outlined in the previous paragraph, namely, to try to ensure that any reductions in complexity and decontextualization are both theoretically justified and visible to the reader. At the end of our endeavours, what we hope to have demonstrated is something of the generalizability of our concept of the psychosocial subject.

Before leaving this chapter we have one final task, namely, to say something about how criminology, which started out being very interested in the criminal subject, has become almost indifferent to the topic. More precisely, in deference to those criminologists who have shown theoretical interest in offenders, why has criminology been so little affected by the new psychosocial developments of the past 20 years?

What happened to the criminal subject?

An implicit answer to this question, as applied to the British context, is to be found in David Garland's (2002) historiography of criminology's 'governmental' and 'Lombrosian' projects. What Garland (ibid: 8) has in mind in talking of 'the governmental project' is the long series of empirical inquiries, which, since the eighteenth century, have sought to enhance the efficient and equitable administration of justice by charting the patterns of crime and monitoring the practice of police and prisons ... [It] exerts the pragmatic force of a policy-oriented, administrative project, seeking to use science in the service of management and control.

His idea of 'the Lombrosian project' is very different. This

refers to a form of inquiry which aims to develop an etiological, explanatory science, based on the premise that criminals can somehow be scientifically differentiated from non-criminals ... [It is] an ambitious ... (and, ... deeply flawed) theoretical project seeking to build a science of causes.

(ibid)

What happened to the originally continentally based Lombrosian project within the UK is that it overlapped with, or found echoes in, 'a new quasi-medical specialism which ... came to be known as psychological medicine or psychiatry' (ibid: 22) focussed on bio-psychological explanations of insanity and the late nineteenth- and early twentieth-century penal and forensic psychiatric work of psychiatrists and prison doctors who were diagnosing, classifying and treating criminals. Indeed, Garland suggests that the psychiatrist Henry Maudsley and the prison doctor J. Bruce Thomson were '"Lombrosian" before Lombroso' having 'written about "the genuine criminal" and "the criminal class"' as early as the 1860s. However, the general thrust of his argument is that the British approach – concerned with therapy and with classifying mental disorders not criminal types; practically connected to the criminal justice system – softened Lombroso's idea of the criminal as a natural type with the result that the interfusion of the two projects produced 'a scientific movement which was much more eclectic and much more "practical" than the original criminal anthropology had been' (ibid: 26). The resulting 'new science of criminology' (ibid: 26) was, thus, also more acceptable to the British.

By the 1920s and 1930s, 'clinically-based psychiatric studies' (ibid: 35) undertaken in the service of treatment and prevention, constituted the criminological mainstream in Britain. Typifying this work was that of W. Norwood East, 'a psychiatrically trained prison medical officer', who, according to Garland, was highly influential despite his 'subsequent neglect' (ibid: 34). Although 'a proponent of a psychological approach to crime' (ibid) and the co-author of a report (with Hubert) 'on *The Psychological Treatment of Crime* (1939)' (ibid: 35), he 'consistently warned against the dangers and absurdities of exaggerating its claims' (ibid), was more interested in practice than 'theoretical speculation' (ibid), and thought that '80 per cent of offenders were psychologically normal' and therefore required 'routine punishment', not 'psychological treatment' (ibid). Although East himself was hostile to psychoanalysis, others were not. Maurice Hamblin Smith, for example, 'Britain's first authorized teacher of "criminology", and ... the first individual to use the title of "criminologist"' (ibid: 33). He wrote a book called *The Psychology of the Criminal* (1922) and 'was ... one of the first criminological workers in

Britain to profess an interest in psychoanalysis … to assess the personality of offenders [and] … for treating the mental conflicts which, he claimed, lay behind the criminal act' (ibid). However, despite some important institutional developments stemming from this interest in psychoanalysis – the Tavistock (1921) and Maudsley (1923) clinics, 'new child guidance centres' (ibid: 34), the Institute for the Scientific Treatment of Delinquency (ISTD) (1932) and its 'own Psychopathic Clinic [1933]' (later to become, in 1937, the Portman Clinic), *The British Journal of Delinquency* (1950) (since 1960, *The British Journal of Criminology*) – psychoanalysis remained 'an important tributary' (ibid: 37) rather than mainstream.

A very different type of criminology was opened up by the publication, in 1913, of Charles Goring's (1913) *The English Convict*. Sponsored by the Home Office and the Prison Commission and based upon a large sample and statistical measurement, and a starting assumption that crime was normal (i.e. common to all, the difference between 'men' being one of degree not a difference of type), it purported to refute 'the old Lombrosian claim that criminals exhibited a particular physical type', only to invent 'a quite new way of differentiating criminals from non-criminals' (ibid: 35). After finding 'a significant … association between criminality and two heritable characteristics, namely low intelligence and poor physique', but no close association between 'family and other environmental conditions' and crime, Goring went on to draw 'a series of practical, eugenic conclusions': criminals were 'unfit' and their propagation should be strictly regulated. As Garland suggests (ibid: 36), this effectively brought back Lombroso 'in some new, revised form' (ibid: 36). Although Goring's eugenicist conclusions seemed to undercut the possibility of reform, and were rejected by the Prison Commissioners, the statistical analysis of mass data as a form of criminological research gradually overtook the clinically based psychiatric study as the preferred form of government-sponsored research, especially after World War II.

Somewhere between the two was a third stream 'best represented by the eclectic, multi-factorial, social-psychological research of Cyril Burt' (ibid: 37), especially his 1925 study of *The Young Delinquent*, which was seen by 'later criminologists such as Mannheim and Radzinowicz … as the first major work of modern British criminology' (ibid). This study

> was based upon the detailed clinical examination of 400 schoolchildren (a delinquent or quasi-delinquent group and a control group), using a battery of techniques that included biometric measurement, mental testing, temperament testing, and psychoanalytic and social inquiries, together with the most up-to-date statistical methods of factor analysis and correlation. Its findings were expansively eclectic, identifying some 170 causative factors that were in some way associated with delinquency, and showing, by way of narrative case histories, how each factor might typically operate. From his analysis, Burt concluded that certain factors, such as defective discipline, defective family relationships, and particular types of temperament, were highly correlated with delinquency, while the influence of other factors, such as poverty or low intelligence … had been seriously overstated in the past.
>
> (ibid: 37–8)

This early period of British criminology – 'between the 1890s and the Second World War' (ibid: 38) – whether clinical, statistical or eclectic was the period of psychology's dominance of the developing field of knowledge. The focus was on individual offenders and their treatment and Durkheim's pioneering sociological work in France, like that of the new Chicago School of Sociology, 'was virtually absent' (ibid). Rather, 'the "social dimension" of crime was conceived as one factor among many others operating upon the individual' (ibid). Garland sees this take-up of sociology as 'a good example of how the criminological project transforms the elements which it "borrows" from other disciplines' (ibid); more charitably, from our perspective, it might be seen as an early, albeit inadequate, attempt to hang on to both the psychological and the sociological dimensions: to be, in our terms, psychosocial. Be that as it may, the crucial point for understanding how this early interest in the criminal subject all but disappeared in the later part of the twentieth century can be traced to the dominance at this stage of 'the governmental project'. As Garland makes clear:

> The governmental project dominated almost to the point of monopolization, and Lombroso's science of the criminal was taken up only in so far as it could be shown to be directly relevant to the governance of crime and criminals.
>
> (ibid)

This domination of the governmental project was to cast its shadow on all subsequent developments in the new discipline right up until the radical challenges of the 1960s and 1970s, spearheaded by the formation of the National Deviancy Conference (NDC) in 1968 and the publication in 1973 of Taylor, Walton and Young's *The New Criminology*. This was broadly true of the institution-building that took place between the 1930s and 1950s, during which time criminology-teaching in universities expanded: the ISTD and its specialist journal was established; and the first British criminology textbook (Jones, 1956) appeared. It is even more evident with the advent 'in the late 1950s' of government 'support and funding' (ibid: 39). Garland sees this development – crucially, the establishment of the government-funded Home Office Research Unit in 1957 and the Cambridge Institute of Criminology in 1959 as 'a key moment in the creation of a viable, independent discipline of criminology in Britain' (ibid: 40). This is because such governmental commitment 'to support criminological research, both as an in-house activity and as a university-based specialism ... marked the point of convergence between criminology as an administrative aid and criminology as a scientific undertaking – the consolidation of the governmental and Lombrosian projects' (ibid). From our point of view, the importance of this convergence is twofold: first, it spelt the death of any serious interest in questions of aetiology and, second, it ensured that when the challenge from sociology eventually came, in the 1960s, the aim was to overthrow the dominant governmental project – specifically its narrow, positivistic, policy-led, correctionalist focus – in the light of the new US-led developments in sociology and the revival of interest in a revisionist Marxism. It was not interested in revamping the Lombrosian project. Let us take both of these points in turn.

Garland notes the divergence that emerged within the Scientific Group for the Discussion of Delinquency (first established in 1953 under the auspices of the ISTD) between the older, clinically minded members and some of the younger ones who 'grew dissatisfied with the clinical and psychoanalytical emphasis of leading (if controversial) figures such as Glover and split off to found the more academically oriented British Society of Criminology' (ibid: 39–40). The ISTD itself, with its commitment to psychoanalysis and 'open hostility to much official penal policy ... remained essentially an outsider body' (ibid: 34), which left it out of the running when it came to the establishment of the first funded university-based Institute of Criminology. The 1959 White Paper which led to the establishment of the Cambridge Institute of Criminology was quite explicit in its rejection of aetiological research – because the problems involved were too complex, answers would not be easy to come by and ' "progress is bound to be slow" ' – and its espousal of ' "research into the uses of various forms of treatment and the measurement of their results, since this is concerned with matters that can be analysed more precisely" (Home Office 1959: 5)' (quoted in Garland, 2002: 43). Unsurprisingly perhaps, this emphasis matched that of Leon Radzinowicz, the Institute's first director. He 'argued in 1961' that '"the attempt to elucidate the causes of crime should be put aside" in favour of more modest, descriptive studies which indicate the kinds of factors and circum- stances with which offending is associated' (quoted in Garland, 2002: 43). This pref- erence for 'modest descriptive studies' was indeed borne out in practice. As Garland says, 'the prediction research that claimed so much attention in the late 1950s ... made little use of clinical information about the offender, and actually discredited to some extent the whole project of etiological research' (ibid: 40). Thus the aetiologi- cal project was undermined, from within: as the younger ISTD members, some influ- enced by the more sociological teachings of Herman Mannheim at the London School of Economics, turned away from clinical and psychoanalytic work; and from without: as government sponsorship put its support (and funding) behind a prag- matic, policy-driven correctionalism.

Why no critical criminological subject?

Opposition to this 'administrative criminology', as it would later be called, was immediate: from 'the psychoanalysts at the ISTD', on the one hand, 'and the group of sociological criminologists that was forming around Mannheim at the LSE' (ibid: 43), on the other. But, it was not until sociology as a university discipline had firmly taken root (massively, a post-World War II phenomenon) that a generation of crimi- nologists would emerge, radicalized by the many critical currents of the 1960s, able to mount a successful challenge to the dominance of traditional, administrative criminology. Not that this new criminology ever supplanted the old. Indeed, the questions asked and the theoretical frameworks deployed were largely very different. Thus, for a while at least, there were two criminologies – old and new; administrative and critical – existing side by side. Those interested in the details of criminology in the 1960s and 1970s should consult Cohen (1981), who picks up the story where Garland finishes. For our purposes, this turn to sociology had many strands: the importance of labelling and social reaction; the politics of crime and crime control; and ethnographic studies of deviants and delinquents designed to 'appreciate' – understand from the inside – their subjective, life-worlds. These latter studies, influenced by symbolic interactionism and the social psychology of George Herbert Mead ([1934] 1967), were where a fresh and properly psychosocial interest in questions of aetiology might have developed. But the move was the other way as symbolic interactionism came under attack from a renewed Marxism. The result was a certain shifting of attention: from micro to macro concerns; from empirically based ethnographic studies to theoretically driven political analyses in which questions of structure and history, not individual biographies, loomed large; from the 'sociology of deviance' to the relations among crime, law and the state. The challenge of feminism, with its concern to establish that 'the personal is political', might have been another opportunity to resuscitate interest in subjectivity, but its main efforts were directed elsewhere: towards establishing the structural or discursive importance of gender rather than its subjective significance.

If the main enemy for the sociologically inspired new deviancy theorists of the late 1960s and 1970s was the governmental project of administrative criminology and its offender-based focus, this goes a long way in explaining their lack of theoretical interest in understanding criminal subjects. But, this is not the whole story. It is also relevant that the emergence of a critical psychology and a feminist-inspired renewal of interest in psychoanalysis came later than the emergence of a critical sociology and was much less far-reaching. In other words, whereas Cohen could talk of 'a whole range of [critical] sociological connections' at the end of the 1970s 'for students of crime and deviance': 'Education', 'Mass media', 'Cultural studies', 'Medicine and psychiatry', 'Law', 'Social policy and welfare' (Cohen, 1981: 238–9) – the same could not be said about critical psychological connections. Thus, one reason for not taking the criminal subject seriously in the 1960s and 1970s was the absence of any adequate (new, critical) theoretical tools from within psychology for so doing.

The rise of Thatcherism in the 1980s and the subsequent upheavals in the funding and administration of higher education in general and the social sciences in particular, as well as more general developments like the collapse of Communism and the inevitable crisis of Marxism that accompanied it, led to further reconfigurings of the intellectual landscape. In broad terms, critical criminologists found themselves pushed, pulled and persuaded towards more policy-relevant research, while policy-relevant research was having to take at least some cognizance of the radical agenda. In other words, the 1980s and beyond have seen some convergence between administrative and critical criminology. The demise of the NDC and the resuscitation of a single body, the British Society of Criminology, with its well-attended Annual Conference acting as an umbrella body for all types of criminology, is some indication of this rapprochement. Illustrative of this new convergence, and particularly relevant for our purposes, was the (short-lived but influential) emergence of 'new' or 'left realism'. Developed from critical criminology, with one of the authors of *The New Criminology*, Jock Young, a leading proponent, its theoretical starting point was the idea that the crisis of criminology was its failure to take aetiology seriously. Coming from someone with impeccable radical credentials, and given that aetiological questions had ceased to interest even the traditionalists, this was a surprising claim. According to Young, this mattered because during the 1970s crime was continuing to rise despite rising incomes, a fact that ran counter to all criminological assumptions about the links between deprivation/disadvantage and crime. Additionally, there was widespread pessimism about treatment: 'nothing', apparently, 'worked' and rehabilitation had ceased to be a goal of Her Majesty's Prison Service. Most alarmingly, neither critical criminology (now referred to as 'left idealism' in contrast to its new 'realist' incarnation) nor what Young called the 'new administrative criminology' (presumably to distinguish it from the old version with its vestigial interest in aetiology, and exemplified by situational crime prevention) had any interest in aetiology.

Young's solution to this crisis was to argue for the development of a:

> realist theory of crime which adequately encompasses the scope of the criminal act. That is, it must deal with both macro and micro levels, with the causes of criminal action and social reaction, and with the triangular inter-relationship between offender, victim and the state.

> ([1986] 2003: 323–4)

Confusingly, Young later went on to talk about a 'square' of crime with 'the public' being the additional element (Young, 1997: 485–6). But, more interestingly for us, 'the criminal act', which obviously entails some attention to the criminal subject, disappeared from view in the actual 'new realist' research that was undertaken. Essentially, these researches consisted of local victimization studies, modelled on the British Crime Survey but with certain changes designed, for example, to improve the returns for sexual offences. In other words, the victim was fairly exhaustively, if conventionally, researched while the state and the offender remain unexamined (except as they manifest in the answers of victims). Here, then, 'taking crime seriously', the project's political starting point, reduced to a now standard element of the governmental project, namely taking victims seriously; and the much-trumpeted aetiological question remained, as before, unaddressed. This expressed concern combined with a practical failure to do anything about it echoes a similar failure in an earlier text co-authored by Young, namely *The New Criminology*. In the final chapter of that book, Young and his collaborators explained the need, for 'a fully social theory of deviance' (Taylor, Walton and Young, 1973: 269), to deal with action and reaction, and to do so at three levels, the actual act (the level of social dynamics), immediate origins (the level of social psychology) and the wider origins (the level of political economy). Yet, 30 years on, realist criminology has provided no real assistance for thinking about the relations among the levels and nothing of substance that might be deemed social psychological. Perhaps, in the light of this brief, schematic history of criminology, it is possible to glimpse why.

2

PSYCHOLOGY AND THE
CRIMINOLOGICAL SUBJECT

In Chapter 1 we introduced the case for a psychosocial approach to the study of crime and its control and explored how it was that criminology became so disinterested in questions of aetiology. Critical to our analysis was Garland's view that the 'science of causes' that became the Lombrosian project is 'deeply flawed' (Garland, 2002: 8). In lumping together psychoanalytical enquiries with medical and psychiatric approaches Garland effectively echoes the sentiments of Radzinowicz and King – key figures in the governmental project – who dismissed psychoanalytic criminology as a system of elaborate excuses invented by uncritical students of Freud:

> Disciples of [Freud] ... who ventured into criminology acknowledged a debt to Lombroso but rejected his classifications and explanations. They used psychoanalytical concepts, particularly to interpret persistent delinquency. Such phrases as frustration, maladjustment, mental conflict, anti-social or a-social attitudes, passed into the currency of diagnosis and treatment ... By way of reaction there grew up suspicion that this whole approach offered elaborate excuses for offenders, implying that they could not help themselves.
>
> (Radzinowicz and King, 1977: 63)

In this chapter we wish to evaluate this claim by looking at the works of M. Hamblin Smith, Edward Glover and John Bowlby. We concede that while each of these authors were reductionist in their approaches – Smith and Glover being particularly doctrinaire in their usage of Freudian concepts – the commitment twentieth-century psychoanalysts made to understanding the unconscious dimensions of criminal behaviour needs reinstating. We go on to consider other psychological approaches to criminology that, to differing degrees, have been more circumspect or critical in their engagement with psychoanalytic ideas. We explain that the turning away from psychoanalysis has been to the detriment of a properly psychosocial grasp of offenders' subjectivities, with little theoretical attention now being paid to the intersubjective dynamics between offenders and their families, their victims, and those who treat them, even less to unconscious motivations. Although not an exhaustive survey, this chapter provides a brief overview of the major psychological approaches to crime that have had a significant impact within criminology, namely, psychoanalytic (Hamblin Smith, Glover, Bowlby), personality-based (Eysenck, Gottfredson and Hirschi), developmental (Farrington) and forensic (Toch). Moreover, many of these theorists (Hamblin Smith, Eysenck, Farrington) purport to deliver a general theory of crime. Control theory and its successor, the life course perspective, situated somewhere between psychology and sociology, constitute our bridge to the chapter on sociological approaches that follows.

Early psychoanalytic approaches: Smith, Glover and Bowlby

First published in 1922 and republished in 1933, M. Hamblin Smith's *The Psychology of the Criminal* was a text 'devoted' to psychoanalysis, defined then as a 'new development of psychology' (Smith, [1922] 1933: v). During his 34 years as a medical officer in Birmingham Prison, Smith became convinced that the 'only hope of solving the problem of delinquency' lay with 'the patient, intensive investigation of the individual offender.' (ibid: vii). Whilst he acknowledged a debt to the works of Dr William Healy of Chicago (who, as we shall see in Chapter 9, had cause to assess Clifford Shaw's miscreant Stanley the jack-roller), Smith made no apology for being an 'unrepentant Freudian' (ibid). He regarded getting into 'the mind of the offender ... [and] the immediate mental mechanisms which produced his delinquency' to be critical to any attempt to understand crime, but particularly so when such understanding was to help devise 'correct methods of treatment' (ibid: 25).

Smith took from Freud the idea that if emotionally charged conflicts were dealt with through 'repression' they could give rise to unconscious 'complexes' of 'infinite variety', some of which would be 'causative' of 'delinquent conduct' (ibid: 97–100). Sadly, this claim was one Smith asserted more than demonstrated. On the few occasions when Smith cited evidence to back up his claims, it was through all-too-brief case summaries, selected almost exclusively because of the repressed sexual complexes of the 'patients' in question. The 'repression of sexual desire' in a man 'separated from his wife', Smith suggested, explained his 'indecent assault on small girls'; whilst 'nervousness' in relation to '[n]ormal sexual desires' had induced a 'complex' conducive to 'larceny' in another man; and the daughter of an adulterous woman had attempted suicide because of the trauma of discovering her mother's infidelity (ibid: 100). In sum, Smith's approach to crime was not only exclusively intra-psychic, but it was also inadequately empirical, with overly firm diagnoses seemingly preceding any critical interrogation of the case material with which he was presented.

A more sociologically inclined, but no less Freudian, approach can be found in the work of Edward Glover, probably the most senior psychoanalytic figure to pursue a career as a criminologist. In his book *The Roots of Crime*, a collection of papers published between 1922 and 1959, Glover (1960) made the case for 'team research' in criminology. By this he meant that sociologists and psychiatrists should conduct criminological research alongside psychoanalytical practitioners, reducing the tendency towards statistical abstraction favoured by the British Home Office:

[T]he most effective way to achieve understanding of delinquency is for the clinical observer to soak himself in his material, and to permit his scientific imagination to play on the impressions he received; for controlled imagination is, when all is said and done, the most potent instrument of research ... It is futile to expect to discover the 'causes' of delinquency by a tip-and-run survey of 100, or for that matter 1000 cases. On the other hand, the happy analysis of an isolated dream fragment in an individual case *may* tell us more about the nature of delinquency than a nation-wide survey ...

(Glover, 1954: 187, emphasis in original)

Glover was as critical of medical psychiatry's biological reductionism as he was of the habit, common amongst sociologists, of borrowing psychological clichés to explain delinquency. He disliked penal-welfare professionals' use of 'derogatory terms' to describe those manifesting 'anti-social behaviours' (as offending was called then and again now), and argued that such derogation often revealed as much about the moral indignation of the observers as it did those deemed pathological (1960: 125). His analysis of prostitution, despite its tendency to over-pathologize, was similarly sensitive to the interrelationships between social reactions to the 'problem' and the reasons why some people regularly bought and sold sex. Without wishing to deny the economically impoverished backgrounds of many prostitutes, Glover disagreed with those who explained the trade purely in financial terms. Harsh moralism, Glover hypothesized, was part of the aetiology of some forms of prostitution, with prostitutes and their clients connected intersubjectively by their reciprocal and 'unconscious' denigration of 'normal sexuality' and/or the opposite sex (ibid: 256). Admittedly, Glover's suggestion that this unconscious attitude of denigration had roots in guilt reactions to 'early sexuality' was no less orthodoxly Freudian than Smith's earlier work. However, Glover also delivered a more properly reflexive analysis, pointing to the need for greater understanding of the 'hopeless' attitudes of many of those who bought and sold sex, the 'emotional disturbances' that blighted some prostitutes' family lives, and the seductions of tabooed desire, symbolized by illicit sex and the 'filthy lucre' involved in its sale (ibid: 253–60).

Expressing his psychoanalytic ideas more sociologically than Smith, Glover argued that punitive attitudes towards sexual deviants and offenders more generally were often more about the punisher's 'need for crime' (ibid: ix) – the public's desire for vengeance – than justice or rehabilitation, an idea central to much recent thinking about contemporary crime control (Evans, 2003; Garland, 2000; Maruna, Matravers and King, 2004). Indeed, Glover's view that 'the so-called normal person has closer affinities with the psychopath than he is willing to admit to himself, much less publicly avow' (Glover, 1960: 295) is contrary to the idea that criminals can 'somehow be scientifically differentiated from non-criminals' that Garland attributes to approaches interested in 'a science of causes'. The infliction of pain, for example, whether through state-sanctioned forms of punishment or a solitary offender's violent assault on another, could be interpreted as a 'symptom equivalent' to psychosis, entailing a process of 'acting out' that spares the punitive individual from experiencing their own psychotic mental symptoms, an idea we draw upon in Chapter 10.

For us though, if not for Glover, it is necessary to go beyond drawing parallels between the cultural and the mental – Glover's sociological analysis of punitiveness, in the final instance, proving little more than the summation of so many unresolved intra-psychic conflicts, and his claims about the aetiologies of violence and prostitution ultimately relying too heavily on the effects of unresolved Oedipal conflicts.

John Bowlby's work, by contrast, is closer to the kind of psychosocial approach we advocate, not least because it was much more closely engaged with rich case material. Bowlby opened up more space for thinking about the intersubjective than Glover and Smith, his reading of Freud being more revisionist, borrowing, as it did, from the ideas of Melanie Klein. In Bowlby's view, Freud had failed to incorporate his most radical therapeutic discovery into his theorizing.

> [The] early formulations of psychoanalytic theory were strongly influenced by the physiology of the day … cast in terms of the individual organism, its energies and drives, with only marginal reference to relationships. Yet, by contrast, the principal feature of the innovative technique for treating patients that Freud introduced is to focus attention on the relationships patients make with their therapist. From the start, therefore, there was a yawning gulf between the phenomena with which the therapist was confronted, and the theory that had been advanced to account for them.
>
> (Bowlby, 1990, quoted in Holmes, 1993: 127)

In his most criminological publication, *Forty-Four Juvenile Thieves*, Bowlby (1946) developed his thesis that there was a link between prolonged separation from maternal figures during infancy and the kind of disturbances that led children into delinquency in adolescence. Bowlby collated and contrasted the clinical case histories of 44 children convicted of theft with those of 44 other children who had also been referred to psychiatric services. Amongst his sample of thieves Bowlby discovered an over-representation of three psychological dispositions. Amongst the 44 thieves there were 9 depressed children, 13 'hyperthymics' – who tended to 'constant over-activity' – and 14 'affectionless characters' – who showed little 'normal affection, shame or sense of responsibility' (ibid: 6). The complex case histories Bowlby constructed depicted children with experiences of severe abuse and neglect; children who were unwanted; children whose parents drank heavily, quarrelled frequently, and abused each other; children whose parents had died or fallen very ill; and children who had spent long periods in institutional care and hospital. Over the six weeks Bowlby and his team spent studying each of the cases they discovered that many of these children also had psychosomatic problems; were stigmatized for being born outside of wedlock; were badly bullied; had been sexually abused; had contracted sexually transmitted diseases; were struggling with religiously inspired guilt; or had been brutally chastised, usually by their fathers. Perhaps unsurprisingly, many of these 'thieves' were also persistent liars, truants, bed-wetters and runaways.

Bowlby noted, however, that his 'affectionless characters' were generally the most recidivist and persistent group of thieves, and thus he devoted particular analytic attention to the characteristics of this sub-group. As it turned out the affectionless characters typically had few real friendships and harboured acute feelings of loneliness and misery, despite their surface-level indifference to the research team. One reason for this was that vast majority of affectionless children had suffered prolonged separations from their parents, or otherwise the complete emotional loss of their mothers and/or other primary carers during early childhood. This was why their stealing – according to Bowlby – was characterized by 'a strong libidinal element' and connected to:

> ... a failure of super-ego development [crudely, conscience] ... following a failure in the development for object-love [love of another]. The latter is traced back to lack of opportunity for development and to inhibition resulting from rage and phantasy on the one hand and motives of emotional self-protection on the other.
>
> (Bowlby, 1946: 55)

As we shall explain in our chapters about Stanley the jack-roller and the serial killer Jeffrey Dahmer, the distinction Bowlby made between physical 'separations' from and the 'emotional loss' of parents can help us understand why some individuals become so callous in their desire to do harm to others and so indifferent with regard to the suffering they cause. It also helps explain why the majority of children who lose contact with a parent do not develop into 'affectionless characters', as Herschel Prins remarks:

> Parents can be physically present, but not in spirit. A child does not have to be separated physically for it to be deprived. For example, there are many fathers ... who may be physically present but absent emotionally ... The reverse of this kind of situation can be true: a parent may be dead but his sprit kept alive successfully.
>
> (Prins, 1973: 68)

In sum, our view is that Bowlby's work was a significant step in the direction of genuinely psychosocial criminology, his research identifying some of the most important connections between the psychic and the social: the significance of childhood attachments to adult forms of relating; the intersubjective and contingent character of these attachments; and the relationships between these attachments and the symbolic, often defensive quality of much juvenile delinquency.

The psychosocial aspects of Bowlby's analysis could have been pushed further however. Despite his attention to the consequences of poor attachment, Bowlby rather foreclosed the question of whether or not the emotionally impoverished child might find new possibilities for developing less destructive ways of relating. Are emotionally deprived children forever damned by their pasts, or can they learn to think and feel differently about themselves? How do the children of physically absent fathers and mothers imagine their mums and dads? And what kind of psychic substitutes do the children with emotionally unavailable parents seek out? With whom or what will the child with poor super-ego development identify? Unfortunately, these were not the questions subsequent generations of criminologists asked of Bowlby's thesis. Those who were aware of it tended to ignore it, partly because its popularization (and over-simplification) in the post-war period lent itself rather too conveniently to a political discourse that blamed working mothers for the problem of wayward youth (Riley, 1983). Others, like Hans Eysenck to whom we now turn, remained deeply suspicious of all psychoanalytic work.

Criminological psychologists: Eysenck, Toch and Farrington

Whilst diligently empirical, Hans Eysenck's thesis is one of a number of biosocial approaches that Lilly, Cullen and Ball (2002: 205) characterize as implicitly 'conservative'. However, as it is 'perhaps to date the most complete *psychological* theory of crime' (Hollin, 2002, emphasis in original) it should not be ignored. Moreover, since it is an explanation 'based on an interaction of biological, social and individual factors' (ibid), we must consider it. For Eysenck, psychoanalysis was symptomatic of the permissiveness that came to demarcate the 1960s. In *Crime and Personality*, for example, he argued that greater lawlessness in the US relative to the UK could be explained in terms of the greater

> stress on social conditioning in England than there is in the United States, where there has been a ... tendency for American parents to take some of the psychoanalytic and Freudian precepts of *laissez-faire* policy too literally.
>
> (Eysenck, 1964: 135)

Eysenck believed that there was a strong genetic component to personality, and adopted a staunchly behaviourist model of human subjectivity. Rejecting the Freudian idea of a dynamic ego, id and super-ego in tension, Eysenck (ibid: 120) theorized the conscience as 'the combination and culmination of a long process of conditioning ... The failure on that part of the person to become conditioned is likely to be a prominent cause in his running afoul of the law and social mores more generally.' To explain the relationship between this failure of conditioning and crime Eysenck (1964, [1987] 2003) developed a two- and later, a three-dimensional model of personality, measured in terms of extraversion, neuroticism, and subsequently psychoticism.

The basic idea linking biological, social and individual factors was that genetic differences in the way that the cortical and autonomic nervous systems function (biology) underpin individual differences in personality types and different personality types respond differently to environmental (or social) conditioning. Extraverts, for example, suffer from cortical under-arousal and thus engage in impulsive, risky and thrill-seeking acts to increase cortical stimulation. This makes them difficult to 'condition'. Introverts, on the other hand, being cortically over-aroused, seek to avoid excessive stimulation by being quiet, reserved and avoiding excitement. In consequence, they are easier to condition. Similarly with neuroticism, the irritable, anxious behaviour associated with neurotics has a genetic basis and social consequences. In this instance, anxiety is a disruptive hindrance to efficient conditioning. The psychoticism dimension and its genetic basis was less clearly articulated by Eysenck (Hollin, 2002: 154). High 'P' scorers, he suggested, were simply more likely to be involved in crime because 'the general personality traits subsumed under psychoticism appear clearly related to anti-social and non-conformist conduct' (Eysenck, [1987] 2003: 92).

Eysenck's personality theory was thus a psychosocial theory of crime, but a reductive one: ultimately, biology determined both personality and conditionability. Moreover, whether it moved criminology beyond the psychoanalytic orthodoxies it tried to surmount is questionable. Eysenck's meta-reviews of psychological studies that were similar to his own found considerable support for the idea that 'personality and anti-social and criminal behaviour are reasonably intimately correlated' (ibid: 105). But few working within more psychoanalytic paradigms would have challenged this assessment, just as Freud himself would have had no problem with Eysenck's claim that 'anxiety' could act as a 'drive', neuroticism turning minor irritations into obsessions. More problematically, the empirical basis of Eysenck's thesis was to prove little stronger than the ones being cited by his psychoanalytic counterparts. As Eysenck himself conceded, 'too little' research had been done 'to be very definitive [as] to one's conclusions' about how 'different types of criminal activity' relate to 'personality' (ibid: 103). Eysenck rather too readily lumped many different forms of crime and anti-social behaviour together, drawing analogies with studies of traffic violators and unmarried mothers in some of his work, and rarely, if ever, attending to the meaning of particular criminal acts committed by particular individuals. In sum, Eysenck was not only uninterested in the unconscious meanings of criminal behaviour; his interest in personality types also made him largely oblivious to the variety of conscious motives that underpin the miscellaneous problem of crime.

In stark contrast, the diversity of motives that contribute to the problem of crime was a starting point for Hans Toch, one of Eysenck's contemporaries (Toch, 1961: 171). In *Violent Men*, Toch (1972) suggested that psychologists should try to understand offenders 'as individuals' and then 'sort them into groups' and 'link them to the rest of humanity, while separating them from their violent acts' (Gibbens, 1971: 11). Ultimately, Toch sought to do this through the construction of typologies, but his analysis, unlike Eysenck's, attended in the first instance, to 'what it feels like to be prone to violence' (Toch, 1972: 27). Toch thought that such feelings would be better captured by ex-offenders than academics, and hence trained ex-prisoners to act as his researchers. The in-depth interview material these ex-prisoners-turned-interviewers generated revealed the diversity of circumstances in which people become involved in violence and the subtleties of meaning that perpetuate violence in some men's lives. Utilizing both parties' accounts of violent conflicts, Toch illustrated how false inferences about another's intentions and/or about what bystanders might think could contribute to a 'cumulative' sense of provocation amongst perpetrators: one man's feelings of threat and violation playing into the other's, intensifying their opposing desires to 'save face', regain a sense of 'respect', or put those they perceived as 'bullies' back in their place. As their egos become 'brittle' (ibid: 231) both protagonists might respond in kind to each other: one of them might become unwilling to concede to the other's demands, whilst the other may come to perceive forcing their will as a moral imperative. Henceforth:

> the violent incident is cumulatively created by persons involved in it. As each
> sequence progresses, it takes on violence-prone connotations and reactions to

match. Violence-prone connotations do not just spring out of the incidents themselves, but pre-exist in the shape of unconscious assumptions. The assumptions are
both personal and social: personal, because they embody stable frames of reference;
social because they take characteristic forms in the minds of violent men.

(ibid: 172)

To some extent, Toch's work anticipated Jack Katz's (1988) viscerally compelling analysis
of the seductions of 'righteous rage'. Indeed, in his attention to the intersubjective dimensions of violence, and in his acknowledgement of the potentially unconscious, often fantastical, dynamics that underpin such violence, Toch superseded Katz's work, which, as
we explain in Chapter 3, is ambiguous on the relevance of the unconscious and its constitution. Toch went further than Katz in this regard, explaining why some men habitually identify with the violence option: some perpetrators interpret their successful
utilization of force as evidence that violence 'works', even though they have to contend
with the perennial 'feelings of guilt, of being scared and of lack of worthwhileness' that
go with inflicting pain on others – feelings that are liable to 'burst forth' in subsequent
conflicts and confrontations (Toch, 1972: 180); while those for whom violence fails resort
to it repeatedly in futile attempts to redeem themselves.

Yet whilst he showed that feelings of inadequacy could both precede and follow
violence, Toch shied away from theorizing the relationship between these feelings
and the 'unconscious assumptions' so evidently at stake in the aggressive behaviour
his research participants described. The foreword to the British edition of his book
highlights why this shortcoming should be considered a missed opportunity:

Ordinary parents tend to relive their own problems in the development of their
children and quite unconsciously foster attitudes of which they do not consciously
approve, at least in the excessive form which their delinquent children display.

(Gibbens, 1971: 20)

For us, Toch's failure to attend to the heritage of unconscious assumptions simply
underlines the point that criminological explanation is impoverished when it lacks
an adequate psychosocial account of the human subject and its development.

Against this backcloth, it is hard to disagree with David Farrington that criminology
needs to take a more developmental perspective, even if this is not quite what
Farrington's own brand of psychological criminology delivers. Much of Farrington's
thinking draws on his analysis of the Cambridge Study of Delinquency, a longitudinal
study of 400 white working-class boys born in Camberwell in London during the 1950s.
This study has not lacked ambition: it draws on diverse elements of existing theories; it
attempts 'to integrate: developmental and situational theories' (Farrington, 2002: 680);
it proposes a dynamic, processual model to link the elements of the theory; and it
purports to explain the five risk factors revealed by the Cambridge Study to be
independently related to delinquency, namely, 'impulsivity, low intelligence, poor
parenting, a criminal family and socio-economic deprivation' (ibid). Once again, we
have an attempt at a general theory that involves both psychological and social
elements. However, the four-stage process linking the elements, what Farrington calls

'energizing, directing, inhibiting and decision-making' (ibid), presumes a subject that is an eclectic mix of the radically different theories the model attempts to integrate, thus reproducing, not transcending, their problems. For example, at the 'energizing' stage, the presumed subject most likely to offend is the one who, in the long-term, desires 'material goods, status among intimates, and excitement' (ibid) and, in the short-term, is easily bored, frustrated, angry and drinks alcohol. This, essentially, is the social subject of 'strain' theory, suffering a disjunction between societal goals (material goods, status, etc.) and the institutional means to achieve them (hence the boredom, frustration, etc.) about whom we shall have more to say in Chapter 3. For now, we need only to point to Farrington's class-based gloss ('The desire for excitement may be greater among children from deprived families, perhaps because excitement is more highly valued by lower-class people' (ibid)) to secure the point.

'In the directing stage, these motivations produce antisocial tendencies if socially disapproved methods of satisfying them are habitually chosen' (ibid: 681). Once again, the socially deprived child with fewer opportunities 'to achieve goals by legal or socially approved methods' (ibid) is the presumed subject. 'In the inhibiting stage, antisocial tendencies can be inhibited by internalized beliefs and attitudes that have been built up in a social learning process as a result of a history of rewards and punishments' (ibid). Here, the presumed subject is the individual subject of control theory (see below), someone with strong or weak self-control depending on how well he or she has 'internalized [socially approved] beliefs and attitudes'. Although the subject is granted an inner world here, it is a very thin one – and one that is produced by a largely behaviouristic view of learning that is not dissimilar to Eysenck's notion of conditioning. 'In the decision-making stage ... whether a person with a certain degree of antisocial tendency commits an antisocial act in a given situation depends on opportunities, perceived costs and benefits, and on the subjective probabilities of the different out-comes' (ibid). At this stage, the presumed subject becomes the rational unitary subject of rational choice theory, weighing up the odds and acting accordingly. The exceptions to the rule are 'more impulsive people' who are somewhat less rational in their calculations (ibid). Finally, the consequences of offending may produce changes in any of the four stages: labelling, for example, may make the socially approved options more difficult and hence increase the antisocial tendency. We shall also discuss in Chapter 3 the inadequacies of the subject of labelling theory.

If the presumed subject is sometimes social, sometimes psychological and broadly rational (when not 'impulsive') he (and despite the references to 'children', the presumed subject is male because the Cambridge Study only included boys) is unremittingly deprived:

> [C]hildren from deprived families are likely to offend because they are less able to achieve goals legally and because they value some goals (e.g., excitement) especially highly. Children with low intelligence are more likely to offend because they tend to fail in school and hence cannot achieve their goals legally. Impulsive children, and those with a poor ability to manipulate abstract concepts, are more likely to offend because they do not give sufficient consideration to the possible consequences of offending. Children who are exposed to

poor parental child-rearing behaviour, disharmony, or separation are likely to offend because they do not build up strong internal controls over socially dis-approved behaviour; while children from criminal families and those with delin-quent friends tend to build up anti-establishment attitudes and the belief that offending is justifiable. The whole process is self-perpetuating, in that poverty, low intelligence, and early school failure lead to truancy and a lack of educa-tional qualifications, which in turn lead to low status jobs and periods of unem-ployment, both of which make it hard to achieve goals legitimately.

(ibid: 681–2)

Thus, despite the dynamism implicit in the processual model and the possibility of things turning out differently, this subject who is an amalgam of risk factors is also a very passive, determined one: given a high loading of relevant risk factors, antisocial tendencies arise early and tend to persist; only the particular manifestations change through the life course. Consequently, in spite of his general endorsement of the 'mater-nal deprivation thesis' (ibid: 675), Farrington tells us little about how developmental processes actually work. This is because, as he himself admits, 'the causal mechanisms linking risk factors and offending' are 'less well established' (ibid: 659). The net result is a theory that emphasizes 'within-individual change over time' – for example, the progress from 'hyperactivity at age two to cruelty to animals at age six, shoplifting at ten, burglary at fifteen, robbery at twenty, and eventually spouse assault, child abuse and neglect, alcohol abuse, and employment and mental health problems later on in life' (ibid: 658) – but explains these different acts in terms of a single 'syndrome of antisocial behaviour that arises in childhood and tends to persist into adulthood ... the antisocial child tends to become the antisocial teenager and then the antisocial adult, just as the antisocial adult then tends to produce another antisocial child' (ibid).

This lumping together of many different crimes as evidence of an antisocial syndrome is a shortcoming we have already outlined in relation to Eysenck's work. In fairness, Farrington defines the syndrome more broadly than Eysenck, including psychological terms like 'impulsivity'; 'attention problems'; 'low intelligence' alongside more socially sensitive measures such as 'school attainment'; 'poor parental supervision'; 'parental conflict'; 'anti-social parents'; 'young mothers'; 'large family sizes'; 'low family incomes'; 'coming from a broken home'; and, the self-evidently biological, 'genetic mechanisms' (ibid: 671–80). But for all the effort to link genetic, social and psychological dimensions the Farrington theory fails to explain how these correlates variously contribute to the 'criminal propensities' the Cambridge Study has purportedly uncovered. Perhaps most oddly for a Professor of Psychological Criminology, what is genuinely psychological, let alone developmental, about Farrington's approach remains unclear even to those most committed to longitudinal criminal careers research (Laub and Sampson, 2001: 44–5).

Control theories: Hirschi and Gottfredson

It is control theory that most problematized the determinism intrinsic in Farrington's formulation. Sampson and Laub (2003: 333) suggest that the notion of an antisocial syndrome, whether or not it is meant as some form of criminological shorthand, tends to 'reify offender groups as distinct rather than approximations or heuristic devices' in the minds of policymakers. It was this kind of reification, they point out, that Hirschi's (1969) classic text, *Causes of Delinquency,* sought to overcome.

Like Eysenck and Radzinowicz and King, Hirschi was deeply suspicious of psychoanalysis. Despite the title of his book, Hirschi's interest was less in what caused people to commit crime and more in the social bonds that fostered conformity and compliance. There were four elements of the 'social bond' in Hirschi's original formulation: 'attachment', 'involvement', 'commitment' and 'belief'. Attachment was the driving force behind the other three elements:

> The chain of causation is thus from attachment to parents, through concern for the approval of persons in authority, to belief that the rules of society are binding on one's conduct.

> (Hirschi, 1969: 200)

Yet what these attachments meant – what they stood for, symbolized, or felt like in the minds of children – was not something that particularly interested him. Hirschi dismissed the research base from which Bowlby's formulations were derived as inadequate (ibid: 87), and argued for a conceptually 'thin' concept of attachment, defined as the child's perception that 'their parents know where they are and what they are doing'. In support of his theory, Hirschi found that the parents of non-delinquents were more likely to know what their children were up to when they were out of view than the parents of delinquents (Downes and Rock, 1998: 241). But Hirschi's data actually suggested that this measure was only a proxy for a more fundamental phenomenon: the child's 'affectional identification' with their parents.

> Perhaps the best single item in the present data is: 'Would you like to be the kind of person your mother (father) is?'... As affectional identification with the parents increases the likelihood of delinquency declines.

> (Hirschi, 1969: 92).

Given his commitment to empirically driven research it is remarkable that Hirschi did not develop his analysis of this 'best single item' further. As we understand it, the issue of 'identification' refers to those mental processes that involve imagining parts of ourselves to be similar to, or compatible with, qualities we perceive in others: 'In identification something of the other gets into the subject, and forms him or her in its likeness' (Hinshelwood, 1994: 70).

This process, which inevitably involves both conscious and unconscious dynamics, helps explain how it is that children, despite their own claims to be different from their mothers and fathers, often adopt attitudes that their parents hold, even when their parents have drummed it into them that they should not make the 'same mistakes' they did. It is also through the process of identification that people form new bonds: bonds that may, in certain circumstances, compensate for the emotional unavailability of primary carers; bonds that might enable the feelings of vulnerability and rage that Bowlby's research suggested emotional deprivation could cause to be redressed.

Hirschi moved even further away from the subjective dimensions of criminal motivation in his subsequent work. Gottfredson and Hirschi's (1990) *A General Theory of Crime*, took up the idea, also manifest in Farrington's work, that something like a stable criminal propensity exists. In *A General Theory*, this propensity was conceptualized as 'low control', defined as a tendency to pursue a range of 'risky', 'insensitive' and 'impulsive' behaviours – driving fast, gambling, truanting and smoking – of which crime is just one manifestation (Gottfredson and Hirschi, 1990: 90). Yet their neglect of the subjective dimension creates a conceptual problem for Gottfredson and Hirschi, who ultimately fall back on 'in-effective child-rearing' defined along four lines for their explanation of 'low self-control':

> First, the parents may not care for the child ...; second, the parents ... may not have the time or energy to monitor the child's behavior; third, the parents ... may not see anything wrong with the child's behavior; finally, even if everything else is in place, the parents may not have the inclination or means to punish the child.
>
> (ibid: 98)

To make this explanation work, the child's own perspective has to disappear from view. In *A General Theory* the child is either acted upon or not acted upon by its parents, depending on their levels of care and energy, moral integrity and/or inclination to punish. It does not matter how the child responds to its parents for it has no agency. And so it no longer matters if there is any attachment, let alone 'affectional identification'. It is not so much that social bonding has replaced the need for an adequate theory of the subject; rather the complexity of both social and psychic dimensions has been unduly neglected.

The life course perspective and the problem of desistance: Sampson and Laub

For Sampson and Laub the age–crime invariance thesis (the idea that criminal propensity remains a stable property of people throughout their lives) is simply not supported by the empirical evidence. Their first study, *Crime in the Making*, demonstrated convincingly that the notion of stable criminal propensities was an over-simplification of most offenders' criminal careers (Sampson and Laub, 1993). Analysing the data sets initially collected by the Gluecks for their study *Unravelling Juvenile Delinquency*, Sampson and Laub explored the criminal careers of 500 men, all born in the 1930s, and identified as delinquents during their childhoods (Glueck and Glueck, 1950). The Gluecks interviewed their research participants at the ages of 14, 25 and 32. Having reanalysed the Gluecks' dataset, Sampson and Laub were able to show that there was both continuity and change in many of the delinquents' lives. As both the Farrington theory and *A General Theory* predict, adolescent problems with drink and drugs, family life and crime tended to continue into adult life even amongst the Gluecks' desisters: 'Those entering adulthood with a history of early trouble and vulnerability exhibit a 70 per cent higher rate of offending than low risk adolescents' (Laub and Sampson, 2006: 262). But even those with a history of early trouble witnessed changes in their criminal trajectories in adulthood – stable employment, military service and marriage, in particular, signalling turning points away from crime and periods of stability.

Sampson and Laub (1993) explained this complexity in terms of what they called an 'age-graded theory of informal control'. Briefly, their central hypothesis was that the social bonds that link people to each other and social institutions change over the life course, and can become stronger when people become invested in their work or their families. Responding to one of their critics' claims that they had remained overly wedded to a 'variable-based analysis' (ibid: 8), Laub and Sampson (2006) pursued life-history interviews with 52 participants from the original sample as they reached the age of 70. Tellingly, this new life-history data revealed the Gluecks' respondents to be a much more troubled population than the previous analyses had acknowledged. Their criminal careers were often much more 'messy and complicated', and the narratives of over one-third of the participants were 'filled with noticeably more pathos, pain and personal destruction' than had hitherto been acknowledged (ibid: 196–7). Laub and Sampson's analysis of this new data set nonetheless confirmed much of their original hypothesis. It also, however, revealed that the particular utility of the notion of 'attachment' in explaining why some men were able to desist from crime whilst their contemporaries, matched in terms of childhood problems and social demographic characteristics, persisted:

> The persistent offender seems devoid of connective structures at each stage of the life course, especially involving relationships that can provide informal social control and social support. Men who desisted from crime led rather orderly lives, whereas the life of the persistent offender was marked by frequent churning, almost as in adolescence. Surely part of this chaos reflects an inability to forge close attachments or make any connection to anybody or anything.
>
> (ibid: 194)

Disappointingly, Laub and Sampson have yet to provide a full theorization of the significance of this 'inability to forge close attachments' and tend to contradict themselves on the extent to which psychological change was involved in the desistance they noticed. Whilst many desisters had acquired a 'degree of maturity' Laub and Sampson perceive the significance of this primarily in terms of 'family and work responsibilities' and the concomitant change of 'routine activities' such responsibilities necessitate (ibid: 147). Likewise, Laub and Sampson note how their desisters 'forged new commitments, made a fresh start, and found new direction and meaning in life' (ibid), but explain this discovery of new meaning almost exclusively in terms of a rational weighing up of the odds, or otherwise 'situated choice': 'Before they knew it, they had invested so much in marriage or a job that they did not want to risk losing their investment' (ibid). We would not want to underplay the significance of such investments nor deny that people routinely and rationally weigh them up. But we would also point out that for most the calculation defies rational logic, such investments being unavoidably emotional. Some of Laub and Sampson's desisters admit as much, highlighting the considerable 'ambivalence' their new statuses as 'family men' aroused in them (ibid). One reason Laub and Sampson do not make more of this is that they expected their participants to be able to explain why they came to 'turning points', a questionable assumption given the revelation that 'unconscious' choices were very often at stake (ibid: 225). As Laub and Sampson later concede: 'We agree that offenders can and do desist without a conscious decision to "make good"... and offenders can and do desist without a "cognitive transformation"' (ibid: 279). What cannot be explained consciously is then attributed to the unconscious without further theorization of the links between the two:

> In our life-history narratives, one thus sees strong evidence for both will/human agency and 'commitment by default' (H. Becker, 1960), often in the same man's life. In other words, there is no escaping the tension surrounding conscious action and unconscious action generated by default.

> (ibid: 281)

Conclusion

We take this admission of the significance of both conscious and unconscious action as evidence that it is necessary to assume a conflicted human subject – not necessarily rational in all their choices and by no means stable in their propensity to act in criminal or non-criminal ways. For us, Laub and Sampson's conclusion underlines the necessity of an adequate account of this conflicted criminal subject. The shortcomings Laub and Sampson identify in more conventional psychological approaches reveals that criminology ought no longer to dodge this issue. When offender types are reified in policy discourses the effects on people's lives are real, unjust and counter-productive, and the positive effects significant others can have on those at risk of criminal involvement are overlooked. As Bowlby pointed out, this was no less true of the earlier Freudian approaches to crime. But whatever the shortcomings of the early psychoanalytic criminology, its sensitivity to the issue of 'mental conflict' was not misplaced. Rather, what was needed was a more thoroughgoing attempt to free psychoanalysis from the discourses of psychopathology; greater commitment to empirical analysis; a more radical rethinking of the relationships between conscious and unconscious dynamics, including 'intra'- and 'inter'-subjective processes and 'identity formation' and 'identification'; and a more complex understanding of the subject's relation to the social world. This last, of course, is the province of the sociological tradition in criminology, to which we now turn.

3

SOCIOLOGY AND THE
CRIMINOLOGICAL SUBJECT

In broad terms we might divide sociological approaches to understanding crime into four: ecological, 'strain'-based, labelling and phenomenological. Ecological approaches, variously embracing the ideas of social disorganization, differential association and cultural transmission, originated in the Chicago School that dominated American sociology in the first part of the twentieth century. Since our chapter devoted to a re-reading of Shaw's *The Jack-Roller* (1930), undoubtedly the most famous of the Chicago School's case studies, commences with a critical look at Chicago School presumptions about the subject, we shall not address the issue here. 'Strain'-based theories start with the work of Merton on 'anomie'. Transforming Durkheim's notion of anomie as 'normlessness', Merton's (1938) idea of anomie as a structurally based 'strain' between means and ends has proved one of the most enduring concepts underpinning explanations of crime and deviance, from subcultural theory to Marxism. Here we critically evaluate Merton's original approach and its adaptation in Lea and Young's (1984) more recent attempt to explain riots and collective violence using the notion of 'relative deprivation'. The biggest challenge to structurally based theories has come from labelling theory. The key thinker behind the symbolic interactionist paradigm, within which labelling theory is situated, is George Herbert Mead ([1934] 1967). Hence, we use his ideas about subjectivity to evaluate the subject of labelling theory before demonstrating his continuing relevance using a classic article, 'Becoming a marijuana user', written by labelling theory's most-cited exponent, namely, Howard Becker (1953). Finally, we turn to the phenomenological challenge to structurally based theories. One of the key thinkers here is Alfred Schuetz, whose short essay on 'The stranger' (Schuetz, 1944) we use to show how it, too, is based in a Meadian view of the subject. We then end with the exciting work of Jack Katz to demonstrate how one of the most innovative, phenomenologically inspired criminological texts of the latter part of the twentieth century, *Seductions of Crime* (1988), which constitutes an explicit and quite particular challenge to Mertonian approaches, still fails to produce an adequately psychosocial 'phenomenological' subject. Although clearly not an exhaustive survey of sociological approaches, we are confident that by covering some of criminology's most influential sociological thinkers, our net effectively covers a much wider area. Our question, the one we put to each of the approaches we consider, is: how adequate is its conception of the subject?

Merton, 'anomie' and 'relative deprivation'

Merton's 1938 article, entitled 'Social structure and anomie', was 'once counted as the single most frequently cited and reprinted paper in the history of American sociology' (Katz, 1988: 313). His theory took issue with the idea that crime occurred because of a failure to control 'man's imperious biological drives', a thesis he attributed to Freud's idea that civilization entails a 'renunciation of instinctual gratifications' (Merton, 1958: 131). Merton was not, however, hostile to psychoanalytic thinking, and cited from the likes of Karen Horney (1937) and Erich Fromm (1941), the latter of whom suggested the need for a psycho-cultural analysis of groups differentially positioned in relation to economic processes and political upheavals. Whilst Merton's focus was more exclusively sociological than Fromm's and Horney's, he never 'denied the relevance of social psychological processes' in 'determining the specific incidence' of cultural 'responses' to social strain (1958: 160) and hoped others would explore these processes empirically. Leaving aside the work of Robert Agnew (1992), which conceives of strain in terms of the loss or anticipated loss of 'positively valued stimuli' (i.e. loved ones, careers, highly valued personal possessions) few of those who drew inspiration from Merton's work took up this challenge. In the US and the UK subsequent reincarnations of 'anomie theory' (e.g. Cloward and Ohlin, 1960; Lea and Young, 1984) attended to group-based cultural responses to relative deprivation to the neglect of a more thoroughly psychosocial focus.

What Merton emphasized, in contrast to orthodox Freudianism and much subsequent criminological psychology, was that crime was an 'expectable' and hence 'normal' response to the social pressures with which people were having to live in rapidly industrializing Western democratic societies. It was therefore wrong to assume that all deviance was a symptom of 'psychological abnormality' (1958: 131–2). Whether or not people turned to crime, Merton argued, depended upon their social position in relation to widely held cultural aspirations and the institutional means of achieving them. Where the populations of less industrialized countries adhered more closely to institutionally prescribed practices and rituals without question, twentieth-century Americans, Merton thought, had not only had their aspirations heightened by 'the American Dream', but had also become preoccupied with monetary success in the context of new forms of consumerism. Differentially positioned in terms of their access to the means of achieving monetary success, American responses tended to take one of five forms, some of which variously lent themselves to crime and delinquency.

1   *Conformity.* Conformists, who constituted the law-abiding majority, were those who aspired to pecuniary success goals and pursued them using legitimate means, such as study and work.

2 *Innovation.* Realizing they were delimited in their capacity to achieve their success goals through legitimate means, a minority tended to innovate, resorting to criminal behaviours or illegitimate business practices to get the things they wanted.

3 *Ritualism.* Ritualists abandoned their desire to get on in the world and instead zealously adhered to bureaucratic rules. Lower-middle-class people, Merton thought, were particularly prone to ritualistic adaptations, and liable to 'carry a heavy burden of anxiety' and/or 'guilt', borne out of their parents' 'strong disciplining' and 'moral mandates' (Merton, 1958: 151–2).

4 *Retreatism.* Retreatists – 'psychotics, psychoneurotics, chronic autistics, pariahs, outcasts, vagrants, vagabonds, tramps, chronic drunkards and drug addicts' – were those who gave up on both goals and means (Merton, 1938: 677). Suffering a 'two-fold mental conflict' in relation to the 'moral obligation' to adopt institutional goals and the 'pressure to resort to illegitimate means', 'Defeatism, quietism and resignation' were the result (ibid: 677–8).

5 *Rebellion.* The rebellious also rejected both the success goals and the legitimate means. However, rebels – often members of a resentful rising class – devised their own goals which they pursued through alternative means.

For Merton, the strength of his theory was that it was able to explain why crime was concentrated disproportionately but not exclusively amongst the lower classes – the most structurally strained – but, given the potentially insatiable character of the desire for monetary success, the better-off could also find themselves prone to feelings of 'anomie'. However, he conceded that his theory applied only to broad social groups within which there would be many exceptions. One reason for this, as he noted in the first published draft of his anomie thesis, was that even the most innovative offenders struggled to free themselves from 'interiorized norms':

> A manifest rejection of the institutional norms is coupled with some latent retention of their emotional correlates. 'Guilt feelings', 'sense of sin', 'pangs of conscience' are obvious manifestations of this unrelieved tension; symbolic adherence to the nominally repudiated values or rationalizations constitute a more subtle variety of tensional release.
>
> (Merton, 1938: 675)

Which particular individuals gave way to their cultural desires could not therefore be explained in terms of structural strain alone. As Merton himself put it: 'Poverty ... and consequent limitation of opportunity, are not sufficient to induce a conspicuously high rate of criminal behaviour'. What mattered was whether or not the 'assimilation of a cultural emphasis on monetary accumulation as a symbol of success' had occurred (ibid: 681). What determined whether or not a person was liable to assimilate this cultural emphasis on monetary accumulation? Merton thought 'the result will be determined by the particular personality, and thus, the particular *cultural background*, involved. Inadequate socialization will result in the innovation response ... an extreme assimilation of institutional demands will lead to ritualism' (ibid: 678, emphasis in original).

So, whilst Merton emphasized the importance of cultural background, he was very clear that 'personality', 'socialization', and the 'assimilation' of success goals made a difference. And, as he explained at the end of his 1958 reworking of his thesis, this difference was a critical one, often complexly related to the intersubjective dynamics between children and their parents:

> *The projection of parental ambitions* onto the child is also centrally relevant … As is well known, many parents confronted with personal 'failure' or limited 'success' may … defer further efforts to reach the goal [and] attempt to reach it vicariously through their children … it is precisely those parents least able to provide free access to opportunity for their children … who exert great pressure upon their children for high achievement.

> (Merton 1958: 159, emphasis in original)

Merton's concern with 'projection' has, to the best of our knowledge, bypassed all of those who have sought to develop anomie theory. As but one example, take Lea and Young's (1984: 218) explanation of 'relative deprivation', which they define, in an echo of Merton, as 'the excess of expectations over opportunities'. What follows is an informed and generally plausible socio-historical account of the difference between the 1930s and the 1980s in order to show why the relative deprivation of the working class in the 1930s did not lead to rising crime rates and riots, unlike the 1980s. The broad explanation is that in the 1930s the working class were politically integrated, which means that despite high levels of unemployment and the relative deprivation associated with class-based inequalities they possessed institutional means – unions, the Labour Party, the National Unemployed Workers Movement, etc. – through which the struggle for improvement in their position could be channelled. Fast forward to the 1980s and, the argument went, relative deprivation had grown – an ironic result of 'the growth of the Welfare State … the mass media and mass secondary education' (ibid: 222) in raising expectations – as had political marginality. Changes in the nature of work, and post-war immigration, had acted to fragment working-class communities and their political and community organizations, and youth unemployment ensured that young people were isolated from whatever remained of working-class political institutions. This rendered the political marginality of the young, including the children of immigrants, especially 'acute': 'It is this volatile combination that underlies the rising street crime and collective violence that we see returning to our cities' (ibid: 220).

Although this proved a controversial thesis at the time, mostly because it failed to question the reality of black crime statistics in making its case, our concern is its failure to address individual level factors that might help explain the different levels of involvement of relatively deprived, politically marginalized youth in crime and rioting. In this particular sense, it constitutes, for us, a retreat from, not an advance on, Merton's seminal notion.

Mead, labelling theory and 'Becoming a marijuana user'

During the 1970s, labelling theory emerged as a very influential antidote to positivist understandings of the causes of crime. According to labelling theory, the causes of crime were not to be sought in the behaviour of individuals but in the processes of interaction between agents of 'social control' (both formal and informal) and individual actors. When the meaning of particular actions was construed by control agents as either unacceptable or law-violating and labelled as such, 'deviance' or crime was the result. In Becker's famous words, 'Whether an act is deviant ... depends on how other people react to it' (1963: 11). This interactionist understanding of deviance has sometimes been read as if there was no need to attend to the meaning of the act since this can only be found in the nature of the (variable) reaction to it: in how it happens to be labelled. The corollary of this for some seemed to be that an understanding of the acting subject was unnecessary. Lemert (1964), for example, saw the initial act (which he called 'primary' deviance) as too commonplace to warrant attention; only the moment of labelling and the actor's response to that (what he called 'secondary' deviance) should be of interest to criminologists.

This is something of a misunderstanding. Highlighting the moment of reaction or labelling should not preclude attending to the act. What an interactionist approach insists upon is that actions, any actions, cannot be understood in isolation: that the meaning of behaviour is always ultimately to be understood in terms of interacting subjects – hence the core, paradigmatic term, symbolic interactionism – even when the act takes place in apparent isolation. Certainly G. H. Mead, by common citation symbolic interactionism's most influential thinker, spent most of his intellectual life grappling with the problem of how human subjectivity emerged out of social interaction. Our task, then, is to describe his efforts in this regard and assess their psychosocial adequacy.

The shorthand version of the subject bequeathed by symbolic interactionism is contained in the idea of the 'looking-glass' self, a phrase usually attributed to the sociologist Charles Cooley (1922: 184), although Miller (1973: xix) insists the honour rightly belongs to the economist Adam Smith: 'Cooley ... was definitely influenced by Adam Smith's looking-glass theory of the self.' What Smith meant by this was that 'in the economic world, the seller must look at himself from the point of view of the buyer, and vice versa: each must take the attitude of the other' (ibid). It is not difficult to see how this notion fits with labelling theory's central idea that we see ourselves through the eyes of others: how others label us, so we are. However, although Mead was influenced by Cooley, he was also critical of him (Miller, 1973: xx; Morris, [1934] 1967: xiii–xiv). Ironically, given that Cooley was a sociologist, Mead's fundamental criticism was that Cooley was not social enough because he followed convention in presupposing an individual self. Mead's concern was the question of how to conceive the relations among 'mind, self and society', to quote the title of his most significant book, in a way that neither presupposed a self – a problem with both Cartesian dualism (self *and* society) and Hegelian idealism (the cognitive self *produces* society) – nor neglected its importance, given its centrality to psychology. This is exactly our problem: how to think the relation between the psyche (self) and the social (society) in a way that recognizes their simultaneous co-presence in any act, but non-reductively.

To avoid presupposing an individual mind or self, Mead insists on a social starting point: 'We must regard mind ... as arising and developing within the social process, within the empirical matrix of social interactions' (Mead [1934] 1967: 133). This social starting point undoubtedly helps explain Mead's popularity with sociologists. However, he does not reduce 'mind' to the social: as a psychologist he insists on the 'indispensable' importance of the inner world, even if, for him, this was conceived in biological not psychological terms: 'While minds and selves are essentially social products ... the physiological mechanism underlying experience is far from irrelevant – indeed is indispensable – to their genesis and existence' (ibid: 1–2). As a further way of escaping mentalistic assumptions, Mead's other starting point was behaviour: 'The act ... and not the tract, is the fundamental datum in both social and individual psychology' (ibid: 8). This did not mean, as it did for the behaviourist John B. Watson, a lack of interest in the 'inner' world (because considered to be beyond 'scientific' investigation); but, rather, an 'approach to all experience in terms of conduct' (Morris, [1934] 1967: xvii):

> even when we come to the discussion of 'inner' experience, we can approach it from the point of view of the behaviorist, provided that we do not too narrowly conceive this point of view ... something of this behavior appears in what we may term 'attitudes', the beginning of acts.

> (Mead, [1934] 1967: 5)

The basic Darwinian notion that Mead developed is that of organisms adapting or adjusting to their natural environments. Transposed to the social realm, Mead regarded the social process as one propelled by mutually adjusting organisms: the behaviour of organism A acts as a stimulus to organism B whose response, in turn, becomes a further stimulus to A, and so on. However, rather than accept the notion that such actions were expressions of (inner) emotions, as Darwin did (thus echoing the conventional psychological attitude that split consciousness and activity), Mead took up Wundt's notion that such acts were primitive forms of communication – 'gestures' – that, once symbolized, would later form the basis of human language. In this way, language becomes 'a part of social behavior' (ibid: 13) and consciousness remains inseparable from the social act:

> When ... [a] gesture means [the] ... idea behind it and it arouses that idea in the other individual, then we have a significant symbol ... Where the gesture reaches that situation it has become what we call 'language'. It is now a significant symbol and it signifies a certain meaning.

> (ibid: 45–6)

Once gestures have become 'significant symbols', communication becomes much more effective. Thinking becomes possible, since this 'is simply an internalization or implicit conversation of the individual with himself by means of such gestures' (ibid: 47) and a conscious mind can develop, which is the ability to take 'the attitude of the other toward one's self, or toward one's own behavior' (ibid: 48). Meaning arises out of these gesture-based conversations: 'The response of one organism to the gesture of another in any given social act is the meaning of that gesture' (ibid: 78). This is not only a thoroughly social and behavioural view of language, it is also, decades before the emergence of discourse theory, a radically constitutive one.

If meaning is constituted within particular situations, how does it escape particularity and become universally understood (within a particular community)? Mead's answer is that through experience we learn to 'respond in the same way to a variety of different stimuli: if there is no hammer to hand, we use a brick, stone or anything having the necessary weight to give momentum to the blow' (ibid: 83). This learning results from what Mead calls 'recognition' – 'a response that may answer to any one of a certain group of stimuli' (ibid) – and this then becomes the basis of habit. Habitual recognition then provides the basis for what Mead, presciently, termed a 'universe of discourse':

> This universe of discourse is constituted by a group of individuals carrying on and participating in a common social process of experience and behavior, within which these gestures or symbols have the same or common meanings for all members of that group.
>
> (ibid: 89–90)

However, for all his concern to spell out what happens internally, given the state of existing knowledge this amounted to little more than speculations about the necessary complexity of the central nervous system. On the other hand, Mead did attempt to articulate the difference between a social 'me' and an individual 'I', a distinction that was both crucial and elusive. At one point, Mead says that 'The "I" is in a certain sense that with which we do identify ourselves' (ibid: 174–5) – but he said nothing further about how he understood the idea of identification. Most often he reverted to the idea of unpredictability: the 'response of the "I" is something which is more or less uncertain' (ibid: 176). This is because, he argued, one never quite knows how one might respond in any given situation; therein lies freedom and novelty:

> [The 'I'] is the answer which the individual makes to the attitude which others take toward him when he assumes an attitude toward them ... His response will contain a novel element. The 'I' gives the sense of freedom, of initiative.
>
> (ibid: 177)

Without both the 'me' and the 'I' 'there could not be conscious responsibility, and there would be nothing novel in experience' (ibid: 178). True, but none of this helps us understand why one individual might respond in one way and another individual somewhat differently. The only other clues Mead offers us are speculative, and reliant on a pathological view of impulsive and violent behaviour. This sort of understanding emerges when Mead, attempting to say a little more about the 'me'/'I' distinction, likens the 'me' to the conventional or habitual dimension of personality and to the Freudian notion of 'a censor' (ibid: 210), what Freud called the 'superego'. The 'I' then becomes the unconventional or impulsive or uncontrolled dimension (the Freudian 'id'?). Within this conception, the person reacting with violence, for example, is seen by Mead as someone for whom the 'I' element has become dominant over the 'me' element. In the only place we can find where he speculates about the origins of such 'uncontrolled' behaviour, he suggests (predictably) a purely social answer, namely, that where opportunities to take the attitude of the other are restricted then 'uncontrolled' reactions can be expected. The social goal – 'the human social ideal' (ibid: 310) – was 'a universal human society' where the 'me' and the 'I' become fused: where 'the meanings of any one individual's acts or gestures … would be the same for any other individual whatever who responded to them' (ibid). In this Mead unwittingly exposed the idealist within the behaviourist.

Mead's notion of an 'inner' world is not only biological rather than psychological, it is largely presumed rather than demonstrated. It is also essentially a cognitive self. Moreover, his notion of the 'I' – of how individuality emerges from the social 'me' – is either unpredictable (hence incomprehensible) by definition, or is the untamed, impulsive individual who awaits 'proper' socialization. Without a more sustained account of an inner world and individuality, including a proper look at emotional life, this remains, essentially, a social account of the self. As Mead himself (self-damningly) put it, 'even its biological functions are primarily social' (ibid: 133). The 'looking-glass self' is indeed a social self, albeit one upset from time to time by unpredictable (and pathological) eruptions of the 'I'. This may help explain Mead's popularity among criminologists, but for us, plainly, it will not do.

Although Mead struggled unsuccessfully to resolve the relation between the 'I' and the 'me', he did at least acknowledge its importance. But, as with later adaptations of Merton's ideas, sociologists adopting Meadian ideas focussed purely on the social 'me'. Take Becker's 'Becoming a marijuana user'. Conscious of his indebtedness to Mead – 'This approach stems from George Herbert Mead's discussion of objects in *Mind, Self, and Society'* (Becker, 1953: 235–2) – Becker started by spelling out what this implied for understanding marijuana usage: 'the motivation or disposition to engage in the activity [of smoking marijuana] is built up in the course of learning to engage in it and *does not antedate the learning process'* (Becker, 1953: 235, our emphasis). He then went on to describe the process through which one learns how to smoke a joint properly, to interpret the effects correctly and thus to enjoy the sensations. Then, and only then, will marijuana-smoking become a pleasurable activity:

> an individual will be able to use marijuana for pleasure only when he goes through a process of learning to perceive it as an object which can be used in this way. No one becomes a user without (1) learning to smoke the drug in a way which will produce real effects; (2) learning to recognize the effects and

connect them with drug use (learning, in other words, to get high); and (3) learning to enjoy the sensation he perceives. In the course of this process he develops a disposition or motivation to use marijuana which was not and could not have been present when he began use, for it involves and depends on conceptions of the drug which could only grow out of the kind of actual experience detailed above. On completion of this process he is willing and able to use marijuana for pleasure.

(ibid: 241–2)

In his anxiety to escape the individualism of a trait-based, motivational account – only those with particular traits will be predisposed/motivated to take up dope-smoking – Becker ended up didactically proclaiming an invariant, purely social route to understanding. In Mead's terms, the marijuana user who has learned to enjoy smoking a joint has learnt the 'me' discourse. But what has happened to the 'I'? While some have taken issue with Becker's phenomenology for ignoring the pharmacology (and hence the biological basis) of drug use, with one respondent memorably suggesting that 'that guy Becker should change his dealer!' (Pearson and Twohig, [1976] 2006: 103), our concern is with the absent 'I'. For what is clear even without systematic research is that people have very different reactions – from mild pleasure to severe paranoia – to smoking marijuana. Whilst both the experience of the smoker (as Becker would contend) and the strength of the drugs (as Pearson and Twohig suggest) have something to do with this, it also seems fairly obvious that person-related differences have something to do with it too. Given the relationship between anxiety and paranoia, one might reasonably hypothesize, for example, that the highly anxious are the ones more likely to develop paranoid reactions. But, this was clearly not a question of interest to Becker.

Schuetz, phenomenology and *Seductions of Crime*

Downes and Rock's (1998: 210) thoughtful overview of phenomenology suggests that it 'came out of a great mass of debates about the character and certainty of knowledge' and that, in consequence, 'it is not always clear what unites those who call themselves phenomenologists' (ibid: 211). However, Downes and Rock go on to offer a very concise definition of the project, and one, moreover, which clearly announces its relevance to our current project: 'The phenomenological project is almost wholly taken up with discussing the manufacture and application of measures to enter and reproduce the subjective experience of others.' (ibid: 215). Although Downes and Rock are unwilling to single out a single father figure for phenomenology, they tend, like others (e.g. Taylor, Walton and Young, 1973: 193–6) to use Schuetz when laying out phenomenological principles. We shall do likewise, using, for brevity's sake, a short essay of his (Schuetz, 1944) to show how his presumed subject is also Meadian. Basically, this is an introspective essay exploring why it is that 'strangers' have difficulty integrating into established social groups. The argument starts by demonstrating how the 'cultural pattern of group life' (ibid: 499) is constituted out of a common-sense knowledge that is heterogeneous, partial, inconsistent and contradictory yet serviceable enough as a guide to action. As such, it 'takes on for members of the in-group the appearance of a *sufficient* coherence, clarity, and consistency to give anybody a reasonable chance of understanding and being understood' (ibid: 501, emphasis in original). This taken-for-granted 'recipe' knowledge (ibid) becomes habitual through ordinary processes of socialization and has the 'function' (ibid) of making life less 'troublesome' (ibid), replacing 'truth hard to obtain ... [with] comfortable truisms', and questioning with 'the self-explanatory' (ibid).

The stranger, by contrast, shares none of this habitual common sense and therefore he 'becomes essentially the man who has to place in question nearly everything that seems to be unquestionable to the members of the approached group' (ibid: 502). He brings his own, different, 'recipe knowledge' to the new group – and finds it is no longer serviceable as a guide to action. Expressed in Meadian terms, the stranger and the in-group member do not share the same 'universe of discourse' because language is more than just words in a dictionary and an agreed grammar:

> Every word and every sentence is ... surrounded by 'fringes' connecting them ... with past and future elements of the universe of discourse to which they pertain and surrounding them ... with a halo of emotional values and irrational implications which themselves remain ineffable.
>
> (ibid: 504)

So, we have a subject socialized into the 'emotional' and 'irrational' complexities of a given (external) 'universe of discourse' (or not, as in the case of 'the stranger'), but no inner world, apparently. The 'universe of discourse' is the only phenomenon accorded any (albeit largely introspective) attention; the phenomenon converting all the inconsistencies and contradictions of recipe knowledge into workable routines for living, learning to make sense of the 'ineffable', is reduced to an 'unquestioning' dummy, someone who simply 'accepts the ready-made standardized scheme of the cultural pattern handed down to him' (ibid: 501) and unthinkingly allows this to become a routinized, habitual guide to action. Ironically, this failure to recognize an active and complex inner world, ends up reductively homogenizing the external world too, making everything all too automatic, and thus less complex:

> the member of the in-group looks in one single glance through the normal social situations occurring to him and ... he catches immediately the ready-made recipe appropriate to its solution. In those situations his acting shows all the marks of habituality, automatism, and half-consciousness.
>
> (ibid: 505)

Katz's phenomenological project within criminology is to reinstate foreground factors – what actually happens in the act of crime; what is its lived reality – as against the discipline's tendency to focus on background 'causes'. Hence his attempt to dethrone what he calls the 'sentimental materialism' of the Mertonian focus on structural factors (Katz, 1988: 313) in order to develop 'a systematic empirical theory of crime – one that explains at the individual level the causal processes of committing a crime and that accounts at the aggregate level for recurrently documented correlations with biographical and ecological background factors' (ibid: 312). So far, so promising (and less introspectively-based than Schuetz). Katz goes on to suggest that this will involve an engagement with the 'moral emotions' (ibid) – like shame and humiliation – and how these are implicated in a variety of different forms of crime. Since these would seem to implicate biographical issues, this focus too would seem to augur well.

Perhaps the most unusual feature of Katz's approach has been to discuss crime in terms of sensuality and pleasure (hence 'seductions') rather than victimhood: criminal as victim of poverty, deprivation, unloving parents, etc.

> [A]s one young ex-punk explained to me [Katz], after years of adolescent anxiety about the ugliness of his complexion and the stupidity of his every word, he found a wonderful calm in making 'them' anxious about *his* perceptions and understandings.
>
> (ibid: 313, emphasis in original)

However, set against this is the importance of 'humiliation':

> Running across these experiences of criminality is a process juxtaposed in one manner or another against humiliation. In committing a righteous slaughter, the impassioned assailant takes humiliation and turns it into rage; through laying claim to a moral status of transcendent significance, he tries to burn humiliation up. The badass, with searing purposiveness, tries to scare humiliation off … Young vandals and shoplifters innovate games with the risks of humiliation, running along the edge of shame for its exciting reverberations … young men square off against the increasingly humiliating restrictions of childhood by mythologizing differences with other groups of young men who might be their mirror image.
>
> (ibid: 312–13)

Here, the criminal-as-victim reappears, but as victim of an immediate 'humiliation' that cannot be contained, not criminal-as-victim of long-standing, background factors such as poverty and social class (although Katz does raise the question of the relation between the two sorts of victimhood: 'Is crime only the most visible peak of a mountain of shame suffered at the bottom of the social order? Is the vulnerability to humiliation skewed in its distribution through the social structure?' (ibid: 313)). There are indeed ethnographies of working-class life that are suggestive of the important role of shame (Sennett and Cobb, 1973; Skeggs, 1997) but Katz suggests that these questions remain open until we have better data about white-collar crime. Be that as it may, the notions of shame and humiliation immediately open up the psychic dimension, as we argue in Chapter 11. Despite explicitly anatomizing shame in a more recent book

(Katz, 1999: 142–74), Katz sticks with his phenomenology. This is not to say that he is unaware of the psychic dimension. This would seem to be implicit in his (reiterated) acknowledgement that different people respond differently to the same situation. For example, in discussing 'righteous slaughter' and the transformation of 'humiliation into rage', Katz says: 'A common alternative is to turn the challenge against the self and endure humiliation' (Katz, 1988: 22). He is also prepared to accept a psychological source to the aggression fuelling the 'righteous slaughter', but still insists on the primacy of the moment: 'Whatever the deeper psychological sources of his aggression, he does not kill until and unless he can fashion violence to convey the situational meaning of defending his rights' (ibid: 31). In many respects, Katz's phenomenological approach to 'righteous slaughter', 'doing stickup', 'senseless' murder and the like are as close as anything in criminology to our own work: he is not afraid to use journalistic accounts as a starting point; he is committed to cases; and he is alert to the smallest of details. His analyses are both brilliant and compelling. But, we feel that, theoretically, it is important to address the question of why only some who experience humiliation become enraged sufficiently to kill. Take the infamous US double murderer, Gary Gilmore, for example. What was it about Gary Gilmore's psychosocial background that turned him into someone *capable* of becoming a cold-blooded, 'senseless' killer, even if particular situationally specific factors were necessary for the actual killings to take place? In other words, we would want to know more about the 'dread' that killers like Gilmore 'seek to represent' (ibid: 276) and their 'paranoic shame in conformity' (ibid), factors that can only be understood biographically. This opening-up of the 'inner world' of offenders, but without losing either Katz's illuminating situational focus or the way these might be shaped by 'background' factors would, we contend, strengthen, not undermine, his analyses. At times he comes close to doing so as the following quote indicates. It comes at the end of his chapter on 'Ways of the Badass'. It is not used biographically but to explain why it is that the badass is a male figure. It has similarities, oddly, to our starting point in the previous chapter, i.e. to the work of Maurice Hamblin Smith. Although not exactly a Freudian reading, it might be seen as a Lacanian one. In any event, it cannot be understood except as a reading of some of the unconscious dimensions of badass behaviour. Echoing our endpoint of the last chapter, it provides a symmetrical point on which to end this one:

> Posed like a phallus, the badass threatens to dominate all experience, stimulating a focus of consciousness so intense as to obliterate experientially or to transcend any awareness of boundaries between the situation 'here' and the situation 'there'. And in this appreciation, the phallus has the further, socially transcendent power to obliterate any awareness of boundaries between the ontologically independent, phenomenal situations of different people. The fascination here is with the paradoxical, distinctively masculine potential of the phallus: by threatening to penetrate others, the badass, this monstrous member of society, can absorb the whole world into himself.

> (ibid: 112–13)

4

TOWARDS A PSYCHOSOCIAL SUBJECT:
THE CASE OF GENDER

In constructing the theoretical contours of a properly psychosocial subject, we have chosen to focus on the issue of gender because of its contemporary relevance to criminology. The advent of a feminist presence within criminology first put the issue on the discipline's agenda, initially through a concern with the fate of women, first as victims and later as offenders (Gelsthorpe, 1997; Heidensohn, 1997). From the early 1990s onwards the fact that offenders are predominantly male generated interest in issues to do with masculinity and crime. Here, more than anywhere perhaps, an opportunity to explore 'why they do it' seemed to present itself. Unfortunately, the sociological straitjacket within which gender was studied within criminology ensured that the masculine subject presumed by such theorizing remained as inadequate as the subjects presumed by the theories discussed in the last chapter (Jefferson, 2002). The same could be said of the subject presumed by the other major figure who addressed the issue of subjectivity and who has been massively influential within the social sciences (including criminology), namely Michel Foucault. This, then, is our starting point: a demonstration of the inadequacies, from our psychosocial perspective, of two influential but purely social accounts of subjectivity – Messerschmidt's (1997) 'structured action' account of masculinity and Foucault's discursive account of the subject. Thereafter we use the work of Wendy Hollway as a bridge to link the work of Foucault with a swathe of psychoanalytic ideas and hence to the construction of a properly psychosocial subject.

Jim Messerschmidt: structure, practice and accountability

Messerschmidt's work on masculinity (1993, 1994, 1997), is a sophisticated attempt to combine Connell's (1987) notion of hegemonic masculinity (broadly, the dominant form of masculinity in a given society at a given historical moment) with the other crucial social structures (namely class and race). The result sees the actor, subject or agent as multiply (and simultaneously) constrained by the structures of class, race and gender. Reconciling this with Giddens' (1984) structuration theory, Messerschmidt suggests that social structures can only be reproduced through the actions of human subjects. In other words, social structures are nothing other than the pattern of constraints produced over time by human actors, thus producing 'structured action'.

The structured action of human beings takes place in specific contexts in which our 'performances' are held to account by others, i.e. in any given social situation we accomplish/do gender (and race and class) through 'accountable' social interaction. To the extent that we perform appropriately (i.e. accountably), we assist the maintenance of existing social structures. Conversely, culturally 'inappropriate' gender performances – men wearing skirts or kissing other men in public, etc. – can threaten the existing dominant gender order. Messerschmidt spells out the connection of masculinity with crime in the following way:

> Young men situationally accomplish public forms of masculinity in response to their socially structured circumstances ... varieties of youth crime serve as a suitable resource for doing masculinity when other resources are unavailable.
>
> (Messerschmidt, 1994: 82)

In other words, those young men unable to compete successfully in legitimate masculinity-accomplishing spheres, like sport and professional employment, for example, may turn to certain forms of crime (those involving aggressive violence, for example) where they are able to compete successfully in 'doing' masculinity. In terms of gendered subjectivity, Messerschmidt provides us with an agentic subject who is also socially constrained. But, the problem is that this subject is still rational and unitary: '[A]ll individuals engage in purposive behaviour and monitor their action reflexively ... we comprehend our actions and we modify them according to (among other things) our interpretation of other people's response' (Messerschmidt, 1993: 77). Mead's social psychology ([1934] 1967) and the idea of the 'looking-glass' self comes back to mind here. As we saw in Chapter 3, this concept struggles to explain those who fail to recognize themselves in the mirror of the other. So, too, with Messerschmidt's account where it remains unclear how, when or why people might 'choose' to act unaccountably. Despite the suggestion, echoing Connell, that 'the cultural ideals of hegemonic masculinity need not correspond to the actual personalities of most men' (Messerschmidt. 1993: 83), in structured action theory the accent is strongly on structural reproduction, not changing structures through unaccountable actions.

Michel Foucault: discourse, meaning and subject positions

The move from structure to discourse, in which Foucault is the central figure, was a significant moment in the social sciences.

> By 'discourse', Foucault meant 'a group of statements which provide a language for talking about – a way of representing the knowledge about – a particular topic at a particular historical moment ... Discourse is about the production of

knowledge through language. But ... since all social practices entail *meaning*, and meanings shape and influence what we do – our conduct – all practices have a discursive aspect' (Hall, 1992: 291) ... Discourse, Foucault argues, constructs the topic.

(Hall, 2001: 72, emphasis in original)

Or, as Michele Barrett (1991: 130) concisely put it, discourse is 'the production of "things" by "words"'. What this means is that we can only know anything about the world – Messerschmidt's structures of class, race and gender, for example – through the discourses historically available to us.

This does not mean that nothing exists beyond discourse, but rather that 'nothing has any *meaning* outside of discourse' (Foucault, 1972, our emphasis). This radically historical view of knowledge makes the truth of anything – madness, crime, sexuality, gender, etc. – historically specific. And, since knowledge is always being applied to regulate social conduct, it is always enmeshed in relations of power: 'There is no power relation without the correlative constitution of a field of knowledge, nor any knowledge that does not presuppose and constitute at the same time, power relations' (Foucault, 1977: 27). Thus truth (or regimes of truth) in any given historical period, is a product of prevailing power/knowledge relations. By the same token, subjects are necessarily caught up in all this: they are constituted by particular discursive formations, regimes of truth, power/knowledge relations, and so on. Put another way, discourses – of madness, crime, masculinity, etc. – construct various subject positions 'from which', as Hall (2001: 80) puts it 'alone they make sense': 'we – must locate ... ourselves in the position from which the discourse makes most sense, and thus become its "subjects" by "subjecting" ourselves to its meanings, power and regulation' (ibid).

Why do particular subject positions make sense to some men but not to others? Why, for example, do only some men identify with the 'hard man' or the Casanova? What makes hegemonic masculinity more important to some men than to others? Why is it that only some young, socially disadvantaged men perceive crime to be a masculinity-accomplishing resource? In both cases then – Messerschmidt's and Foucault's – we get a strong sense of the social dimension of gendered subjectivity: in the former, through the situational accomplishment of masculinity through accountable practices that reproduce the social structures of (class and race and) gender; in the latter, through discursive formations providing gendered subject positions. But in neither case do we get any sense of why *individuals* might take up (or identify with) particular subject positions or accomplish masculinity in accountable rather than unaccountable ways. Here, then, is where a notion of the psyche is indispensable; which brings us to the work of Wendy Hollway.

Wendy Hollway and the importance of investment

Hollway's 2001 article represents an attempt to work specifically with Foucaultian notions of discourse within a particular area – sexuality – *and* to address the issue of identification (or what she calls 'investment'). Broadly, Hollway's account starts by identifying three contemporary discourses of sexuality: 'male sexual drive', 'have/hold' and 'permissive'. The central notion in the male sexual drive discourse 'is that men's sexuality is directly produced by a biological drive, the function of which is to ensure reproduction of the species' (Hollway, 2001: 273). The 'have/hold' discourse subordinates sexuality to committed, faithful love of the relationship, partnership, marriage or family life, which is seen as the only proper location for reproduction. In the permissive discourse, sexuality is divorced from both reproduction and relationships and is regarded simply as pleasurable activity to be pursued for its own sake. In all three discourses, it should be added, heterosexuality is presumed.

Hollway also addresses the issue of gender differentiated subject positions in each of these discourses (or, how power/knowledge relations produce different, and unequal, positions for men and women to 'occupy'). Thus, only men, by definition, can occupy the subject position in the male sexual drive discourse; for women, the only available position is to be 'the object that precipitates men's natural urges' (ibid: 274). In the have/hold discourse, the subject position is, in theory, equally available to men and women: both are enjoined to engage their sexuality only within the confines of the relationship, marriage, etc. However, men's failure to live up to the ideal by being sexually unfaithful is tolerated more as the male sexual drive discourse provides ready-made excuses for male promiscuity. The permissive discourse is similarly egalitarian in theory, offering both men and women the opportunity to indulge in sex as pleasurable fun. However, because it is based on the idea 'that sexuality is entirely natural and therefore should not be repressed' (ibid: 275), it favours a version of sexuality that is not unlike that in the male sexual drive discourse. This makes it easier for men to adopt. In other words, existing power/knowledge relations, such as the masculine version of sexuality embedded in the male sexual drive discourse, constantly operate as a brake on the transformation of gender relations. New, apparently more egalitarian discourses never appear in a historical vacuum but jostle and commingle with older, more traditional discourses: 'practices', as Hollway reminds, 'are not the pure products of a single discourse' (ibid: 276).

Crucially for our purposes here, Hollway does not overlook the importance of a *biographical dimension* – 'Practices and meanings have histories, developed through the lives of the people concerned' (ibid: 277). This biographical dimension underpins a critical development of Foucault: the notion that practices and meanings are invested in, psychosocially.

> By claiming that people have investments (in this case gender-specific) in taking up certain positions in discourses, and consequently in relation to each other, I mean that there will be some satisfaction or pay-off or reward ... for that person.
>
> (ibid: 278)

Importantly, Hollway observes that 'satisfaction ... is not necessarily conscious or rational. But there is a reason' (ibid). Using case examples, Hollway shows how people's investments in social discourses are the complex outcomes of the following processes:

- retaining a feeling of being powerful or avoiding feelings of vulnerability or powerlessness;
- the suppression of significations/subject positions that threaten to make subjects feel deprived of power;
- defensively projecting these suppressed feelings onto the other. For example, male fear of commitment – of taking up a subject position in the have/hold discourse – is a product of the powerlessness that getting close to someone can entail. The idea of commitment, and the closeness and security it promises, is then disavowed or suppressed, and projected onto a female partner; and
- this suppressed desire for intimacy is desire for the other.

In much psychoanalytic work this desire for the other is conceptualized as originating from a repressed Oedipal desire for the child's mother (or substitute), a notion we elaborate in the next section. For the moment, an illustration may help us understand this notion. Using an extract from her own diary to illustrate the intersubjective dynamics that were at play in the relationships of couples she was studying, Hollway refers to how 'Jim'

> got at me twice, about tiny things, in a way that I felt to be antagonistic. When I pointed it out we tried to do some work on it. Blank. Then he came up with the word 'oranges' as if from nowhere. When he thought about it a bit he said it had something to do with his relations with women. If a woman peeled an orange for him, it showed that they cared about him. Then he said that his mother used to do it for him, even when he could do it himself.
>
> (Hollway, 1989: 58)

Incorporating this psychic dimension enables a thoroughly psychosocial, not merely discursive, subjectivity to be posed:

> What makes this analysis different from one which sees a mechanical circulation of discourses through practices is that there is an investment which, for reasons of an individual's history of positioning in discourses and consequent production of subjectivity, is relatively independent of contemporary positions available. According to my account this is an investment in exercising power on behalf of a subjectivity protecting itself from the vulnerability of desire for the Other.
>
> (Hollway, 2001: 282–3)

With her examples of how the desire for unconditional love informs what heterosexual couples struggle to say to each other, particularly in relation to the decision as to whether or not to use contraception and/or try for a baby, Hollway (1989: 47–66) succeeds in demonstrating both the unconscious reasons for her subjects' investments in powerful, rather than vulnerable, gendered subject positions and the unique, biographical origins of these particular investments. As we shall see in later chapters, this notion of a vulnerable subject, investing in empowering discursive positions whilst projecting vulnerabilities onto others and attacking them there, provides a critical part of the answer to the criminological question: why did they do it? However, there is one issue that Hollway's work leaves unresolved for us, namely, whether there is something specific to the biographies of boys and girls that affects their responses to their parents. Are there sex-specific developmental processes that explain how gender is implicated in the pattern of investments made by boys and girls and men and women? To answer this question requires a longish detour via psychoanalysis.

Psychoanalysis and the origins of our investments in our gendered identity

Freud, the Oedipal complex and sexual difference

For Freud, civilization is founded on the repression of libidinal instincts. The infant is a bundle of libidinal (or sexual) and aggressive instincts, a polymorphously perverse pleasure-seeking organism. Since infants inevitably come up against an obdurate reality that often opposes their libidinal pleasure-seeking – the breast is not always available to be sucked, the thumb may be removed from the mouth, etc. – this sets up a conflict between an inner world of instincts and the external, sensory world. Out of this conflict a primitive consciousness, or ego, which is at first a 'bodily ego' (Freud, [1923] 1984: 364), perceiving the world through the bodily senses, emerges. It develops gradually by controlling or inhibiting instincts (ibid: 397). During this period the child discovers the erotic potential of different body parts – the mouth through sucking, the anus through defecation, the genitals through masturbation, which Freud conceptualized in terms of oral, anal and phallic stages.

Having reached the phallic stage, sometime between the ages of two and five, the boy child falls victim to two fantasies: that he can become the mother's lover; that the father's revenge will mean the boy losing his penis. This fear of castration, and the consequent loss of pleasure, become imaginable after the discovery of sexual difference: the realization that girls have already been 'castrated'. These fantasies are properly psychosocial: they emerge from within and invest the external world with meaning; and the realities of the external world – discovering the pleasures of the penis; noticing girls do not possess one – help shape the nature of the fantasies.

Freud claimed that these fantasies precipitate the Oedipal crisis, a momentous turning point both in relation to a boy's sexual development, but also more generally in the development of selfhood, or identity. The painful realization that his father, not he, is his mother's primary love-object and the terrifying threat of castration combine, with the result that 'the child's ego turns away from the Oedipus complex' (Freud, [1924] 1977: 318) – a process Freud also describes as repression – and 'the object cathexes are given up and replaced with identifications' (ibid: 319). In other words, desire for the mother – object love – becomes repressed into an unconscious realm (what Freud was to call the 'id') and the libidinal energy fuelling that desire is transformed into a partly desexualized and sublimated form of desire, a desire to be like – to identify with – the father. This transformation not only founds the unconscious but also the super-ego:

> The authority of the father or the parents is introjected into the ego, and there it forms the nucleus of the super-ego, which takes over the severity of the father and perpetuates his prohibition against incest, and so secures the ego from the return of the libidinal object-cathexis.
>
> (ibid)

In terms of sexual development, this 'process ushers in the latency period': the genital organ has been saved but its function 'paralysed'. In terms of psychic development, the formation of the super-ego (or the 'ego ideal' as Freud sometimes calls it) sets up an internal storehouse (a 'conscience') where the injunctions and prohibitions of the father and, later, other authority figures, and, more generally, religion and morality, become internalized. It also establishes a structure of mind – the id, the ego and the super-ego – where conflicting and contradictory demands implicating the internal and external world are inevitable:

> Whereas the ego is essentially the representative of the external world, of reality, the super-ego stands in contrast to it as the representative of the internal world, of the id [being 'the heir of the Oedipus complex']. Conflicts between the ego and the ideal will … ultimately reflect the contrast between what is real and what is psychical, between the external world and the internal world.
>
> (Freud, [1923] 1984: 376)

In our terms, Freud's theory was properly psychosocial. It theorized a self negotiating an irreducible inner world together with an obdurate social one. But it is difficult to know what the implications of Freud's thinking are for the question of gender/sexual development. On the one hand Freud suggested that the repression involved in the boy's resolution of the Oedipus complex and the resulting identification with the father was an inherently gendered process. On the other hand, such a reading over-simplifies his position; not only because Freud slipped rather too easily between using the terms 'father' and 'parents', as we saw above, but also because gender is not a term he ever used. Look in an index to his writings on sexuality and you will find plenty of references to 'genitals', none to 'gender'. This distinction is important. Although Freud used the terms 'masculinity' and 'femininity', his interest lay in understanding the different development of sexuality in boys and girls, not what we now understand as gendered identity. And even when he used the terms 'masculinity' and 'femininity', Freud acknowledged how confusing they could be:

> 'Masculine' and 'feminine' are used sometimes in the sense of *activity* and *passivity*, sometimes in a *biological*, and sometimes, again, in a *sociological* sense.

> The first of these three meanings is the essential one and the most serviceable
> in psychoanalysis ... The third, or sociological, meaning receives its connotation
> from the observation of actually existing masculine and feminine individuals.
> Such observation shows that in human beings pure masculinity or femininity is
> not to be found either in a psychological or a biological sense. Every individual ...
> displays a mixture of the character-traits belonging to his own and to the oppo-
> site sex; and he shows a combination of activity and passivity whether or not
> these last character-traits tally with his biological ones.

> (Freud, [1905] 1977: 141–2n1, emphases in original)

Despite these provisos, there is no doubt that Freud's account of sexual development
takes the boy child as the standard and, when thinking of girls, he failed to question
what we now see as the masculinist assumptions of his day. Crucially, the penis and
anatomical sexual difference was accorded a central role in what we would now see as
his attempted explanation of gender difference: women's 'sense of inferiority'; tendency
to jealousy; lesser attachment to her mother; and disinclination to masturbate are all
'psychical consequences' of the notorious 'penis-envy' (Freud, [1925] 1977: 337–39).
The little girl's turning against masturbation is seen as particularly important:

> This impulse ['an intense current of feeling against masturbation'] is clearly a
> forerunner of the wave of repression which at puberty will do away with a large
> amount of the girl's masculine sexuality [active clitoral masturbation] in order
> to make room for the development of her [passive, vaginal] femininity.

> (ibid: 339)

To be fair, Freud ends his paper with the repeated proviso that actual men and
women 'combine in themselves both masculine and feminine characteristics' and all
this is based on 'a handful of cases' and may not be typical (ibid: 342–3). However,
in wanting it both ways, Freud revealed awareness of a problem that his latent biologism could not solve. The best that may be said of this, as others have (Mitchell,
1975: 377–81), is that Freud's is an account of gender development under patriarchy.

Another way of making the point about all of us being mixtures of masculine
and feminine would be to say that the pattern of identifications of actually existing boys (and girls) is far from straightforward, the case of the homosexual male
being but one obvious example that has given psychoanalysis problems over the
years (Lewes, 1989). Freud understood this since he recognized the necessarily
ambivalent feelings caused for boys by having to identify with someone who
inspires love, guilt and fear simultaneously. He also knew that this crisis could be
resolved more or less successfully, positively or negatively, meaning that some boys
would fail to identify sufficiently with the father to enable successful separation
from the mother, and hence could store up problems for subsequent relationships.
But, 'the very fact that Freud admits a positive and negative Oedipus complex
immediately begins to undermine the complex as an account of sexual difference'
(Hood-Williams, 2001: 53).

Where, then, might one look for an adequately psychosocial account of gender development? One place where people have begun to look for an answer is the work of Melanie Klein.

Klein, the pre-Oedipal period and anxiety

With the interchange between post-structuralist and feminist thinking, there has been a move away from the equation 'penis = sexual difference = gender' and a refocussing on the pre-Oedipal period and the role of the mother, especially the moment of an infant's beginning to distinguish its own boundaries from those of its mother's. Here, the work of Melanie Klein (1988a and b) has been central, especially her attention to how infants defend against anxiety. In some respects Klein retained Freud's biologism: she thought 'that "masculinity" and "femininity" are … biologically determined but reinforced during early childhood' (Minsky, 1998: 34) and made the death instinct, not the sexual instinct, primary. But, in other respects, the Kleinian object relational perspective is an approach that frees itself of Freud's biological reductionism, thus paving the way for a more adequately psychosocial theory of development.

Where Freud made sexuality, desire and the father central to his account of Oedipal conflict, the child's acquisition of identity and its entry into culture, 'Klein argues that it is the baby's anxiety arising out of its instinctive emotional ambivalence towards the mother … that is the major problem with which the small baby, and later the adult, have to contend' (ibid: 33). Coping with this anxiety arising from the struggle in relation to the mother (and later, others), leads to the construction of phantasies of love and hate, driven by the primitive defence mechanisms of splitting and projection, which provide the basis of an early fragile identity. The breast rather than the penis is central to this process:

> Loving and hating phantasies of the breast are the baby's first experience of relating to the mother and (since the baby's identity is fused with the breast because it does not have an identity of its own) of filling itself up with a good or bad phantasy of the breast thus creating a primitive sense of having a self.
>
> (ibid: 35)

Thus, feelings that become too distressing may be split off as 'bad', separated from both the internal and external 'good' phantasy objects, and projected onto the mother's breast, which then becomes 'bad'. Such defences, stemming from persecutory anxiety, are characteristic of a baby's early months and what Klein called the paranoid-schizoid position (although anyone can operate from such a position). As the baby learns to take in whole objects, to perceive the mother as the source of both love and hate and to live with the resulting ambivalence, Klein talks of the baby entering the depressive position. Such an achievement is never absolute; we never entirely relinquish paranoid-schizoid defences, although our particular experience of early nurturing will affect both our level of general anxiety and our characteristic ways of defending against it.

This Kleinian understanding of development enables us to break with the idea that masculinity is something essentially, biologically or psychically, to do with actual men. Where Freud's Oedipal moment implicated gender, albeit unsatisfactorily, Klein's conceptualization of 'anxiety', 'splitting' and 'ambivalence' was gender-neutral (Hood-Williams, 2001). Masculinity, conceived in Kleinian terms, does not therefore have to assume a set of attributes possessed by men. Consequently, Kleinian thinking effectively *forces* us into the realm of the social to explain sexual difference, without denying the (irreducible) significance of the psyche, i.e. into an explanation that is psychosocial. In so doing, it also begins to provide important elements that enable possible answers to the 'why did they do it?' puzzle, as well enabling us to acknowledge the possibilities for change. For example, the notion of psychic positions draws our attention to the psychic conditions that evoke the kinds of emotions that can, given unfavourable social conditions, motivate hateful attacks on others – envy, spite, greed, disgust – as well as the kind of individuals (the traumatized, the unloved, the estranged) likely to have trouble containing these feelings (Brown, 2003). Concomitantly, the notion that people can move from a paranoid-schizoid mentality to more depressive modes of thinking takes us into the criminological domain of guilt, shame and reparation and the positive contribution the intersubjective working through of these emotions, under favourable social conditions, can make to human development across the life course. However, the (now reposed) gender question remains, namely: how does a (biologically sexed) individual's anxiety, arising as it does from a unique mixture of the constitutional and the biographical, relate to social discourses of gender difference? Nancy Chodorow has provided one very influential answer.

Chodorow and early psychic separation

Nancy Chodorow is a Professor of Sociology who later trained as a psychoanalyst. Her most influential book, *The Reproduction of Mothering* (1978), was primarily interested in understanding why girls take so readily to mothering despite the fact that motherhood operates to reproduce the gendered division of labour in so many ways (e.g. by disadvantaging women in the world of paid work). Her core argument concerned differences in the way mothers separated from their daughters as opposed to their sons. Because mothers found it harder to separate from their daughters, girls remained psychically connected to their mothers for longer, a process that prepared them well for the crucial mothering task of connecting and relating to others but less well for dealing with independence. With sons, the process was reversed: mothers found it easier to separate from them and, in consequence, pushed them into an early psychic separation. This made boys better at the (culturally masculine) task of being independent but less good at the (culturally feminine) task of connecting with others and relationships. As Craib (1987: 729) concisely put it, 'the core of Chodorow's argument is that the little boy is pushed into an early psychic separation from the mother'. The effect of this early separation on boys is the development of 'well defined and rigid' ego boundaries and an unwillingness to 'risk themselves in relationship' (ibid: 730). In Kleinian terms, social manifestations of 'masculinity' can be conceptualized as defences against the (psychic) anxieties attendant upon an early separation.

In terms of advancing a psychosocial approach, Chodorow's thesis had considerable merit. Widespread and deeply entrenched cultural norms about masculinity and femininity were connected with the psychic process of acquiring a separate sense of selfhood. As a general theory of gender difference this may well help explain the defensive quality of many acts of male violence: from teenage conflicts over turf, to the domineering violence of the wife batterer. However, by explaining gendered identity in terms of a process of individuation that plays out differently for boys and girls, Chodorow more or less substitutes Freud's anatomical appendages with separation processes. In other words, Chodorow amended the Freudian thesis but did not transcend it. With Chodorow, as with Freud, it remains impossible to explain the many exceptions to the rule: the girls unsuited to mothering and the caring boys. Chodorow herself recognized this problem of overgeneralization and strove to address it. But, her later work (Chodorow, 1994) wrestled only inconclusively with the problems of a more multiple, less generalized understanding. The writer who has most consistently addressed this problem in a resolutely non-reductive fashion is Jessica Benjamin (1995, 1998), another social theorist turned psychoanalyst who, along with Chodorow, is part of the distinctively North American, contemporary relational school of psychoanalysis.

Benjamin, overinclusive bisexuality and gender complementarity

Jessica Benjamin differs from Nancy Chodorow in seeing what Chodorow saw as something that happens to all boys as but one possible outcome. Where this early psychic separation happens, Benjamin talks of a situation where the boy has 'repudiated' his identification with his mother 'and the elements associated with his own babyhood are projected onto the girl, the daughter' (1998: xvii). But, Benjamin argues, it is possible to retain and acknowledge identification with the mother. Where both Freud and the object relational theorists (like Chodorow) go wrong, Benjamin suggests, is in falsely splitting the desire to be like (identificatory love) from the desire for (object love). Thus, the binary logic of Freud's account of the Oedipal complex – desire for the mother being replaced by desire to be like the father – is not fundamentally challenged by Chodorow's account of separation processes.

Benjamin's radical suggestion is that the pre-Oedipal phase is characterized by multiple identifications – with father as well as mother (or substitutes) and what they symbolize culturally. These multiple, bisexual identifications Benjamin, following Fast (1984, 1990), calls 'overinclusive' (Benjamin, 1998: 60). From this perspective, what determines Oedipal outcomes is the extent to which this overinclusive bisexuality is given up. When it is given up decisively in favour of the mutual exclusivity of gender difference, with its overvaluation of the masculine and denigration of the feminine, Benjamin reasons that this Oedipal posture is built psychically on a foundation of defensive repudiation:

> without access to the overinclusive identifications, the oedipal renunciation [of the possibility of being both sexes] inevitably elides into repudiation, splitting the difference, rather than truly recognizing it.

(ibid: 64)

But, things need not turn out like this if one can hang on to pre-Oedipal overinclusive identifications through the Oedipal process of becoming aware of gendered oppositions. Then it becomes possible to tolerate gender ambiguity and uncertainty, to recognize gender difference and the inevitable separation involved without resorting to defensive splitting and 'projecting the unwanted elements into the other' (ibid: 69). From the social side, the nature of the parental relationship, how gender differentiated it is and how well each parent has managed to hang on to their overinclusive identifications will also play a part in determining which outcome – splitting and defensive repudiation, or bridging and tolerant recognition – is the more likely.

Benjamin's approach therefore offers us the chance to show how biography and gender difference are related in a non-reductive, psychosocial fashion. It does so in a way that is capable of encompassing the messy reality of actually existing gender relations, the diversity of actual men and women's relationships to discourses of masculinity and femininity, and the underlying psychological processes. For Benjamin, a person's biography might be summarized as the result of having to separate from a particular mother or substitute (and her particular relationship to gender) and having to learn to share her with a particular father or substitute (and his particular relationship to gender). This takes place against a backdrop of managing the inevitable excitement and anxiety generated by loving attachments, both the desire for (object love) and the desire to be like (identificatory love). The timing and management of these universal (and irreducibly psychic) tasks will determine how any particular individual relates to questions of (socially produced) gender differences. On the question of the social origins of masculinities and femininities, Benjamin convincingly demonstrates the essential 'ambiguity of gender' (ibid: xvi), that gender has no essential content even though 'patriarchal culture has historically given certain contents to … gender categories' (ibid). So, there remains the possibility of changing the content of gender categories. However, she is clear that, because identification and a tendency towards splitting are unavoidable psychic processes, gender categorization itself is inevitable.

Conclusion

We have travelled a long way from Messerschmidt's account of 'doing gender'. But, throughout, we have tried to hold firmly in mind our objective: to understand better the psychosocial production of gendered subjectivity. We do not claim that this journey has resolved all the issues raised by a psychosocial approach to gender. But, we have the elements of an explanation: a way of thinking about the social dimension of gender through notions of power, discourse and subject positions and about the psychic dimension through the idea of investing in subject positions that avoid feeling vulnerable or powerless, often through defensive splitting and projection. We also have a sense of how these feelings of vulnerability and defences against them originally become tied to more or less polarized views of gender depending on one's early love relations with parental figures before and during the Oedipal moment.

For criminology, Benjamin's non-reductive approach to gender helps us grasp why it is that crime is so often a male activity (via the defensive repudiation of femininity by men in social situations where gender polarization is normal) but also why some women identify with certain crime options, despite the cultural proscriptions of appropriate feminine behaviour. Indeed, as we will show in relation to some of our cases, Benjamin's twin focus on the fixity and fluidity of identification – its constraining and enabling potential – not only helps explain why some people persistently victimize others, but also why it is that most of us do not commit crime most of the time, and why even those who do perpetrate unthinkable acts of harm are sometimes able to change with the help of significant others. We now have enough of a theoretical framework to begin to make some psychosocial headway with our fundamental question, namely, 'why did they do it?' With this in mind, we turn, in the next chapter, to the first of our case studies.

5

ANXIETY, DEFENSIVENESS AND THE FEAR OF CRIME

How scared are we?

(Guardian 2 headline, 13 February, 2003)

It's a panic for sure. But it's a calm panic

Since the [US] government issued its guidelines for families to prepare a 'disaster supply kit' in case of chemical, biological or nuclear attack ... the nation's DIY shops have become the epicentre for a wave of subdued but nonetheless palpable panic ... 'We've had three times the amount of business we normally have in a day,' said Bill Hart, at a hardware store in Bethesda, Maryland.

(Guardian, 14 February, 2003)

Public blind to fall in crime

The crime rate in England and Wales is falling again but most people do not believe it, according to the latest Home Office figures. The results of the British Crime Survey, published yesterday, suggested that crime fell by 9% during 2002 ... The BCS ... shows that the risk of becoming a victim of crime fell slightly, from 28% in 2001 to 26% in 2002 ... Nevertheless, the results show a sharp rise in the number who believe crime is getting worse in England and Wales: the proportion rose from 56% in 2001 to 71% last year.

(Guardian, 5 April, 2003)

Open any daily newspaper on almost any day and the chances are you will find an article related to 'fear of crime'. In the wake of 9/11, such articles are probably on the increase. Some, like the first *Guardian* article extracted above will try to assess, in the words of its headline, 'How scared are we?' Others, like the second extract, seem to recognize the issue of overreaction. Still others, like the final extract, draw attention to the disjunction between fear and risk – in this case to the fact that despite the falling crime rate in England and Wales increasing numbers of people 'believe crime is getting worse'. What these and other similar articles reveal, if nothing else, is that the issue of fear of crime is more complex than might appear at first sight. Our intention is to show how and why our present knowledge of the topic is so muddled, and what is necessary to clarify matters. The latter point involves showing how the adoption of a psychosocial approach to the topic manages to do this.

The articles featured above could be said to be operating at either the level of the individual – asking how scared we are or exploring the disjunction between an individual's risk and an individual's fear – or at the level of the social, i.e. as contributions to public discourses about fear of crime. With this distinction in mind, we aim to approach the topic both in terms of what is known about the fearful individual, and of what is known about the social meanings of fear of crime. Although this may look like a consideration of the matter moving from psychology to sociology, both sorts of approach have been sociological rather than psychological. This is because there has been little interest in the psychology of crime fears, only in the social demographic characteristics associated with the fearful individual. The real difference between the two sorts of approach then resides in whether fear is seen as arising from within individuals, albeit individuals who are only of interest as group members: young/old, male/female, black/white, etc., or is seen as a consequence of the way politicians or the media sensationalize particular problems.

Our concern will be to show how neither approach is adequate to the task of understanding fear of crime *fully*, that is, both its socially constructed meanings *and* how particular individuals relate to such meanings. To do so requires transcending this fearful individual/constructed discourse dichotomy psychosocially. This entails both a theoretical and a methodological shift: from fearing individuals as constellations of demographic characteristics to defended subjects; and from decontextualized survey-based information to biographical interviewing designed to illuminate the connections between defended subjectivity and investments in the fearful subject position within fear of crime discourses. We end with case-study material designed to exemplify our argument. In this instance, we examine the case of one highly fearful elderly man, showing how the threat of criminal victimization had become a repository for other anxieties pertaining to his life, and how the positioning of the interviewer functioned, intersubjectively, to inhibit this elderly man's capacity to surmount, however temporarily, his identification with the position of the crime-fearing subject.

What do we know about the fearful individual?

Although there has been a great deal of research into fear of crime – Hale (1996) refers to the presence of over 200 reports, and a recent online search dredged up 837 entries – surprisingly little can be said conclusively about fear of crime.

(Ditton and Farrall, 2000: xxi)

Ditton (2000) also suggests that the field is riddled with contradictory findings. Threading through this morass of inconclusive contradictions is what has been called the 'fear–risk paradox' (Hollway and Jefferson, 2000: 12), namely, the tendency for fear and risk (of criminal victimization) to be inversely related. The most at risk group, young men, tend to be least fearful; whilst women, especially older women, tend to be more fearful than men but less at risk. From the first British Crime Survey (Hough and Mayhew, 1983) onwards, this finding has been 'discovered with monotonous regularity' (Gilchrist et al., 1998), thus contributing to, if not actually creating, the common stereotype of the old woman too fearful to go out after dark. Given these findings, to the extent that we can conclude anything at all about who is most likely to be fearful of crime, the answer is that the most fearful individuals are those least at risk of becoming victims of crime. How can we explain this paradoxical, apparently irrational, finding?

A start can be made by looking at the way in which this knowledge was produced, namely, by aggregating the answers given by survey respondents to a single, standard question: 'how safe do you or would you feel being out alone in your neighbourhood at night?' (Ditton and Farrall, 2000: xix), with potential responses confined to 'very safe', 'fairly safe', 'a bit unsafe' or 'very unsafe'. Rather than start with a theoretically informed definition of what fear of crime might be before proceeding to measure it, in producing this standard question, crime-survey researchers clearly assumed this was unproblematic. As a result, what exactly was being measured is anybody's guess, as various critics have implicitly recognized. Ditton and Farrall, for example, have this to say about the question:

> Kenneth Ferraro and Randy LaGrange [1987] ... criticize it (rightly in our opinion) for failing to mention the word 'crime', for relying upon a vague geographical reference, for asking about something they may do very rarely, and for mixing the hypothetical with the real. In addition, we would add that the use of the word 'how' at the start of the question is leading in the extreme.

> (ibid)

Hollway and Jefferson (2000: 8–9) are similarly scathing about the question, suggesting that this scenario probably means different things to different people, assumes a consistency to feelings of fear and, in conjuring up a generalized threat, not specific fears, may 'be eliciting more about general anxiety than the "fear of crime"'.

In order to demonstrate more generally the symbiotic relationship between survey questions and the knowledge produced, some researchers have tried asking different questions, changing the question order, or even asking the same question more than once in the interview. Each change has produced different results. For example:

> One well-known piece of American research showed that if you ask people '*which* of these is the most important problem facing this country at present?' and then show them a short list which includes 'crime' as a possibility, 35% will pick crime as the most important problem. But if you ask them, as they did, the open question, '*what* do you think is the most important problem facing this country at present?', and *don't* give them a list to choose from, only 15% will

suggest crime. So, 60% of the apparent 'importance' of crime as a problem is created by the way the question is asked.

(Ditton, 2000, emphasis in original)

The underlying problem clearly rests with the nature of survey-research interviews and their Likert scale responses. As a methodology for studying something as complex as fear of crime, it is simply inadequate to the task. Basically, this is because respondents' answers are thoroughly decontextualized: their meanings in relation to either the interview itself or the life world of the interviewee are unsought; their subsequent coding renders them even more abstract. With no knowledge of the situated meanings of the responses being coded and with the coding process adding a new layer of artificiality, the aggregated data, suitably broken down by age, sex, race, area, etc., is then presented as a real world picture of who is and who is not fearful of crime. Small wonder that the results of such research are so inconclusive, contradictory and paradoxical. As Josselson (1995: 32) neatly put it: 'when we aggregate people, treating diversity as error variable, in search of what is common to all, we often learn about what is true of no one in particular'.

If survey-based methodology is responsible for the extraordinarily muddled findings about the fear of crime, perhaps a better starting point would be an attempt to define 'fear of crime' *theoretically*? In attempting to do so, we come up against Ditton's (2000) provocative statement that 'fear of crime doesn't exist'. This is not intended to mean that nobody is worried about crime; rather, it is a short-hand way of saying that the *meaning* of fear of crime 'doesn't exist' at the individual level. Because meaning is established at the social not the individual level, we must attend first to the *social* origins of the term. So, if we wish to understand what fear of crime is, we shall need to shift to what is known about the topic at the social level: the social construction of discourses relating to fear of crime.

What do we know about the social construction of fear of crime?

The fear of crime debate within criminology is dominated by the attempt to produce more accurate measurements of the numbers of fearful individuals. The literature on the social construction of fear is broader, less focussed exclusively on crime and criminal victimization. Law and order is an issue, but as part of broader processes of politics and change. Examples of such approaches can be found across a wide spectrum of sociological work. We focus on three distinct but related such approaches: Zygmunt Bauman's thesis on the insecurities of postmodernity; the work on moral panics; and Murray Lee's exploration of the discursive origins of the current debate about fear of crime.

Bauman on the insecurities of postmodernity

Bauman argues, broadly, that today individual freedom is evaluated more highly than collective economic security and this produces widespread fear and anxiety:

> [W]hether or not Sigmund Freud was right in suggesting that the trading off of a considerable part of personal liberty for some measure of collectively guaranteed security was the main cause of psychical afflictions and sufferings, unease and anxiety in the 'classic' period of modern civilization – today, in the late or postmodern stage of modernity, it is the opposite tendency, the inclination to trade off a lot of security in exchange for removing more and more constraints cramping the exercise of free choice, which generates the sentiments which seek their outlet (or are being channelled) in the concerns with law and order.
>
> (Bauman, 2000: 213)

Bauman's argument is that the trade-off between economic security and the desire for free choice, in terms of employment and cultures of consumption, has given rise to pervasive fears and anxieties that find sanctuary in the authoritative interpretation of social ills, most notably, the demand for greater law and order. Bauman goes on to argue that for many of us the sanctuary of our homes – conceived as a kind of 'body-safe extension ... has become the passkey to all doors which must be locked up and sealed' as we find ourselves bereft of safety, security and certainty (ibid).

Work on moral panics

Stan Cohen famously started his classic book *Folk Devils and Moral Panics* (1972) with a definition of a moral panic. The idea of societies undergoing profound changes being prone, periodically, to overreact to 'old' threats as if they were new and unprecedented, to scapegoat a few to protect threatened ways of life and to call for firm measures, has become, now, a core sociological concept. Hall et al. went on to develop the idea in their book *Policing the Crisis* (1978), by suggesting that moral panics were part of the political scene when governments were suffering a 'crisis of hegemony' (unable to rule through the routine production of consent). Later, Pearson was to use the notion in his book, *Hooligan: A History of Respectable Fears* (1983), to show how moral panics about the 'hooligan' were a regular feature of the social landscape because of the way nostalgia for the 'good old days' vitiated past wrongs and relocated them in certain kinds of contemporary youth.

In each of these examples – and countless other works too numerous to mention – there is a notion of overreaction to an imagined threat of some kind, and a sense that the threat (or 'folk devil') being responded to is being used as a scapegoat for some other issue. Some level of social flux plus the existence of relatively powerless groups who are available for scapegoating, and threatened groups who have sufficient power successfully to label others are all prerequisites. From this baseline, fear of crime can be understood as a specific variant of this prototype moral panic.

Lee on the discursive origins of fear of crime

Lee's discursive understanding of the origins of fear of crime is an attempt to trace, specifically, 'The genesis of "fear of crime"' (2001). In a cogently argued piece, Lee concludes that fear of crime, or what he calls, 'a self-sustaining *"fear of crime" feed-back loop'*, is a product of the politics of law and order in the USA since the 1960s.

> [T]he constitutive discursive elements of fear of crime's genealogy could be listed as – although not exclusive to – the following: the increasing sophistica-tion of statistical inquiry; criminological concern with new forms of crime statistics; the emergence of victim surveys; rising rates of recorded crime in the USA and new attempts to govern this; racialized concerns about 'black rioting'; a particular form of populist political discourse; and a historical moment where the conditions of possibility were such that these seemingly diffuse discourses could converge – the debating and passing of *The Omnibus Crime Control and Safe Streets Act 1968*. All the sites of power/knowledge and the discursive arrangements required to set in train a self-sustaining *'fear of crime' feedback loop* fell into place in the USA at this point in its history, and 'fear of crime' emerged as a legitimate governmental and disciplinary object of calculation, inquiry and regulation.
>
> (ibid: 480, emphases in original)

Lee goes on to say what he means by the term *'"fear of crime" feedback loop'*:

> By *'fear of crime' feedback loop*, I mean, inter alia, that the constituent elements I have listed above operate symbiotically to produce and intensify crime fear and the research related to it; that research into victims produces and maintains the criminological concept of 'fear of crime' quantitatively and discursively; that this information operates to identify fear as a legitimate object of governance or governmental regulation; that the techniques of regulation imagine partic-ular types of citizens – *fearing subjects*; that these attempts to govern 'fear of crime' actually inform the citizenry that they are indeed fearful; that this sen-sitizes the citizenry to 'fear of crime'; that the law and order lobby and pop-ulist politicians use this supposed fearing population to justify a tougher approach on crime, a point on which they grandstand, and in doing so sensi-tize citizens to fear once again; and that this spurs more research into 'fear of crime' and so on.
>
> (ibid: 480–1, emphases in original)

More brusquely, Ditton and Farrall (2000: xv) suggest that 'what we now rather blandly refer to as fear of crime began life as the "fear of blacks"' and, slightly more extensively, that:

> '[P]ublic alarm' about crime emerged, via the manipulation of the Nixonian silent majority, from right-wing concern about the extension of rights to the poor and the black. Indeed ... one of the very first academic essays on the subject – Frank Furstenberg [1971] comments, 'fear of crime is the symptom of the silent majority's lashing back'.
>
> (ibid: xvi)

Lee and Ditton and Farrall acknowledge the importance to their work of a book by Harris (1969) that details the 'senatorial shenanigans' (ibid: xv) preceding the passage of the *Omnibus Crime Control and Safe Streets Act*. Ditton and Farrall (ibid: xvi) end their overview of work on the topic by linking the social and the individual levels. It is a fitting endpoint for us, too: 'In sum, gradually over that 30-year period, general – if bigoted – societal concern about crime has been transmuted into a personal problem of individual vulnerability' (ibid: xvi).

If we want to understand fear of crime, the sociological work briefly glossed here offers important pointers to its social and political dimensions. It is in and around issues such as these that offer the essential social starting point for criminological work on fear of crime. But what this work fails to do is to discuss which particular individuals are vulnerable to the new insecurities consequent upon the transformations of post- or late-modernity, are susceptible to the blandishments of a moral panic, or are likely to become invested in the predominant discourse about fear of crime. The discourse of fear of crime may produce or make possible 'fearing subjects' as Lee suggests, but he cannot explain why some people become 'fearing subjects' – at least some of the time – and others do not; why it is, for example, as Ditton et al. (1999) argue elsewhere, many people are more angry about crime than afraid; and why it is that the conventional social discriminators of age, class and risk of victimization largely fail to predict which kinds of emotional reactions people are likely to express.

Approaching fear of crime psychosocially

We need, then, to bring the feeling individual back in, but without losing sight of this understanding of fear of crime's social origins. In other words, we need to understand the relationship between individuals, with their unique biographies and what Lee calls the '"fear of crime" feedback loop'. How might this new knowledge be produced? We have already established the inadequacies of the survey-based methodology to do so. What are the alternatives? Broadly speaking, those wishing to explore the meanings people attach to their experiences in a properly contextualized fashion, have turned to qualitative research. Here, the in-depth or semi-structured face-to-face interview is usually the method of choice. For example, feminist critics of early work on fear of crime, who thought women's experiences of sexual harassment or rape were not properly taken into account (Junger, 1987; Riger et al., 1978; Stanko, 1990), often used such interviews to ask women (and men in some cases) about their fears (Gilchrist et al., 1998; Stanko, 1990).

However, despite a lot of work trying to produce an interview instrument adequate to the task of capturing people's experiences and the meanings these held for them (Maynard and Purvis, 1994; Mishler, 1986), the qualitative research interview remained deficient in several respects. It continued to assume that the interviewer's questions meant the same thing to the interviewee as they did to the interviewer asking them, and vice versa, i.e. that both shared a common understanding of the words used. It also assumed that interviewees knew themselves well enough to be the faithful chroniclers of their own experiences and that interviewers knew themselves well enough to understand what was being said. In other words, qualitative researchers tended to operate with the same assumptions about subjectivity as survey researchers. Subjects were rational unitary beings, transparent to themselves and able to be transparent to another when given a chance to tell their stories.

But, as we have been arguing throughout this book, subjects are not rational unitary beings with full self-knowledge, but psychosocial subjects with a split consciousness, constantly unconsciously defending themselves against anxiety. This unconscious defensive activity affects what and how anything is remembered, with painful or threatening events being either forgotten or recalled in a safely modified fashion; it also affects how such memories are communicated to any interviewer, given that the context of the interview may be more or less threatening. At both stages, the act of remembering and the act of communication, meaning is rarely straightforward – and never wholly transparent. The interviewer too is a defended subject, and so the same applies: the meanings – of the questions asked and how answers are understood – will also be affected by the interviewer's dynamic unconscious with its own 'logic' of defensive investments. What are the implications of this version of subjectivity for the research interview? Two things seem central: the importance of trying to understand something of a person's whole biography in order better to understand how any remembered part might best be made sense of; and the importance of the psychoanalytic idea of free associations as a way of trying to glimpse what might lie behind communicated meanings.

The biographical-interpretative method and the importance of gestalt

The biographical-interpretative method was first developed by German sociologists producing accounts of the lives of holocaust survivors and Nazi soldiers (Rosenthal, 1993; Rosenthal and Bar-On, 1992; Schutze, 1992). It is a disarmingly simple method. It starts with a simple invitation to respondents: 'please, tell me your life-story' (Rosenthal, 1990). This open invitation allows the respondent to start where they wish and to fashion their story (or stories, since lives usually consist of multiple accounts) as they wish. The importance of this attempt to elicit stories is that life-stories refer to things that have actually happened to people. While these are rarely the whole story, the way that people tell their stories – remembering particular details, drawing particular conclusions, etc. – will be revealing (more so than the teller realizes), once we know how to 'read' them. Once the initial story has been told, the interviewer, who has listened attentively and taken notes, follows up the emergent themes – in their narrated order – using the respondent's own words and phrases. This invitation to elaborate on themes is effectively an invitation to tell further stories. No attempt is made to evaluate or judge the material, nor to get respondents to explain themselves. Thus 'why' questions, often the staple of semi-structured interviews, are eschewed. This has the advantage of ensuring people stick to their revealing stories and avoids the premature closure, and intellectualizations, which explanations tend to promote.

This, in essence, is the way the biographical-interpretative method produces the data that, when analysed and written up, becomes someone's life-story. This is not the place to appraise the analytic procedure of 'objective hermeneutics' preferred by the German biographers, except to refer the reader to other sources (Flick, 1998; Oevermann et al., 1987; Wengraf, 2001) and say that the whole process is guided by the theoretical idea that people's lives, however apparently disjointed and contra-dictory, have a 'gestalt': a whole that is greater than the sum of its parts. Wertheimer, the founder of gestalt psychology, thought that it was impossible to 'achieve an understanding of structured totals by starting with the ingredient parts which enter into them' and that 'parts are defined by their relation to the system as a whole in which they are functioning' (cited in Murphy and Kovach, 1972: 258). Following this gestalt principle, and assuming the interviewer has managed to elicit appropriate sto-ries and not destroyed them by clumsy intrusions, the analytical task is to reveal the whole that enables sense to be made of the various parts. It is this principle of the importance of the whole that makes decontextualized data – from the Lickert-scale tick-box response to the coded themes abstracted from their texts of origin – so prob-lematic for us. Whole lives, whole texts, have to be the starting point, not abstracted parts – a point we observe in the subsequent chapters of this book.

Interpreting the gestalt: the importance of free associations

The German biographical-interpretative tradition remained agnostic about the value of psychoanalytic concepts, despite the fact that their material, not surpris-ingly, contained examples of 'defended' story-telling (Gadd, 2004a). Schutze, for example, revealed that elicited accounts such as those of Nazi soldiers would be highly defensive ones, given the difficult and painful subject-matter. This needed a methodological strategy to uncover 'faded-out memories and delayed recollections of emotionally or morally disturbing war experiences' (Schutze, 1992: 347). As we have seen, this strategy was guided by the principle of gestalt. Given our under-standing of the role of unconscious defences against anxiety in people's lives, and hence in the stories they tell, we needed to give the gestalt principle a central role in producing and analysing data.

One of the methods Freud used to understand unconscious defensive activity was 'free association'. This involved him allowing the patient to 'choose the subject of the day's work' in order that he could 'start out from whatever surface [the patient's] unconscious happens to be presenting to his notice at the moment' (quoted in Kerr, 1994: 98). This starting point is remarkably similar to the gestalt-inspired invitation to 'please, tell me your life-story'. The difference is that by asking the patient to say whatever comes to mind, the psychoanalyst assumes that the narrative thus elicited is structured by unconscious dynamics; that is, the 'logic' is emotionally motivated rather than rationally intended like the logic guiding consciousness. Once this unconscious activity is better understood, and its relationship to the conscious self and behaviour, one can begin to make sense of the 'whole' person in all of their contradictoriness: how what we say is so often at odds with what we do; how our rational self co-exists with a self capable of all kinds of apparently irrational behaviour.

So, the key to a person's gestalt, if one assumes a defended subject, is to be found in expressions of anxiety and the unconscious defences and identity investments these give rise to. And the free associations made in interviewees' narratives provide the key to accessing these expressions of anxiety. This route to a person's gestalt has the added advantage that it is alert to a story's incoherences (e.g. its contradictions, elisions, avoidances), in a way that many more conventional approaches are not.

Hollway and Jefferson (2000) used just such a method, the biographical-interpretative method modified by free-association narrative interviewing, in a research project investigating the fear of crime of men and women, young, middle-aged and old, on two estates in a northern English city. The initial invitation to respondents to tell their life-story was modified to reflect the core theoretical concerns of the project; so respondents were invited to tell the interviewer about their experiences of crime, risk, safety and anxiety with follow-up invitations shadowing the associations they had made. Hollway and Jefferson's argument, broadly, is that the already anxious are most likely to become the highly fearful subjects of fear of crime discourse (thus helping to explain the fear–risk paradox). In a paper attempting to explain why fear of crime was such a powerful vehicle in the contemporary period, Hollway and Jefferson (1997: 260) argued that because the fear of crime discourse produces risks that are (potentially) knowable, actionable and controllable, this makes it a 'powerful modernist tool in the quest for order, in contrast to Beck's unknowable risks of late modernity'. They went on to show how, at the level of the anxious individual, crime, and the potential for victimization associated with it, 'could actually serve unconsciously as a relatively reassuring site for displaced anxieties which otherwise would be too threatening to cope with' (ibid: 264). This, then, was a psychosocial account of fear of crime: what fear of crime meant as a socio-political discourse of late modernity; for whom it might provide a suitable identity investment. To render all this more concrete, we end with a case study from Hollway and Jefferson's project, together with some reflections on how both the interviewee's biographically laden anxieties and the interviewer's inability to identify wholly with them, colluded to produce an unshakeably fearful subject.

Anxiety and fear of crime: a psychosocial case study of Hassan

Hassan was a 68-year-old man who lived alone. An immigrant to Britain in the 1940s, he remained single until his forties, then had a marriage arranged with a much younger woman who joined him in England, with whom he raised five children in quick succession. These were happy years; everything was 'smashing'. Hassan was fulfilled as husband, father and provider – and unafraid. Then his wife listened to her communist brother and challenged Hassan's authority, eventually leaving, taking the children. Later Hassan was persuaded to sign over his half of the house to his wife and children, leaving him with nothing. Soon after, Hassan's health gave out. He was forced to retire early from his job as a nursing assistant and 'now' spends his days in considerable pain.

'Now' – which seemed to refer generally to his years as a divorced, retired man, living on the estate – everything was 'terrible'. Hassan felt frightened to go out at all, especially after dark – and rarely did except to pray during Ramadan.

> I mean I don't go out at night at all. I'm frightened if I go out, if somebody pinch me, or hit me, or – and I don't open the door to nobody. I'm frightened to death. I wish the government do something about it.

Even at home, where he claimed to feel safest, Hassan jumped when the fridge made a noise and found watching television scary, especially because of the stories of old people getting killed (unable to read English he was spared lurid press accounts of crime). Yet despite his repetitive talk of all this 'pinching and killing' frightening him and all the elderly 'to death' Hassan had few experiences of criminal victimization. The examples he could recount included: an experience of racially abusive behaviour (two men calling him a 'black bastard' from their car window and throwing eggs and bottles at him when he was returning from the mosque one evening) and the mischief-making of local children (ill-behaved kids ringing his doorbell and running away, and on one occasion, throwing a stone at his window and cracking it). 'Now' Hassan is reluctant to go on holiday through fear of being burgled and often feels fearful for his life – 'I don't like somebody to kill me if they hate me' – even though, since the racial harassment, his nephew and a friend drive him to the mosque.

Judged against either his present experience of life in a fairly protected corner of the estate in purpose-built accommodation for the elderly, or his 'smashing' past experience as a happy family man and worker, Hassan's present fears could, from a rationalistic, risk-based perspective, be construed as excessive. Coupled with his appraisal that the crime situation was getting 'worse' and merited immediate government intervention, his fears are perhaps better conceived as quite heavily invested, the 'upset' of the racial harassment notwithstanding. Clues as to why this might be so could be found both in Hassan's account of his marriage breaking down and the fact that his vehement tirade against crime was part of a general tirade against the ills of modernity, including sexual permissiveness and drugs. He sometimes interjected that life was better in Saudi Arabia, where people did not steal from each other because they were afraid of having their hands cut off. A traditional, conservative, religious man, Hassan's marriage broke down when his wife challenged his traditional patriarchal right to order her life. A younger woman who picked up the language quicker than him, she chose modern independence over traditional religious and patriarchal authority – as did their children (to the extent that they were in a position to choose freely) in going with her. The loss of all he ever worked for (his years as a single man seem to have been spent largely saving and preparing for his future marriage and family: he bought and fully furnished a house, 'everything new', to the wide-eyed bemusement of his young wife) left him disappointed, with only a painful old age ahead. His family – now all living in London – like many of those living in his community, were too busy to make much time for him: 'nobody bother … nobody wants to know you'. Hassan's devout and fatalistic religious Muslim beliefs had helped him come to terms with some of these worries. Yet, there was ample evidence in his account that his underlying anxieties had not been eradicated. The more Hassan insisted otherwise the more it became clear that he could not 'forget' the emotional pain of his separation from his family:

> I left the house, I left the wife, I left the kids. That make me a bit worried at first, you know. But I forgot about it. Tell you true. I forgot about – it's no good to kill myself about that, you know. It happened, it happened, it finished … And from that – I forgot about everything, you know what I mean? The kids ring me up, the girls are talking to me and that's it. And I forgot about everything …

The strength of Hassan's investment in the position of the fearful subject is indicative, we suggest, of how deep was his loss and how unbearable it felt: unbearable enough to bring to mind the notion that it might have killed him, and dominant enough to need to be consciously driven from memory (witness the constant reminder that he 'forgot about' it all). Unsurprisingly, then, the memories refused to go away. As Hassan surmised, late on in his second interview, he would sometimes find himself talking to himself about the very things he wanted to forget:

> Sometime[s] I – I forgot the things that past, you know, but sometime it there … I used to talk to myself sometime[s]. I say, 'Well I've been 49 years, and I bought the house … and I lost everything … [and am] now lonely' and things like that … Always I want to forgot things like that, you know? [T]: Mmm] But sometime[s] you can't help it, you know what I mean? Is a bit hard for me, you know what I mean? It's a bit hard. When I'm lonely now or … when my health is not really well, you know?

Might Hassan's fear of someone killing him because of hate, which had become consciously associated with racially motivated harassment, also be unconsciously connected to the inevitable turmoil of being spurned by a loved one and all the hate, self-hate, denial and regret that can entail? Likewise, Hassan's repetitive 'you know' that punctuates the passage above can perhaps be read as an implicit request for some recognition of the many difficulties that made up his life: his losses, his loneliness, his poor health. His plaintive 'is a bit hard', also repeated, seemed to ask for an acknowledgement that was not forthcoming from the interviewer. One important reason for the interviewer's [TJ] reticence had to do with the prescriptions of the Free Association Narrative Interview method: to be non-intrusive in the interests of eliciting the respondent's story in their own words. However, there was probably more to it than that, given that, in any interview situation, the interviewer with his or her own pre-existing prejudices, concerns, anxieties and investments is also positioning the interviewee, consciously and unconsciously, as well as being positioned by him or her.

In Hassan's case, my [TJ] first conscious impressions were of a rather anxious man (needing to check me out from an upstairs window before letting me in), in poor health (he walked with a stick). Inside, his house was full of stereotypically feminine touches: it was neat and tidy; he served me tea in dainty teacups; evidence of his sewing was strewn around. As the interview progressed, it was hard not to feel sorry for this lonely, ageing man in poor health, often in physical pain and with a store-house of painful emotional memories, growing old far from home and without even the solace of the written word, for the most part. On the other hand, he was quite a difficult interviewee whose repetitive complaints had a slightly self-pitying tone. This, combined with an apparently inordinate fear of everyday occurrences like untoward household noises and badly behaved kids, made him seem, at times, stereotypically weak and effeminate, notwithstanding the fact that he was an ageing man whose physical powers were indeed weakening.

In addition, Hassan's experiences of racist abuse were completely beyond my direct personal experience, even though as an academic who had spent a long time research-ing and writing about racism I had had a lot of indirect experience of it. It may have been the case, therefore, that although, consciously, I identified with him and his very difficult life, I may have been less well-equipped, unconsciously, to fully identify with what he was feeling. What for him, from a culture with long experience of racial vic-timization, must have felt generally frightening – having eggs and bottles thrown at him, for example – perhaps sounded to my less identified unconscious like a nasty but fairly isolated example (in his case) of racial violence and thus an inadequate basis for his general fearfulness of crime. Similarly, although I am consciously aware of the importance of cultural differences in story-telling, and the role these may have played in the production of what I saw then as his self-pitying tone, I may well have been less attuned at an unconscious level. In other words, although it is possible, in general, con-sciously, to identify across very different positionings in discourses of gender and race, particular situations and circumstances may well trigger defensively motivated uncon-scious responses. With my own conscious investments in a strong and stoical mas-culinity, for example, it may well have been the case that the manner of Hassan's story-telling made it difficult – at that time – to fully identify with Hassan's fearfulness and his weak, somewhat self-pitying effeminacy. Moreover, this unconscious failure to fully identify with Hassan had considerable discursive support. Where Afro-Caribbean males have to contend with a discursive stereotype of themselves as tough, macho and sexy, the discursive construct of the Asian male (at least until comparatively recently) was almost the reverse (plus a notion of deviousness). To the extent that Hassan's behaviour chimed with discursive stereotypes and, perhaps, with my lingering uncon-scious identification with them, it becomes possible to read Hassan's apparently exces-sive identification with the fearful subject of the fear of crime discourse as a contingent co-production of both interviewer and interviewee.

Conclusion

In essence, then, what we are arguing is that subject positions are negotiated in relation to the individual's biography and attendant anxieties, the discursive fields available to the individual (often constrained by their class, ethnicity and gender), and intersubjectively through the responses of others. Whether someone invests in the position of the fearful subject preoccupied with the ever-growing threat of victimization depends in part on how available that position is to him or her. This availability is partly a consequence of how social researchers pose and follow up questions as well as how the individual feels about crime. Of course, sometimes people's feelings about crime – or other matters – are so strong or entrenched that it matters little how they are asked about them. Hence, some people, probably a minority, will say they feel fearful about crime no matter how the question is posed or who is doing the asking. That said, most people are not completely fixed into the subject positions they occupy and thus – as we will show in subsequent chapters – can be enabled to occupy other positions if their anxieties can be sufficiently contained through identification with and recognition by another person. This, it appears, was not something the interviewer managed to do for Hassan, partly because of the injunctions of the FANI method and partly because of the interviewer's own positionings at that time. This reduced the possibilities for Hassan to step outside the position of the crime-fearing subject and thus, perhaps, become more conscious of his ulterior motives for being so afraid.

Our approach is consistent with Lee's and Ditton and Farrall's arguments that the fear of crime has only become an issue since there has been a widely available public (or social) discourse about fear of crime; an argument that is not the same as suggesting that people are not fearful of crime. What we add to this approach is the recommendation that criminologists should re-include the individual, but without simply returning to the traditional individualist approach underpinning most of the research on this topic. This means not seeking out the fearful individual but attending to the question of why some individuals and not others come to be heavily invested in the fear of crime discourse. Risk levels are not able to account for this differential investment, but theoretically attuned case analyses, like the one we have presented above, can. Through the case of Hassan we have shown how anxiety is crucial to understanding the appeal of the fear of crime, albeit mixed in its psychological benefits. That is to say, for the highly anxious, fear of crime is one discourse (amongst many) which can provide a ready vehicle for feelings that are difficult to face up to simply because within this discourse crime is depicted as knowable, actionable and controllable. This helps us explain why it is that law and order, as Bauman highlights, has become one of the primary outlets through which postmodern insecurities are worked through – and hence why talking tough about crime currently appears to politicians so critical to their electability. It also – to continue the theoretical engagement with Bauman – helps explain why the home, the place in which we invest so much of ourselves, can often be imagined as a kind of 'body-safe extension', the infiltration of which by strangers, irrespective of whether they take anything of value, seems so threatening to our sense of bodily integrity. This is why Kearon and Leach – in an analysis informed by the work of the psychoanalyst Winnicott – liken burglary to an 'invasion of the "body snatchers"':

> [T]the significance of the invasion is problematized by the embodied nature of the relationship to home and things: by their very nature, familiar objects are conceived of and lived as extensions of the body … things that are so close to the body … that they feel amputated by burglary … The loss of objects, crucially, is much more than the loss of part of a cognitive, discursive identity … Objects are valuable because they are rich with sensory and memory-laden experience, as well as representing identity… Thus the experience of loss is often experienced retrospectively in burglary (people do not always know what something means until it is gone) and this loss can be of apparently unsentimental items.
>
> (Kearon and Leach, 2000: 467)

Thinking again about Hassan, this may be one further reason why he was so afraid of crime. Having lost the family home in which he invested so much, not just financially but also emotionally in terms of his dreams and expectations, for him 'pinching and killing' had become synonymous: invoking a potential loss of self, the psychical amputation of the few remaining remnants of all he had ever hoped and striven for.

6

FEMINISM, AMBIVALENCE AND DATE RAPE

Traditionally, rape – non-consensual sexual intercourse – is regarded as a rare event committed by an abnormal or psychopathic stranger. A violent sexual attack by an unknown male leaping out from the bushes captures the stereotype. Today, rape is likely to be seen as less rare, commonplace even, often committed by known, 'normal' men, and able to take a variety of forms, including that associated with the consensual activity of dating. In terms of explaining the causes of rape there has been a shift from the traditional individualistic focus – identifying the psychological/behavioural profiles of convicted rapists and their differences from normal men – to a focus on the social factors that encourage the denigration of women and thus render them 'rapeable' objects. The purpose of this chapter is to chart this shift, made possible by contemporary feminism, and detail its advantages over the traditional understanding, but also its limitations: what it has difficulty explaining on account of its 'oversocial' approach. Addressing these limitations through a case study of date rape will conclude the chapter.

Feminism and rape

Feminism first noticed and made visible the maleness of the perpetrators of certain violent acts such as domestic violence and rape. This noticing was intimately connected with feminist activism on behalf of victimized women. In 1971, Erin Pizzey helped found the UK women's refuge movement (which established safe houses for women victims of domestic violence and their children). She then went on in 1974 to write a book on the same topic. In the US, Susan Griffin's famous 'Ramparts' article (1971) and Susan Brownmiller's path-breaking classic *Against Our Will* ([1975] 1976) accompanied the movement to establish Rape Crisis Centres. Thereafter, feminists started to redefine other activities – such as pornography and sexual harassment – as acts of violence against women: in the former case, famously seeing porn as the 'theory' for which rape was the 'practice' (Morgan, 1982).

What this new feminist approach to rape did, most comprehensively in Brownmiller ([1975] 1976), was to draw attention to:

- the maleness of rape;
- the large number of unreported rapes;
- rape by troops during wartime;
- the narrowness of the legal definition, e.g. rape only being possible outside of marriage (eventually rectified in Britain in 1991 as a result of feminist campaigning);
- the double trauma of rape victims: first attacked by the rapist and then handled insensitively by a patriarchal legal system; and
- date rape.

In sum: feminists drew attention to the widespread nature of rape, to its acceptability (to the extent that it was often not taken seriously unless it conformed to the 'stranger rapist' stereotype) and hence to its normality. Brownmiller, in probably the most influential of radical-feminist redefinitions, even went as far as to indict *'all men'*: 'Rape ... is nothing more or less than a conscious process of intimidation by which *all men* keep *all women* in a state of fear' ([1975] 1976: 15, emphases in original). From being a problem implicating a few psychopathic men, rape was thus transformed into a social problem implicating all men – a solution that bears all the hallmarks of a (too) simple inversion. Interestingly, having apparently shifted the debate to the social level, Brownmiller went on to argue that men rape because they possess a penis and superior physical strength, an explanation couched in terms of individual biology. More commonly, however, feminists have tended to explain the 'normality' of rape in terms of 'patriarchy' (strictly speaking, an unequal social system dominated by the father but more generally understood as an unequal social system which advantages men, economically, politically and socially) and the accompanying sexist culture that systematically privileges masculinity over femininity and allows men to behave in possessive, domineering and objectifying ways towards women (Dworkin, 1988; MacKinnon, 1987; Roberts, 1989; Scully, 1990).

The advantages of such an approach over the traditional pathologizing one should, we hope, be obvious:

- it refocussed attention on 'normal' men;
- it drew attention to the various types of rape other than (the comparatively rare) stranger rape, including acquaintance rape; and
- it established a link between normal male sexuality (aggressive, competitive, phallic) and rape.

However, despite these considerable advantages, which over the years have had considerable practical effects in the way the authorities now handle the crime of rape, problems remain:

- The different types of rape, from brutal sadistic stranger rape to drunken date rape, are all given the same explanation: the 'baby' of difference, we might say, was run off with the 'bathwater' of similarity.
- Women are transformed into passive victims and are thus robbed of all agency.

- Overprediction. Despite the widespread nature of rape, the majority of men do not rape and the majority of women do not become rape victims. Estimates of women who have been raped vary from 1 in 6 in the US to 1 in 4 in England and Wales (Finney, 2006; Tjaden and Thoennes, 2006).
- The focus is purely on the violence of rape and not at all on its specifically sexual nature.

Post-(radical)-feminist approaches

The early radical-feminist approach probably now constitutes the starting point within criminology for thinking about rape. For some it is also the endpoint. However, we can cite various attempts to address the problems just noted.

Different types of rape

Stephen Box (1983: 162) distinguished five types of rape ('sadistic', 'anger', 'domination', 'seductive' and 'exploitation') and explained each type in terms of the relative importance of four factors: 'economic inequality', 'the utilization of techniques of neutralization', 'the law's "unwitting" encouragement' and 'acceptance of the "masculine mystique"'. This multi-factorial explanation suggested that for each different type of rape, a different combination of the four explanatory factors is needed. So, for example, the extreme brutality of 'sadistic rape' – rape where 'both sexuality and aggression become fused into a fury of violent, mutilating acts' (ibid: 127) – was explained largely in terms of 'the acceptance of the "masculine mystique"' – 'the offender's attachment to being "manly" and his location within the distributive system of social rewards' (ibid: 161). In other words, in relation to this type of rape economic inequality between the sexes is relatively unimportant, the law does not 'unwittingly' encourage nor are techniques of neutralization (rationalizing justifications or excuses) much in evidence. By contrast, Box's explanation for 'exploitation' rape – 'any type of sexual access gained by the male being able to take advantage of the female's vulnerability because she is dependent upon him for economic or social support' (ibid: 128) – was much more dependent on these latter three factors and only 'to a lesser extent, his mesmerization by the "masculine mystique"' (ibid: 161).

Box's typology remains an important attempt to hang on to the 'baby' of difference even if the figuring of a general notion of 'manliness' in 'each type of rape' is too reductive:

> each type of rape is primarily committed by men from that population who are relatively more attached and identified with notions of 'manliness' and feel the need to demonstrate this essentializing view of themselves whenever they experience some identity doubts or anxieties.

> (ibid: 161, emphases in original)

Moreover, Box's analysis was ultimately oversocial. For Box, 'rape is fundamentally a cultural expression, a means by which "stressed, anxiety-ridden, misogynist" men can assert their "cherished notions of masculinity"' (ibid: 161). Thus, despite this acknowledgment of psychic anxiety and different types of rape, cultural misogyny remains ultimately determinant. Hence, the criminal subject is still a relatively passive, unitary respondent to opportunity and sex-role conditioning. And the population at large is all too tidily divided into victims and villains, with little overlap or scope for ambiguity.

The passivity of female victims

Radical feminists dominated the early stages of the debates about sexuality and violence against women. More recently, new 'power' or 'post'-feminist voices have emerged, partly as a consequence of some of feminism's successes, and partly in response to what was regarded as a stifling and retrogressive 'political correctness' on US campuses. Kate Roiphe (1994) and Camille Paglia (1992) in particular took it upon themselves to combat what they saw as the new, campus-based political correctness on date rape, which they argued had extended the definition of rape to include verbal as well as physical coercion and any sex that was *felt by the victim to be violating*. They saw these developments as a retrogressive product of 'victim feminism', the new orthodoxy that, for them, robbed women of an active sexuality and of any responsibility for their own actions in dating scenarios (such as getting blind drunk), and failed to take sexuality (as opposed to male power) seriously.

This was an important attempt to open up the question of female agency in relation to sexuality. It also has parallels in other feminist debates (the role of 'choice' in the relations between career and motherhood, for example). However, both Roiphe and Paglia were based in the humanities and were not specifically addressing the weaknesses, from a social-science perspective, of 'victim feminism'. The result was that they ended up inverting their opponents' notion of subjectivity: from passive victim of male power to active, responsible agent whose destiny lay in their own choices. Simple inversions, as we said earlier, do not transcend a given position. The agent envisaged, in consequence, was still too rational, too unitary, especially in relation to something as emotionally difficult as dating.

Overprediction

The question of who is more or less likely to rape still tends to be answered, if at all, using traditional theorizing, albeit acknowledging feminism's case in this area. Ellis' social learning theory of rape is one of these. Ellis (1989: 12–13) suggests that rapists, like all of us, learn through imitation and intermittent reinforcement. He then argues for a social learning theory of rape that sees rape basically as a form of aggressive behaviour towards women learned through the imitation of real life or mass media 'rape scenes', their reinforcement through association (of sexuality and violence), the perpetuation of various 'rape myths', and the desensitizing effects of the constant viewing of sexual aggression: 'these four hypothesised effects may be called the *modelling effect*, the *sex-violence linkage* effect, the *"rape myth" effect*, and the *desensitisation effect*, respectively' (ibid: 13, emphases in original). His suggestion is that his theory, by focussing on the cultural traditions that link interpersonal aggression and sexuality, supplements the feminist accent on socio-economic and political exploitation.

Yet despite its attempt to take seriously the issue of overprediction, Ellis' thesis is still oversocial and, as with social learning theory generally, deterministic. As Ellis himself puts it, his analysis had 'roots in research ... which determined that repeated exposure to almost any type of stimulus tends to promote positive feelings toward it'. Any research tradition that produces such a plainly fallacious result is clearly in need of an overhaul. As Stan Cohen (2001) has demonstrated, exposure to other people's violence induces many different responses in us: identification with the perpetrators' aggression or the suffering of the victims; standing by, doing and feeling nothing; or, assuming a state of denial.

The question of sexuality

Although sexuality was acknowledged by Roiphe and Paglia, its complexity was not. Taking sexuality seriously, in all its complexity, demands a psychosocial account involving non-unitary, split subjects and unconscious processes. As we shall see, this is essential if we are to make sense of date rape.

Distinguishing between inner and outer worlds: the relation between vulnerability and power

Although there is very little literature on men talking about rape, what there is reads very differently from feminist accounts. Where feminists talk of *male power* – a reference to men's social power over women, generally, in a male-dominated world – men talking of times when they have raped tend to talk of their felt sense of inadequacy or vulnerability vis-à-vis women. For example, 'Jim', a 36-year-old convicted rapist who had been imprisoned three times for sexual offences, said that 'women often made me feel inferior' (quoted in Levine and Koenig, 1983: 84). 'Jay', a 23-year-old file clerk who had not actually raped a woman but only felt like doing so, adds a further twist: 'A lot of times a woman knows that she's looking really good and she'll use that and flaunt it, and it makes me feel like she's laughing at me and I feel *degraded*' (quoted in Beneke, 1982: 42, emphasis in original). 'Jay' recognized that his feelings of inadequacy could turn into anger and then be used to reassert power over women: 'Just the fact that they can come up to me and just melt me and make me feel like a dummy makes me want revenge. They have power over me so I want power over them' (ibid: 44). Reading events from this point in the process might seem to reinforce the feminist notion that rape is a manifestation of male power. But, this reading misses the connection to feelings of inferiority and degradation and thus the difference between inner feelings (of vulnerability) and wider social patterns (that men are powerful) and, importantly, the painful conflict between the two 'worlds'.

Contradictory feelings and confusion

These contradictions, between how one is expected to feel and how one actually does feel, are painful partly because they are confusing. 'Rick', a 32-year-old man who resented the way women could lump together all men 'as oppressors and rapists', (ibid: 48) certainly found it so:

> You're torn between the precepts you as a man were raised with, that you're supposed to be dominant and a provider and be very deferential and respectful to women. If you're deferential to women it may be accepted graciously or you may get put down for it.
>
> (ibid: 47)

'Mike' thought similarly. He was a 30-year-old man 'seeing' a woman to whom he was very attracted, a feeling he thought was reciprocated even though she said she did not wish to be 'sexually involved'. During one of their dates, Mike and this woman were sharing a bed:

> She took my hand and said, 'I don't want to lead you on.' It was said in a way that confused me. I didn't take it as a sexual rejection. Then she was intensely affectionate with me. She started hugging me and kissing me intensely. I didn't quite know what was happening. I felt intensely passionate and I think she did, too.
>
> (ibid: 51)

However, in case it be thought that these contradictory feelings and the resulting confusions are restricted to men, an interview-based study (Phillips, 2000: 8) with young women reflecting on the relations between 'sexuality and domination' revealed that this is not the case: 'throughout their interviews, women spoke of confusion, of contradictory emotions, of not knowing what to think'. This study, by 'a feminist researcher, teacher and advocate' (ibid: ix), bravely (and uniquely, as far as we can tell) addressed the feminist shibboleth about rape, namely, 'no means no', from a starting position of agreement with the sentiment behind the (apparently simple) question addressed to men on the feminist-inspired lapel badge: 'What is it about "no" that confuses you?' After listening to women's '*own* answers to the question', Phillips was forced to concede that these were 'often multiple, murky, and dauntingly complex' (ibid: x; emphasis in original):

> [F]or many of the young women in this study, rape *is* about sex, *as well as* about violence. Often it involves coercion, manipulation, or threats, but falls short of physical aggression. Many women report saying yes when they want to say no, and saying no when they want to say yes or maybe. And some say nothing, even when they want a painful encounter to end.
>
> (ibid: 14, emphases in original)

In a sideswipe at those feminist voices that are afraid to confront this issue for fear that to admit complexity may end up blaming women for their own victimization,

Phillips (ibid: 10) insists on the 'need to carve out spaces in which we dare to talk about agency, confusion, power, desire and the murkiness of consent, without blaming women for their own violation.' We hope that this chapter will be seen as one of those spaces.

Contradictions and the limits of discourse

Some have addressed the issue of contradictory messages and confused feelings at a different social level, that of discourse. In an interesting analysis, Kitzinger and Frith (2001) suggest that the problem of mixed, contradictory messages between men and women will not be successfully addressed by urging women to 'just say no' more assertively. They point out that conversation analysis has revealed that refusals or saying 'no' are much harder to articulate than acceptances because of the implicit message of rejection they carry. However, Kitzinger and Frith go on to suggest that we make ourselves understood well enough by saying 'no' in other areas of life, i.e. by saying 'no' in a roundabout way and, therefore, the root of the problem is not male misunderstanding because women do not say 'no' clearly enough.

> We claim that both men and women have a sophisticated ability to convey and to comprehend refusals, including refusals which do not include the word 'no', and we suggest that male claims not to have 'understood' refusals which conform to culturally normative patterns can only be heard as self-interested justifications for coercive behaviour.
>
> (ibid: 168)

What starts out as interested in addressing contradictory messages and confused feelings ends up, once again, in a very definite place: no means no whether articulated directly or indirectly. Such certainty retains feminist credibility, but at the expense of the multiplicity, murkiness and 'daunting' complexity of the answers Phillips (2000) elicited from her interviewees. Put another way, the subject implied by Kitzinger and Frith's discursively based analysis of conversations is too 'knowing', too rational; s/he is without an inner world.

Linking inner and outer, contradictions and discourse, psychosocially

> [Y]ou sort of expect rejection, really, when you're out with the girl. And yet when she does reject you, it complicates it. It multiplies your feelings, and you take your anger out on her in that way. I'm most angry at myself for my own lacks. There's sex involved, of course, but I think it's brought on by the hostility.
>
> ('Jim' quoted in Levine and Koenig, 1983: 83)

'Jim' is the 36-year-old convicted rapist that we encountered earlier. This particular quotation of his seems to sum up all that we have been trying to say about date rape – if we know how to read it. But first a reminder of what we hoped to have established in Chapter 4, namely, that the elements of an adequate psychosocial explanation are: an 'outer' world comprising various social discourses – of masculinity and of sexuality, to cite the two of most relevance to date rape; an 'inner' world beset by nameless anxieties that will be unconsciously defended against in various ways, often by splitting off the 'bad' feelings and projecting them onto others; and, linking 'inner' and 'outer', a set of 'investments' – the adoption of particular subject positions in particular discourses because they provide some kind of satisfaction or protection. Applying this approach to 'Jim's' words, we can make some sense of his anguish and confusion.

He starts by expecting rejection. Read discursively, this is a version of 'nice girls don't' (at least on a first date). In other words, Jim expects his date to reject his sexual advances (which as a male are expected of him) otherwise she risks being labelled 'easy' or a 'slut'. However, when she does what Jim expects her to, 'it complicates it' because Jim has strong feelings about rejection: 'It multiplies your feelings.' We would say he is strongly invested in those discourses of masculinity and sexuality that, like Hollway's 'male sexual drive' discourse, indissolubly connect the two (Hollway, 1989). In other words, Jim's masculinity is bound up with sexual activity. Because of his investment in such a discourse, the feelings of rejection are particularly painful and these feelings make him angry ('I'm most angry at myself for my own lacks'). But, rather than deal with 'his own lacks', Jim unconsciously defends against this painful situation by splitting off the anger directed at himself (a realization that seems to come only after the event) and projecting these angry feelings on to his hapless date: 'you take your anger out on her'. When not confronted with a rejecting situation, Jim is able to face up to the real problem of his 'own lacks'. In other words, to quote from something he offers as a general explanation of his date rapes:

> I wouldn't take no for an answer. I think it had something to do with my acceptance of rejection. I had low self-esteem and not much self-confidence and when I was rejected for something I considered to be rightly mine, I became angry and I went ahead anyway. And this was the same in any situation, whether it was rape or something else.
>
> ('Jim' quoted in Levine and Koenig, 1983: 83)

'Low self-esteem' and a lack of 'self-confidence' make for anxiety in men surrounded by discourses of masculinity that demand the opposite. This raises the issue, posed by Messerschmidt (1994) in Chapter 4, of the legitimate resources available to build masculine esteem and confidence. Patently, 'Jim' lacked these. Hence he regarded sex with a woman, one area where he could hope to accomplish something to enhance his masculinity, as 'rightly mine'. When this 'right' was denied him, the blow to his already low self-esteem and confidence proved too anxiety-invoking. Anger is a common form of defence to cope with such anxieties. As Jim explained this anxiety-induced anger found expression in sex ('There's sex involved, of course'), thus ensuring that the sex was intertwined with a more general sense of 'hostility'. At this point, the feminist understanding that says rape is about power, not sex has some validity: but we need a more complex theorization of power in order to capture the intersubjective dynamics being alluded to here. Moreover, to focus only on the question of power, as we have tried to show in this short deconstruction, is to ignore much else that is also implicated and risks building a politics of rape on very shaky foundations.

The Donnellan case

The case we have chosen as a test of our theory is one that involved two students who had been close friends for two years prior to the rape allegation. It achieved a high public profile at the time of the trial, which resulted in the acquittal of the defendant, Donnellan, and has been written about more extensively elsewhere (Hollway and Jefferson, 1998; Lees, 1996: 79–85). Our procedure, as with the theoretical literature we have been considering, is to use an existing account, in this case that provided by Lees (1996), to describe the contours of the case, to demonstrate how the limitations of the feminist theoretical framework prevent it noticing certain things, and to show how the case (implicitly) raises questions that are not subsequently addressed. Our contention is, in line with our psychosocial orientation, that such questions can begin to be answered by addressing the 'inner' world vulnerabilities, anxieties and confusions of the various participants, something that can be better understood biographically and inter-subjectively, as well as the sometimes contradictory external, social world of power relations and discourses they inhabit. We then briefly indicate the contours of our answer to the unaddressed questions, drawing on the work of Hollway and Jefferson (1996; see also Jefferson (1997b) for a psychosocial analysis of the Tyson date rape trial).

In her book on rape trials, Sue Lees (1996: 79–85) spends a few pages on 'The Donnellan Case'. She has two main concerns: the press coverage, and why the case was ever allowed to proceed to trial. Concerning the former, she notes the celebratory tone that the press used to greet Donnellan's acquittal and the facts that he was described as 'the perfect gentleman' (ibid: 80) and she, Ms X, was depicted as 'a campus wild child' (ibid) – despite the fact that 'she was reported to have been a virgin on arrival at university, unlike Donnellan, who ... had a previous sexual history' (ibid). Lees also notes that 'the medical evidence presented in the trial went well beyond professional judgement and joined in condemning the complainant' (ibid) by detailing how much she had drunk, how drunk she was and how 'very, very sexy' this would have made her (ibid: 81). As for why the case was allowed to go to trial, Lees details Donnellan's insistence, in contrast to Ms X and the university who wanted the matter dealt with internally. Lees expressed surprise that the Crown Prosecution Service would take such a weak case, given her 'inebriated state' (ibid: 83) and the delay between the event and it being reported to the police, and speculates about the reason: 'public interest, with the encouragement of [the legally well-connected] Lord Russell [Donnellan's personal tutor], may well have been the main reason' (ibid). Lees also notes that 'some newspapers drew the totally false conclusion that too many rape cases were proceeding to trial' (ibid: 84). By focussing on the effect of all this on Donnellan's reputation, Lees thought that the case promoted reactionary thinking.

In between her concerns with the press coverage and how the case ever got to trial, Lees (ibid: 81) sandwiches the 'bare facts of the case', which were 'as follows':

> The couple, both twenty-one years old, had not had a previous sexual relation-ship but had been seen kissing at a Christmas party, where they were both very drunk. According to Donnellan's evidence, the complainant had taken him back to her room and had consented to sex. Donnellan claimed that their on-off non-sexual relationship (as she had refused to sleep with him) had fizzled out after five months. The alleged rape happened after this. The complainant, on the other hand, could not remember exactly what happened as she had passed out, but the next day had accused Donnellan of rape.
>
> (ibid: 81)

These then are the relevant 'facts' of the case as Lees sees them. Every selection of what is relevant (and exclusion of what is not), every act of noticing (and failing to notice), is the beginning of an interpretation, however implicit. As a feminist researcher, it is hardly surprising that what attracted Lees' attention was also, implic-itly, a feminist interpretation. Both the media coverage that sullied the complainant's reputation but not Donnellan's and the perversity of proceeding to trial with such a weak case effectively damaged the feminist cause on rape. However, what Lees missed as a result of her particular theoretical starting point is crucial, we contend, if we are interested in understanding what happened on the night of the rape allegation. Lees seems remarkably incurious about these details. But, as we intend to show, the details missing from her account recast somewhat her analysis of the media coverage and the decision to proceed to trial. What follows is an attempt to reinstate some of the details that Lees failed to notice, and a demonstration of how such noticing, informed by our psychosocial approach, offers a more fruitful theoretical avenue.

Lees' desire to rectify what she perceived as the media's attack on the character of the complainant actually constitutes a significant distortion. For example, her attempt to 'balance' the press coverage of Ms X as the 'wild child' and Donnellan as 'the perfect gentleman', by suggesting that he, not she, was the sexually experienced one, is actually misleading. The complainant may have been a virgin on arrival at university but, on her own admission, she was sexually promiscuous as a university student whilst Donnellan, who had had one sexual encounter prior to university, had spent most of his time at university in love with the complainant and hoping to start a serious relationship with her. Indeed, the newsworthiness of the item stemmed in large measure from just this apparent reversal of traditional roles in the rape scenario: not predatory rapist and virginal victim but 'Mr Nice Guy and Ms Voracious Vamp' (Hollway and Jefferson, 1998: 409). It was the kind of 'man bites dog' story of which newspapers dream. Moreover, this newsworthy role reversal was itself embedded within a larger, (post)feminist metanarrative about contemporary changes in gender relations: she, not he, was the sexually active one; she, not he, was into casual sex. This role reversal, and what it meant for gender relations and for feminism – was this a sign of progress, regress, or what? – informed much of the surrounding commentary (Hollway and Jefferson, 1998). In other words, even in its own, feminist, terms, the attempt to 'rescue' the complainant by redefining her as a traditional victim missed the social significance *for feminism* of this shift and thus produced an analysis that lagged behind much of the press commentary. Arguably, by failing to engage with the complainant's professed sexuality, Lees' account may be of less relevance to young women than she would undoubtedly have wished.

This failure to take seriously the role reversal, and the (fitful and partial) shift in gender relations of which it is symptomatic, rendered Lees blind to a whole host of related details that, once noticed, shed light on the dynamics of the relationship of this couple and, hence, offer important clues as to why it ended so tragically for both of them. One of the reasons Lees was blind to the details of this couple's relationship prior to the night of the rape allegation is that, from her feminist perspective, they are irrelevant. Feminists have worked long and hard to prevent a woman's prior sexual history, with the defendant or with anyone else, being relevant in the adjudication of rape cases: what happened on the occasion in question, and only that, is to be considered as relevant. Did he proceed with intercourse against her will? Was she in a position genuinely to give her consent? And did he knowingly proceed without it? Whether or not this is the best way to proceed in relation to deciding rape cases, what is certain is that the removal of information about the participants, their personal and relational histories, renders it impossible to make sense of this particular 'date rape' allegation. But, using what we know of their past histories and of their relationship at the time of the allegation, the event begins to make some sense. In so doing, it may also help us think through other date-rape cases, each time respecting their own particularities.

So, what should we notice about the protagonists, their biographies and their relationship, and about the night in question? Although not exhaustive, the following broad list contains the key details, obtained from a fairly exhaustive reading of the press coverage (see Hollway and Jefferson, 1998):

- The two had been very close, trusting friends prior to the allegation.
- For much of this time, Donnellan was in love with her and wanted a serious, love relationship.
- Ms X constantly refused the relationship he wanted but she spent much time with him, in night clubs, passionately kissing and 'necking'.
- She told her friends she did not fancy him.
- She confided in him about her drunken 'one-night stands'.
- By the time of the party on the night it happened, he said he was no longer in love with her.
- What happened that night, according to him (because she remembered nothing between getting drunk and waking up to someone having sex with her) was that she got very drunk and was kissing him and two other men. She fell over several times and Donnellan helped her home to bed where she initiated further kissing and the subsequent 'energetic' sex. He questioned her willingness, but she dismissed his doubts.

> After sleeping a while, she initiated a second bout of sex but virtually fell asleep in the middle of it so he stopped. Shortly afterwards, she awoke, jumped out of bed and accused him of trying to 'screw' her. The next day she rebuffed all his approaches at contact, screaming at him not to touch her.

What are we to make of this host of seemingly contradictory details? They clearly raise a number of questions. However, for brevity's sake, we intend to reduce these to two compound ones: one addressed to her behaviour, one to his. To make sense of her relationship with him, we need to answer the following question:

- Why did this sexually adventurous young woman spend so much time in the company of a man with whom she did not want a serious relationship, passionately kiss him when she did not fancy him, and become freaked out after a night of drunken sex with him yet not when it happened with other men, whom she knew less well?

As for him, the following question needs an answer:

- Why did this shy young man looking for a serious relationship become drawn to such an unlikely mate (one who passionately kissed him but had sex with others), continue in the relationship after she refused him the committed relationship he wanted and then passionately kiss and eventually have sex with her after he had fallen out of love with her?

Let us start with her own response as to why she spent so much time kissing a young man she did not fancy since it is the closest we get to her answer to the question. She said, memorably: 'A kiss is just a kiss: to me it means nothing' (quoted in the *Guardian*, 20 October 1993). Like many utterances, as we have been arguing all along, it can conceal as much as it reveals, because its motivational source has unconscious as well as conscious origins. However, let us see first what it reveals. Expressed discursively, she is saying that she can choose the meaning she attaches to a kiss. She need not be saddled with any of the meanings it has acquired inside traditional discourses where a kiss can signify anything from polite greeting between comparative strangers to the ultimate expression of intimate love. In other words, control of the meaning of practices associated with sexuality is vested in her, an independent woman: a kiss can mean something or nothing; it has no fixed meaning; she makes the choice. By implication, control of the meaning of sex is vested in her: it means whatever she wants it to – love, friendship or drunken romp; and she can do it with whomsoever she pleases, and whenever she pleases. We talked in Chapter 4 about Hollway's three discourses of sexuality – 'have/hold', 'permissive' and 'male sexual drive' – and the different significance of sex within each: love and commitment; pleasurable fun; natural (male) desire (Hollway, 1989, 2001). What the complainant seems to be articulating with her 'a kiss is just a kiss' statement, and in her sexual behaviour (by no means confined to the complainant as the young people interviewed in connection with the case made clear), is a new (post-)feminist discursive position on sexuality. This is a version of the permissive discourse shorn of its implicit patriarchalism (that is, promiscuous sexuality modelled on the 'male sexual drive' discourse). This, to recap, is what seemed to lie behind the story's newsworthiness – and why it posed a challenge to traditional feminism.

But her conscious identification with a (post-)feminist discourse is not the whole story. For what her statement concealed is why she would want to spend so much time doing something so meaningless *with this particular man* yet refuse him the meaningless sex she indulged in with other men. Here the question of desire, something beyond conscious choice, is implicated. To understand this, we will need to look elsewhere, piece together other bits of evidence. She was a convent-educated girl who was a virgin when she entered university. Friends said the ending of her first love relationship had left her devastated and she said that sex unconnected with love was preferable because nobody got hurt that way. Here, then, is a clue, gleaned from knowledge of her particular biography, as to why she preferred the casual sex of one-night stands, why she chose such sex rather than sex as part of a committed relationship: casual sex protected her from hurt, from feeling the vulnerability implicit in the emotional dependence on another whom one loves.

However, the fact that Ms X spent so much time with Donnellan, as friend, trusted confidante and quasi-lover, suggests she also still desired the emotional closeness of a proper love relationship, but without the risk of hurt. Hence the defensive need to split sex from love: to keep sex emotionally safe by restricting it to casual encounters; to keep love emotionally safe by restricting it to platonic friendships. Passionate kissing was what, for her, marked the border between the two, signifying neither sex nor love. But from our perspective, this was wishful thinking. Like all borders between two dangerous territories, it was always unsafe because always potentially under threat from either sex or love. In other words, being the point where love and sex meet, at least within traditional discourses, passionate kissing actually has a surfeit of potential meanings – and can thus be a very confusing practice when undertaken in denial of any meaning whatsoever. This has implications that we return to later. The defensive splitting of sex from love also entailed splitting men into two categories: those she had sex with because there was no danger of her falling in love with them; and those she did not because of the danger they presented of becoming a love relationship. Perhaps the appeal of Donnellan is revealed, paradoxically, in Ms X's claim that she did not fancy him. This made him a perfectly safe friend who was neither a potential sexual partner nor someone with whom she might fall in love: more like a brother, perhaps (except that he had declared his desire for the kind of committed relationship she feared). His very safety as a man who transcended both categories is what enabled her to allow him to occupy both categories, as quasi-sexual partner and quasi-love relationship. This enabled them to 'play' at both sex and love, using passionate kissing as their boundary marker. But, for her to remain feeling safe, this situation had to stay frozen in time: passionate kisses could only ever be that – just kisses and nothing more; they must not develop into real love or real sex. This helps explain Ms X's extreme distress when she realized that sex with Donnellan had taken place. In doing so, he had effectively dismantled the category distinctions that were so important to the maintenance of her emotional safety, unconscious distinctions that she expected him, her attentive, loving friend, to recognize and observe no matter how passionate the kissing and, according to him, no matter that she might have drunkenly asked for sex with him. In this way, and however inadvertently, he had ruined her trust in him, a trust that, however unreasonably, expected him to understand her conscious desires (for kissing, sex) through her unconscious needs (to stay safe from hurt) – to second-guess her contradictory desires – whilst also grappling with his own. This is, concretely, what we mean by the confusing surfeit of meaning in passionate kissing.

But why was the night of the rape allegation different to all the others when passionate kissing had occurred, apparently without the tragic outcome of this particular night? Certainly, if we are right about the inherent instability of their chosen solution of intimate friendship stopping short of sexual intercourse, a tragic outcome was always a possibility. However, what had changed by then was that Donnellan had said he was no longer in love with Ms X. Perhaps this helps explain the timing. Certainly, by her own admission, she got drunker than usual that night. That led to him taking her home and, according to him, her sexual come-on. Since getting drunk disinhibits, thus allowing the usually inhibited parts of the self (parts denied, repressed or otherwise inaccessible to consciousness) freer rein, perhaps both getting extra drunk and the subsequent sexual advance were, unconsciously, a way of keeping Donnellan's apparently waned interest alive.

If she consciously identified with a (post-)feminist version of the 'permissive' discourse, where sex meant whatever she wanted it to mean, Donnellan consciously identified with the traditional 'have/hold' discourse of sexuality, where sex forms part of a meaningful, committed, monogamous, long-term relationship. Yet he chose to spend many nights in the company of a woman who explicitly refused him the meaningful sexual relationship he craved, having a quasi-sexual relationship with her and, later, listening to her accounts of meaningless, casual sex with men she did not love. As we did with her, let us start to situate biographically these apparently contradictory desires. On arrival at university, this shy young man with little sexual experience encountered a highly sexualized culture in which casual sexual encounters seemed to be commonplace. For young single men, an active (hetero)sexuality is not only permissible discursively but also culturally valued as a sign of masculinity (unlike the case for single women for whom an active sexuality, even in these postfeminist times, still has only limited discursive warrant). It is highly likely, therefore, that a part of him would be attracted to the idea of the casual sexual encounter (but also threatened by it, since incompatible with his identification with 'sex-as-commitment').

Donnellan's relationship with the young woman was apparently able, not without tension we would hazard, to reconcile these conflicting identifications and desires. His passionate but restricted sexual 'flirting' with a desirable and sexy young woman was able to secure his masculine desire to be (hetero)sexually active without compromising his (conscious) commitment to meaningful sex inside a loving relationship. His open, trusting relationship with her had many of the advantages of a committed sexual relationship, but without the risk of hurt that an actual sexual relationship with her, given her casual approach to sex, was liable to produce. His indirect participation in her casual sexual encounters through the confidences she shared with him, enabled him to identify, albeit vicariously, with a permissive version of sexuality, without compromising his positioning within the 'have/hold' discourse, and, again, without risk. In other words, the pattern of his identifications and desires seemed to complement hers in a way that satisfied both their conscious commitments and their unconscious desires. By providing her with a sexualized loving relationship but without 'proper' sex (sexual intercourse) he satisfied her unconscious desire for love in a way that protected her vulnerability. By accepting her casual sexual relationships he assisted her conscious commitment to the idea of sexual freedom. In his case, her willingness to share her liberated sexual lifestyle while stopping short of direct participation in 'proper' sex enabled him to satisfy an unconscious desire to be more permissive but without risk. Her willingness to behave rather like a girlfriend assisted his conscious commitment to the idea of a steady, loving relationship. These complementarities were, we suspect, the basis of their mutual attraction. And passionate kissing – that empty but very discursively available signifier – was the practice that best expressed this tangle of conflicting emotions.

Why then did it unravel on the night in question? The likeliest answer, as we saw from her side, was that he was no longer in love with her. Expressed discursively, he no longer positioned himself in the have/hold discourse in relation to her. This also meant that sex with her, now freed from any desire for a long-term relationship, no longer carried with it the risk that he might be hurt by it: that she had the power to make him feel vulnerable. Consequently, he was freed up to fully position himself within the permissive discourse, like one of her one-night stands, a position that he had been half engaged in so often through their 'meaningless', passionate kissing. This enabled him to 'hear' only her conscious desire for sex with him, not her unconscious need to be protected from herself. As her quasi-boyfriend he had responsibly looked after her many a time in the past, ensuring the boundary between love and sex remained intact: now he was 'anyman', just one of the three men who she was kissing that night, and the one she had invited to have sex with her; now, he too could be 'irresponsible', one of her 'bits of rough', no longer 'Mr Nice Guy'.

Conclusion

In this chapter we have critically reviewed the literature on rape from the time when radical feminists challenged the traditional idea of the rapist-as-psychopath. We identified several inadequacies in these early feminist accounts, namely: their failure to distinguish different kinds of rapes, their presumption of female passivity; the problem of overprediction; and the failure to take seriously the issue of sexuality. Under these four headings we looked at more recent attempts to address these deficiencies, but found these wanting. What was needed, we argued, was to take seriously both 'inner' world issues of anxiety and vulnerability as well as 'outer' world issues of power relations and the discourses through which these are mediated. Doing so entailed attending to the sometimes painful confusions that result from the contradictions among and between 'inner' feelings and wider social patterns. Such confusions are not resolvable at the level of discourse, as some have attempted. (Nor, sadly, are they likely to be resolvable through legislation, as recent attempts to clarify the relationship between consent and intoxication seek to do (Office for Criminal Justice Reform, 2006).) Rather, we suggested that only a psychosocial approach is adequate to the task. Crucially, this means attending both to the discursive positions that are available to people and what motivates them to take up particular positions: why they are 'invested' in particular positions (and not others). Understanding people's discursive investments, which are always a complex product of unique biographical histories, requires exploring how unconscious defences designed to protect oneself from feeling anxious, vulnerable and out of control are implicated in such discursive 'choices'. Investments are, then, the psychosocial link between 'inner' and 'outer' worlds. We then looked at a particular case of date rape: first through Sue Lees' account, noting what it failed to see as a result of its particular feminist approach; then, using our psychosocial approach, trying to show how it could offer a more plausible account of a rather unlikely friendship and how, tragically, it ended with a rape allegation.

7

VULNERABILITY, VIOLENCE AND SERIAL MURDER: THE CASE OF JEFFREY DAHMER

Whether serial killing is a relatively new and growing problem, or something that has recently come to be seen as a problem, is still a moot point (Coleman and Norris, 2000: 93–4). What is undeniable, however, is the growth of criminological interest in the topic in the last 20 years or so (cf. Holmes and De Burger, 1988; Holmes and Holmes, 1998; Lester, 1995; Levin and Fox, 1985). There is broad agreement as to what it is – multiple murder committed over a relatively long period of time – and that this is different from 'mass murder' (multiple murder in a single episode) and 'spree murder' (multiple murder committed over a restricted time period in numerous locations). 'Jack the Ripper' and Peter Sutcliffe, the 'Yorkshire Ripper', are both examples of serial killers; Thomas Hamilton, who burst into a schoolroom in Dunblane and killed 16 children, their teacher and then himself, was a mass murderer; and Michael Ryan, the man who ran amok in Hungerford killing 16, would be classified as a spree killer.

When it comes to explanations, details may differ but the approach, with some notable exceptions, is very uniform, namely, the production of a *multi-factorial profile*. The notable exceptions are feminist accounts like those of Caputi (1988) and Cameron and Frazer (1987) that make connections between serial killing, specifically sadistic, sexual murders, and 'contemporary patriarchy' (Caputi, 1988: 3). Cameron and Frazer (1987: 166–7) in particular make an extremely thought-provoking argument, suggesting that the 'common denominator' of sex murderers is 'a shared construction of … masculinity' in which 'the quest for transcendence' is central. This notion is able, importantly, to accommodate the fact that many victims of serial killers (as was the case with this chapter's chosen example, Jeffrey Dahmer) are men, something that Caputi's notion of sex crimes as a manifestation of 'gynocide' – 'the systematic crippling, raping and/or killing of women by men' (Dworkin quoted in Caputi, 1988: 3) – simply cannot. However, it remains trapped, along with the radical feminists we discussed in the previous chapter, within an exclusively social account, and hence, for our purposes, is inadequate.

Multi-factorial profiles are problematic for a number of reasons. Take, for example, the one suggested by Norris (1989) and discussed by Lester (1995: 93–101). This has '21 elements':

- 'ritualistic behaviour'
- 'masks of sanity'
- 'compulsivity'
- 'search for help'
- 'pathological liars'
- 'suicidal tendencies'
- 'history of sexual assault'
- 'deviant sexual behaviour'
- 'head trauma or other injuries'
- 'history of chronic drug and alcohol abuse'
- 'drug and alcohol abuse by the parents'
- 'physical and psychological abuse'
- 'unwanted pregnancy'
- 'difficult pregnancies'
- 'unhappy childhoods'
- 'cruelty to animals'
- 'firesetting tendencies'
- 'neurological impairment'
- 'genetic disorders'
- 'biochemical symptoms'
- 'feelings of powerlessness or inadequacy'.

Taken altogether, the discussion of these elements embrace a hodgepodge of descriptive characteristics and explanatory notions that are not so much wrong – Jeffrey Dahmer could have ticked many of these boxes – as far too commonplace, as Lester noted:

> Norris saw the profile he presented as defining a new syndrome ... However, what Norris has actually accomplished is to make the serial murderer seem quite similar in many ways to the average murderer.

> (ibid: 101)

Behind this problem is the cross-sectional method used to produce 'typical' profiles. In cross-sectional analysis, the elements of the profile are derived from looking across a sample of cases to see what is recurrent or common as opposed to rare or idiosyncratic, since only the common features are thought to need explanation. But, having been taken out of the context of particular cases, the explanations then offered tend to be equally context-free: hence, too general. In broad terms, such a procedure tends to emphasize structure over process and to downplay the merely contingent.

The result of this sort of approach is that we get a sense of the kinds of factors associated with serial killing in general, but disappointment when we come to match any particular case up against the profile. Take, for example, a necrophiliac killer like Jeffrey Dahmer. Lester says of necrophilia:

> Some serial killers have necrophiliac tendencies (that is, sexual attraction to corpses), but necrophilia is quite uncommon and we have little idea about how

such desires develop. Sears discussed the possible involvement of the need for power, the excitement of the hunt and the social pressure on men to be strong and 'manly'. Sears also noted that the media may play an important role in shaping the serial murderer's behavior.

(1995: 87)

The 'need for power', 'excitement', the pressures of masculinity and the media are all, somehow, involved; and such issues do indeed arise in the Dahmer case, as we shall see. But, without spelling out how they are connected to produce a specifically necrophiliac outcome, it can hardly count as an incisive explanation. After all, such issues are also implicated in a whole range of highly acceptable forms of human behaviour, such as playing football and bungee jumping.

In Chapter 1 we made a general argument justifying the use of case studies in terms of their ability to further the development of theory. This is what is so lacking in accounts of serial murder, including the generalized, overly social feminist explanations and the mixtures of psychological, sociological and biological factors – part description, part explanation – that constitute the typological basis of 'profiling theory'. By contrast, attending to the particularities of case studies necessarily involves drawing on theory, but always constrained by the details, contexts and contingencies of the specific material in question. Statements like Lester's (above) on the nature of necrophilia have constantly to be related to case details. In that way, and only in that way, can theory be developed that is robust enough to explain the idiosyncratic – and Dahmer's case is as idiosyncratic as they come – while also advancing a more general theoretical understanding of necrophilia. It is time to put all this theory into practice in attempting to understand, as best we can, the serial killer Jeffrey Dahmer.

In what follows we draw heavily on Brian Masters' (1993) detailed and imaginative engagement with the Dahmer case, as well as Dahmer's father's soul-searching autobiography (Dahmer, 1994). In combination, these texts provide the material from which we have constructed our 'pen portrait', and the seeds of an explanation of Dahmer's serial killing with which we wish both to engage and transcend.

Jeffrey Dahmer: a case study

A pen portrait

Jeffrey Dahmer was born in 1960, the first child of a difficult marriage. His mother, the daughter of an alcoholic, suffered constantly from depression. Her pregnancy was difficult, entailing two months in bed with nausea. She disliked breastfeeding Jeffrey and soon gave it up. Jeffrey's father was first a student, then a research chemist, who spent much of his time working. His work, and his wife's sensitivity to noise, led to several house moves in Dahmer's early years. At nursery school, Dahmer was shy and awkward and found it difficult to relate to other boys.

At the age of four, Dahmer had a double hernia operation that he remembered, 27 years later, as extremely painful; so painful that 'he thought his genitals must have been cut off' (Masters, 1993: 30). The pain lasted for about a week but, at the time, he made little fuss: his mother noted he was 'so good in hospital' (ibid), whilst his father remembers him as 'a quiet little boy' who sat 'quietly for long periods, hardly stirring, his face oddly motionless' (Dahmer, 1994: 60). Dahmer was fascinated by animals, insects and bones (his 'fiddlesticks'). When he was five or six, his mother gave birth to his brother, Dave. Then the family rows got worse and his mother became more depressed.

Dahmer disliked school and, according to his father, was 'frightened and unnerved' by it, 'as if he had come to expect that other people might harm him in some way' (ibid: 62). On the few occasions when he did make friends he became extremely sensitive to being let down. A friend 'betrayed' him by telling a teacher Dahmer had strangled him, a 'pretend' game that the friend had agreed to keep to himself. His teacher 'betrayed' him by giving away his present of tadpoles to her. He subsequently 'poured motor-oil into the container and killed all the tadpoles' (Masters, 1993: 36). Dahmer's father, by his own admission a man averse to social contact and overly committed to his work, became concerned about his son's lack of interest in social activities and his preference for undertaking solitary, secretive pursuits – such as dissecting dead animals and keeping their skeletons. Although Dahmer passively accepted his father's attempts to interest him in regular activities like tennis and the Scouts, he did so without enthusiasm. His solitary pursuits were invested with fantasy. His favourite fantasy was an invented game he called 'Infinity Land' involving bone-like stick men who would be annihilated if they came too close together, a fantasy he enjoyed all by himself for years, 'telling nobody' (ibid: 38). When he did finally entrust his secret to another boy, the boy's parents stopped their son seeing Dahmer.

During his early teens Dahmer started drinking, put on weight, played the fool at school and made his teachers anxious as his grades deteriorated. His fascination with dissecting animals led to him looking out for 'road kills': animals killed by vehicles on the roads. By the age of 16 he was a morose, sullen, uncommunicative loner, often drunk, who had become 'transfixed' by human skeletons. He was also masturbating three times a day to images of male nudes, especially their chests and abdomens. He fantasized about 'possessing' a male body, to control, kiss and have sex with, and decided, aged 17, that he could only do so by capturing one. A fit, muscular jogger who passed his house regularly was to be his prey; but, despite on one occasion awaiting him armed with a baseball bat, the jogger failed to appear.

An acrimonious divorce following his mother's affair led to his father moving out and his mother – by this time assessed by her doctor as 'constantly angry, frustrated and demanding' and generally very unreasonable (ibid: 56) – leaving with Jeffrey's younger brother, in contravention of a court order. Over the years there had been many arguments, but only Jeffrey's brother had noticed Jeffrey respond to these by angrily slapping at trees 'with branches he'd gathered from the ground' (Dahmer, 1994: 89). Aged 18, Jeffrey was left behind in the parental home. He started drinking more and became subject to more insistent masturbation fantasies. These involved the sexual exploration and ownership of dead men after having killed them.

Dahmer's first killing soon followed. He picked up a bare-chested hitch-hiker, Steven Hicks, about his own age (19), in his father's car, invited him back for beers and a joint, discovered he had a girlfriend, and then, as Hicks decided to leave, clubbed and strangled him with a barbell. Dahmer then enacted his fantasies with the dead body before masturbating over it. Fear quickly followed – 'I was out of my mind with fear that night' (Masters, 1993: 67) – and the next day he dismembered the body, bagged it and left it under the house – but not before examining the insides, penetrating and masturbating with the viscera and masturbating in front of the severed head.

It was to be eight years before Dahmer killed again. At first, he attempted to live a 'normal' life, using alcohol to forget the killing. He enrolled at Ohio State University, partly to please his father. But he soon dropped out, a 'weird' and friendless alco-holic. With his father's assistance, he enrolled in the army, trained as a medic and spent two years in Germany – but still spent most of his time alone and depressed. He was still drinking to erase the memories of Hicks' death. Drinking on duty led to his early discharge. Now 21, he relocated to Florida working seven days a week in a sandwich bar and drinking away all his money, eventually becoming homeless. His father gave him the money to return to the family home in Ohio where his father and second wife now lived. There, Jeffrey dug out the remains of Hicks' body and 'smashed them ... with a large rock', scattering the fragments in an attempt to oblit-erate the 'sin' that still tormented him (ibid: 80). But, after a drink-related arrest, he was sent by his father and stepmother to live with his grandmother in Wisconsin: 'six years of apparent stability and concealed turmoil' followed (ibid: 82).

Dahmer got on well with his 'perfect grandmother' whom he thought was 'very sweet'. He got a job – extracting blood from volunteers – and became interested in Satanism; but after ten months he got the sack, for poor performance, and was con-victed on a charge of disorderly conduct (urinating in public). Determined to change his ways, he started to spend more time with his Grandma, including church-going and Bible-reading, and less time masturbating and fantasizing about men. This 'good' period lasted about two years, during which time he was less haunted by his first killing and even spent a Christmas – his first contact in five years – with his estranged mother and his brother. He got an unskilled job as a mixer working nights in a chocolate factory in Milwaukee. Then, following the offer (which he resisted) of a blow job by a man in a library, he recommenced masturbating four times a day and felt stronger and stronger urges for a man until, two months later, 'his control broke down' (ibid: 88).

Around this time, Lionel Dahmer tried to encourage his son to pursue a relation-ship with a young woman in the church congregation, never suspecting that his son was homosexual 'despite the fact that he had ... never expressed the slightest inter-est in a woman' (Dahmer, 1994: 187). When Jeffrey stopped attending church regu-larly, he started drinking again. He also began having anonymous sex in the back rooms of porn shops, exposed himself in public, and would rub himself up against unsuspecting men in crowded settings. Once he stole a male mannequin from a store and enacted his sexual fantasies with it, until his Grandma made him get rid of it. Dahmer even tried (unsuccessfully) to initiate sex with his brother. Eventually, Dahmer discovered the bathhouses, but the anonymous sex there was too energetic for his taste. So, he started to drug men, using sleeping pills. He would then enact his sexual fantasies on their inert bodies for 'up to eight hours' (Masters, 1993: 93). When this led to the hospitalization of one of his drugged partners, Dahmer's bathhouse membership was revoked and he continued the practice in hotel rooms with men he picked up in gay bars. Dahmer fantasized that the men belonged to him and would masturbate several times before fondling them and falling asleep with his head on their chest or stomach listening to their bodily sounds. When they were awake, by contrast, he found it difficult to get an erection.

By his mid-twenties and still living with Grandma, Dahmer's sexual behaviour was hyperactive, his fantasies more elaborate and his desire – for lifeless male bodies – more intense. His behaviour became more erratic, including making obscene gestures to police officers and masturbating in public – an offence for which he was arrested, convicted and forced to undergo counselling. This counselling revealed an uncommunicative, disconnected, isolated, powerless, controlled, intolerant, lethargic man who lacked the ability to concentrate, was virtually incapable of showing emotional affect, felt worthless and 'when angry … becomes almost delusional in his paranoid beliefs' (ibid: 104). During this period Dahmer killed again.

In November 1987 Dahmer picked up a 'youthful and engaging' (ibid: 106) 25-year-old, Steven Tuomi, outside a gay bar, took him back to a hotel room and then woke up the next morning with Tuomi dead beneath him with his chest caved in and with bruises all over his arms. Dahmer could not recollect having killed Tuomi and was shocked, horrified and panic-stricken – having successfully fought the urge for so long. Afterwards, he hid the body in the family home for a week, then dismembered it and smashed up the bones, binning everything except the head. This he kept for a short while for masturbation purposes before it too was thrown out having become brittle. From then on '[h]e gave up the struggle' (ibid: 111) to suppress his fantasies and desires, and began to see them as a 'compulsion' that he was powerless to fight. After a month or two, the fear of what he had done left him: '[F]rom then on it was a craving, a hunger … and I just kept doing it, doing it and doing it, whenever the opportunity presented itself' (ibid: 113). Yet, Dahmer was still capable of stopping short of killing. For example, shortly after the killing of Tuomi, he took Bobby Sampson, a 23-year-old black man, to his home, 'drugged him and masturbated four times with him' (ibid: 118), and stopped there.

Over the next few months Dahmer killed and disposed of two more men, James Doxtator, a tall, attractive, 14-year-old 'Native American' (ibid: 118) and 23-year-old Richard Guerrero, in similar fashion. He paid them to come and spend the night with him, had sex with them, drugged them and enacted his masturbatory fantasies with their inert bodies, strangled them, had more sex with their actually dead bodies, dismembered them while continuing to masturbate with and penetrate particular bodily organs, and then disposed of the parts, usually keeping the head for a while, partly for masturbation purposes and partly as a memento. In the next three-and-a-half years until his arrest for murder in July 1991, by when he had killed 17 times, this pattern was to become his hallmark. Occasionally, something happened to interrupt the killing. After one such occasion, when an intended victim, 'Ronald Flowers, a handsome, broad black man of twenty five' (ibid: 122), was drugged and molested but not strangled – an incident that led to a complaint and a visit from the police – Dahmer's family decided that Grandma had had enough of Dahmer's drinking and night-time male 'guests' and he moved into his own apartment. His father booked him in for treatment for his alcoholism, but this only lasted for four sessions. Dahmer, meanwhile, had become obsessed with the video *The Return of the Jedi*, identifying strongly with the all-powerful Emperor. He was also planning to make some kind of temple, for which purpose he bought a black table, to be the altar, and two statues of griffins – mythological creatures – to be protectors.

A second botched killing involved a 13-year-old 'healthy and athletic' (ibid: 133) Laotian student called Somsack Sinthasomphone managing to escape after being drugged. Sinthasomphone's escape was followed by Dahmer's arrest and confinement for 'Second Degree Sexual Assault and Enticing a Child for Immoral Purposes' (ibid: 129). The ensuing psychological reports echoed the earlier ones, only worse: 'a seriously disturbed young man' for whom 'the pressure he perceives seems to be increasing' concluded Dr Goldfarb; 'he must be considered impulsive and dangerous' (ibid: 131). Between conviction and sentence, after pleading guilty but saying the drugging was an accident and the complainant's age a complete shock, a depressed and suicidal Dahmer killed again: 'twenty-four-year-old half-caste, Anthony Sears [who was] ... attractive ... extrovert and friendly' (ibid: 135), and saved both his head and genitals in a case in his locker at work. He was sentenced to twelve months in the House of Correction with work release (plus five years probation), and served nine months.

On release, Dahmer told his probation officer his problem was drink and a lack of friends. He secured a new supply of sleeping tablets (to drug his victims) from his doctor, rescued the head and genitals from his locker, defleshing the former and keeping only the skull and scalp, and moved into an apartment in a poor, deprived and dangerous neighbourhood, 'almost the only white person in the block' (ibid: 139). The skull of his fifth victim (Anthony Sears) was painted and put on display. Weeks later Dahmer killed again, Raymond Smith, 'a thirty-two-year-old black man ... [who was] short, well-built, muscular' (ibid: 140–1). This was to be the first of twelve murders in 14 months, a sequence ending only with Dahmer's arrest and subsequent confession. It was also the first time Dahmer photographed his victim, having first laid him out on his 'altar' table. During his probation-ordered group-therapy sessions, Dahmer was becoming more and more uncommunicative, unkempt and unclean; and a further psychological evaluation thought 'a major relapse ... just a matter of time' (ibid: 144).

The photos of Dahmer's seventh victim, 'Eddie Smith, a 27-year-old black man ... well-built and attractive' (ibid: 144, 146), proved unsatisfactory and he cut them up. Dahmer tried different ways – freezer for the skeleton, oven for the skull – to preserve the defleshed remains, but these too proved unsuccessful. Another intended victim, 15-year-old Luis Pinet, managed to escape – Dahmer having run out of sleeping tablets had attempted to use a rubber mallet instead; but this was after spending the night with Dahmer and voluntarily returning for more. Even after this second escape the victim returned – for his bus fare – and after a struggle, a failed attempt at strangulation by Dahmer and further talk, during which the victim promised not to tell anybody about the incident, Dahmer walked him to his bus stop and paid for his ride home. Later, Dahmer was to say that he lacked 'the ability to do him any harm' (ibid: 149), but didn't know why. Dahmer's victim did tell the police, who filed a 'false imprisonment' complaint, but they dismissed Pinet's changing stories of the event.

Dahmer's next two killings, Ernest Miller, 'black, twenty-three-years-old and well built' (ibid: 153) and David Thomas, a black 22-year-old, took place in the same month, September. The killing of Miller exhibited two innovations: the use of a knife to kill because the use of two rather than the usual three sleeping pills left Dahmer afraid his victim might awake during strangulation; and that he ate some of the victim's flesh. Dahmer also tried, unsuccessfully, to reassemble the defleshed skeleton for use in his Temple; instead the skull was spray-painted and added to his growing collection. Between February and May 1991, three more men, all black, were to die at Dahmer's hands: 17-year-old Curtis Straughter, 19-year-old Errol Lindsey and Tony Hughes, a profoundly deaf 31-year-old with little capacity for speech. By this time, Dahmer's daily life consisted of work, watching *Exorcist II* on return from work, followed by drinking in bars and searching out victims. Once, Dahmer let a man escape, because, he said, 'he realised he did not like him as much as he had thought' (ibid: 157). But other victims were subjected to novel indignities. He started to use handcuffs to enhance the fantasy of control and a leather strap for quicker strangulation. He completely removed the skin of one victim to keep for his shrine. Most hideously, he attempted to create a 'zombie', a lifeless person with no will of their own, by performing a crude lobotomy – by drilling a hole in the victims' skulls and injecting muriatic acid into what he thought were the frontal lobes – in the pathetically vain belief that this would give him what he wanted without having 'to keep killing people and have nothing left except the skull' (ibid: 176). One of his victims given this treatment was a Laotian schoolboy, 14-year-old Konerak Sinthasomphone, who happened to be the younger brother of Somsack who had luckily escaped Dahmer's clutches three years earlier. Konerak too escaped briefly, but, unfortunately for him, Dahmer managed to persuade the police that the naked, disoriented man was his drunk lover. Back in his apartment, Dahmer administered a second injection.

This killing by injection of a young schoolboy took place some three days after the killing of Tony Hughes, whose decomposing body was still in Dahmer's bedroom. Dahmer then took a day off work, for which he got a warning, to dispose of the two bodies. His landlord threatened eviction unless Dahmer did something about the 'intolerable … smells emanating from his apartment' (ibid: 182). And his probation officer sent him back to the doctor who 'prescribed some powerful anti-depressant pills' (ibid). But the killings continued. A month later Dahmer killed three men in the space of 15 days: a 20-year-old black man, Matt Turner; a 23-year-old 'Puerto

Rican, half-Jewish man', Jeremiah Weinberger (ibid: 183); and 24-year-old Oliver Lacey, a 'handsome black body-builder' (ibid). One of these victims, Weinberger, suffered a protracted death, the result of having boiling water injected into his brain (the earlier muriatic acid experiment having failed). On the day of the last of these three killings Dahmer was suspended from work 'pending a review of his record on attendance' (ibid). He told his probation officer he was unable to afford his apartment and was contemplating suicide. She sent him to the doctor who prescribed more antidepressants. Dahmer tried, unsuccessfully, to pick up another man. The next day he was fired from work; Dahmer picked up, murdered and dismembered 25-year-old Joseph Bradehoft, a white, 'married man [with] ... bisexual inclinations' (ibid: 184). Dahmer's flat was now full of bodies and parts of bodies in various stages of decomposition and dismemberment.

According to Dahmer, during this period nothing but his insatiable desires gave him pleasure. Without a job or money, and on the brink of losing his home, he continued to try to pick up men, eventually succeeding. But, without sleeping pills to drug what was to be his final victim, the victim realized he was with a mad man and escaped, alerting the police, who came back to Dahmer's apartment and arrested him. The next day Dahmer's confessions began.

During his pre-conviction imprisonment, 'Dahmer pleaded guilty to the facts and waived his right to a first trial' (ibid: 215). All that remained was the second trial, to decide his sanity and hence the appropriate sentence. This meant endless psychological and psychiatric examinations. This process he found upsetting, humiliating and depressing; but it left him free of his compulsions. The trial lasted a little over a fortnight. Prosecution and defence were agreed that Dahmer had a severe personality disorder, but then they differed: prosecution thought that his disorder was not a mental disease and that he had exercised free will; the defence thought Dahmer was mentally ill and unable to help himself. The jury took little time to come to a majority (10–2) verdict on all 15 counts: they judged that Dahmer was not suffering from a mental disease when he committed his murders. His sentence amounted, theoretically, to a total 'minimum' sentence 'of over nine hundred years' (ibid: 274). However, within three years, Dahmer's oft-expressed death wish was granted when he was murdered by a fellow inmate in prison.

A psychosocial reading

Commencing any attempt to understand a particular case involves adopting a particular focus. This means deciding which of the case's core details are salient to one's interpretation, and which are superfluous or incidental. In this case, since we are dealing with a homosexual, necrophiliac serial killer whose victims were mainly black (12 out of 17), we need to justify our focus on Dahmer's necrophilia, rather than the race of his victims or the fact of his homosexuality. On the issue of Dahmer's victims being mainly black, his father reminded us that many saw this as the appropriate focus: 'this fact had made a great many people see him as a race-killer, someone who had purposely chosen black victims' (Dahmer, 1994: 191).

Leaving aside the fact that such a focus overlooks the victims who were not black, we agree with his father's assessment that there was no racial motivation (ibid). Jeffrey Dahmer's choice of mainly black victims, we would argue, was a function of opportunity and attraction. In support of the importance of opportunity, we note that most (12) of the killings took place after he had moved to North 25th Street, a desperately poor street in a deprived, largely black district of Milwaukee. It seems not particularly surprising, therefore, that most of his victims were black. As for the question of attraction, if Dahmer was particularly attracted to black male bodies, it was their attractiveness as bodies, rather than their blackness, which seems to have been at stake. Both Lionel Dahmer (1994) and Brian Masters (1993) agree on this: '[h]e had wanted bodies, muscular, male bodies ... it was as simple as that' (Dahmer, 1994: 191–2); where Masters mentions the attractiveness of particular victims, it was always in terms of their muscularity or build, as we have noted in the pen portrait. For these reasons, then, our attempted explanation will not focus on the race of the victims.

What about his homosexuality? How relevant was this to Dahmer becoming a serial killer? Should this be our focus? As we saw in our brief look at feminist approaches in our introductory section, questions of masculinity are seen as a key element in understanding serial killing, even in the unusual case of a man killing men and not women (Cameron and Frazer, 1987). And it is certainly the case that the issue of homosexual desire implicates masculinity, given that the dominant versions of masculinity everywhere make heterosexuality so central. However, it is hard to see how Cameron and Frazer's (ibid: 166–7) idea of sex murderers as sharing a masculine 'quest for transcendence' could be used to shed much light in this case. Yet this, as we pointed out earlier, is the best general explanation of the serial sexual murderer currently available. The truth is that the topic of sexual desire – heterosexual or homosexual – is huge, diverse and contested. Moreover, it is not a criminological topic but becomes so only when that desire becomes linked to coercion and violence. So, explaining how Dahmer became attracted to men rather than women, even were there adequate theoretical models to assist us, cannot be our focus. Ours must be: how did that desire become dangerous? How did it become linked to the willingness to do harm in seeking its satisfaction?

So, it is specifically necrophiliac killing that concerns us in what follows. As we know from our brief look at the typological profilers in the opening section of this chapter, they are interested only in lists of associated factors – power, excitement, masculinity and 'the media' were those mentioned by one author as associated with necrophilia you may remember – but not in how these might produce the *desire* to have sex with the dead. This seems to us to be the crucial issue.

Let us admit from the start that, given how little is known about necrophilia, the extent of disagreement among the seven psychiatrists used during Dahmer's trial, and the sheer complexity of a case like that of Dahmer's, we will not be able to resolve all the relevant issues. Even were that possible, it would take far more space than we have here. What we can do, though, is to demonstrate why a case such as this makes *necessary* a psychosocial approach such as ours and indicate some of the ways such an approach illuminates features of the case that presently remain largely unlit. It is a way of thinking about cases such as this as much as what exactly gets thought that we are trying to promote in the analysis that follows.

Let us start with the pattern of the murders and the changes in their nature over time. Briefly, there is an eight-year gap between the first and second killing, after which they become much more regular and, towards the end, even more so with the time interval between killings dropping sometimes to days. As for the method used, the pattern of drugging followed by sexual activity, strangulation, more sexual activity, dismemberment, keeping the head as token and sexual aid undergoes several modifications over time, most notably the use of photography and the injection of acid or water into the brain to create a 'zombie'. Relevant here also is the fact that not all of the men Dahmer picked up with a view to murder suffered that fate. However we understand these changes, they immediately undercut the idea of a fixed profile, fully formed at the outset. What they suggest, rather, is a man going through changes: some external, such as his living arrangements and the degree of privacy they afforded; others internal, such as the strength of his cravings, the depth of his depression, the morbidity of his fantasy life.

Brian Masters' attempt to make sense of this process is captured in his chapter headings: 'The Fantasies'; 'The Struggle'; 'The Collapse'; 'The Nightmare'; 'The Frenzy'. The notion of a man struggling with but eventually overcome by an irresistible compulsion is certainly an improvement on the static notion of a profile and is certainly in accord with how Dahmer himself claimed to experience his 'disintegration'. But, it remains too general an understanding. Undoubtedly Dahmer did struggle after the first killing not to give in to his desires and things certainly got worse, harder to resist, after the second killing. But there is some evidence that this general escalation in Dahmer's compulsive behaviour was capable of being 'interrupted' by various contingencies. Take the period between the first and second killings. Much of this time – the 'years of apparent stability and concealed turmoil' – Dahmer lived with his grandmother, who was undoubtedly the relative with whom he got on best. Although, significantly, he 'could not bring himself to say that he loved her' (Masters, 1973: 82–3), he did describe her as 'a perfect grandmother, very kind … easy to get along with, very supportive, loving, just a very sweet lady' (ibid: 83). For two years he spent a lot of time with her, attended church and read the Bible with her, and severely restricted his time spent masturbating. In the light of what went on to happen, it would be foolish to make too much of this. But, this interlude does demonstrate it could have been different, under certain highly favourable conditions. In the event, the (refused) offer of a blow job by a man in the library set Dahmer off masturbating many times a day and, subsequently, to exposing himself in public; frotteurism; anonymous sex in porn shops and bathhouses; and on to the killings. Masters conceptualizes this, echoing Dahmer's own understanding, as a breakdown of control. But we still need to ask, if we wish to understand the loss of control, what was it about the good times with Grandma that kept his morbid desires under control?

A similar point could be made about the times when Dahmer failed to kill the men he had brought home for that purpose. Take Dahmer's failure to kill what would have been his eighth victim, 15-year-old Luis Pinet, a part-time worker at the gay club Dahmer frequented. It is a convoluted tale involving Pinet agreeing to be paid $200 to go home with Dahmer for a nude photo session followed by sex. Unusually, Pinet stayed the night and agreed to return. After a misunderstanding about times, Pinet returned for a second session. Meanwhile, Dahmer, having run out of sleeping tablets, had purchased a rubber mallet with which to knock out his victim. Dahmer's unsuccessful attempt to do this led to Pinet storming out in anger without the money Dahmer had offered, but then returning for his bus fare. Dahmer became panicky, 'either because he would lose the boy again, or because the boy might report the incident; perhaps a little of both' (ibid: 148–9), and tried, unsuccessfully, to strangle Pinet. Dahmer then persuaded Pinet to talk and to have his hands tied. Pinet managed to get free and tried to leave, at which point Dahmer produced a knife. They continued talking through the night, after which Dahmer took Pinet to *a bus stop and paid for his ride home*, having first secured a promise of silence from him.

Dahmer claimed he didn't know why but he 'just didn't have the ability to do him any harm' (ibid: 149). Masters offers two possible explanations: the 'obvious' one that 'he [Dahmer] was sober and the victim was awake' (ibid); and the 'more subtle' one that 'The length of time … [they] were acquainted' (ibid) meant Pinet was transformed from fantasy object into 'a human being' (ibid). These are not mutually exclusive explanations of course: the first is a recognition of necessity; the latter a possible insight into Dahmer's state of mind at the time. We think Masters' 'subtle' answer is on the right track, but it is not just about the length of time Dahmer and Pinet were together. It must also be to do with the quality of that interaction: the ability of Pinet, somehow, to talk and behave in such a way as to dissolve Dahmer's murderous fantasies.

A final example of contingency interrupting his compulsions occurred after Dahmer's arrest and confession. After the long talks about himself with psychiatrists and police officers, in contradistinction to his earlier sullen, uncommunicative exchanges with psychiatrists, Dahmer claimed that, although he still felt guilty, the compulsions had left him: 'I'm free of the compulsion and the driving need to do it' (quoted in ibid: 220). This has to be seen as a revealing change since it occurred when Dahmer was in an almost manically frenzied killing phase. Masters attributes this change to the 'connectedness he had always lacked' (ibid), something the lengthy talks and interviews centred on Jeffrey Dahmer provided. We do not disagree, but would also point to the importance of the quality of these interactions. In all these cases then – living with Grandma, certain interactions with victims, the lengthy confessional and post-confessional evaluative interviews – there is evidence of a crucial shift, albeit only temporary in the earlier examples, in Dahmer's inner world. Dahmer's inability to understand (and hence benefit from) these shifts is an indication of an unconscious dimension to them. If we want to understand these shifts, as we have argued all along, it will be *necessary* to proceed psychosocially.

In his attempt to find an origin for the journey into the darkness of necrophiliac murder, Brian Masters settles on the traumatic event of Dahmer's hospitalization for a double hernia operation at the age of four, something that the young Jeffrey was too young to understand or control:

Suddenly, his embryonic autonomy is shattered by a rude invasion; his little powers of decision are roughly withdrawn and he becomes an *object* in the hands of strangers. *His ability to maintain control* is undermined, disregarded, even perhaps cancelled ... Not knowing why, he will wonder and invent. His capacity to handle his emotional reactions to trauma and threat *when alone* is still very insecure and his understanding of this, his body, how it works and what one may do with it, is tiny ... Jeff Dahmer's own imaginings about the insides of people's bodies began with his hernia operation and the intrusion into his.

(ibid: 202, emphases in original)

There are several things that need to be said about this argument. The first, as John Bowlby's early work showed, is to agree that early hospitalization is, undoubtedly, a traumatic event for a young child. But, second, as Duncan Cartwright (2002: 149) – a therapist and academic who has systematically analysed cases of 'rage-type' murders – reminds us, 'how the effects of trauma are internalized' is 'a more important question to ask'. Third, and following on from this, we need to know something of the specific quality of Dahmer's 'embryonic autonomy'. In other words, adopting our object relational focus, Dahmer's traumatic event will have taken on particular meanings depending upon the nature of his actual relationship with his significant 'objects' (mother, crucially, but also father) and how these had been internalized. It is, then, these significant mediations of the trauma that we must first address.

Masters does not entirely neglect these. At one point, he suggests the possible explanatory importance of Dahmer's relations with his depressed mother, only to retract the idea on evidential grounds: 'There is ... no evidence whatsoever to support this idea' (Masters, 1993: 172). Masters is mistaken in thinking there is no 'evidence' linking the depressed mother and the reproduction of 'deadness' in children. Hence, we do think the issue of depression is central to understanding Dahmer's murderousness. In talking about the internalization of the dead mother, the psychoanalyst, A. H. Modell draws attention to the imagined nature of the process: to the distinction between the 'internal representation of the mother' and the 'conscious memory of the historical mother' (Modell, 1999: 77). What this distinction does is to enable us to accommodate Dahmer's memories of his mother, which refused to blame her (despite the fact that he barely kept in contact as an adult), with his unconscious, or phantasy, construction of her. In other words, it is her appearance in Dahmer's inner world, her *imago*, not how she might actually have been, that is our concern. Modell then goes on to suggest the potentially 'devastating' consequences of internalizing such an *imago*:

The mother was experienced as if she lacked the capacity to recognise other minds. The consequences of experiencing the failure of the mother to acknowledge the child's inner life can be devastating. For recognising the uniqueness of children's inner life is equivalent to recognising that they are psychically alive.

(ibid)

This experience of the mother's failure to acknowledge the infant's otherness, despite efforts on the part of the infant 'to invite and solicit' such recognition, can result in a form of identification by imitation as a substitute for love: 'It is as if the patient is saying: "If I cannot be loved by my mother, I will become her"' (ibid: 78). Becoming her involves not only identifying with her inner deadness, but also internalizing her 'murderous envy' and 'killing rage' (Sekoff, 1999: 121). Phenomenologically speaking, these ideas about the consequences of identifying with a 'dead' mother predict very accurately the persona of the young Jeffrey Dahmer: painfully shy, socially awkward, solitary, withdrawn, apathetic, uncommunicative – all possible indicators of an identification with depression – but capable of great rage when he felt 'betrayed' (e.g. the killing of the tadpoles incident). But as we have argued throughout this book, children have the potential to make many identifications. Given the many similarities between them, from their difficulties in social relationships to their shared interest in science, it would be negligent not to ask why Dahmer could not have escaped the full consequences of imitating his mother's inner deadness through identification with his father. This is especially important when the mother–infant relationship, as seems to be the case here, is pathological.

Lionel Dahmer's autobiography suggests that there were, in fact, many points of identification between him and the young Jeffrey. Lionel also suffered depression as a child, a problem he associated with 'a profound sense of isolation and abandonment' arising from his mother's hospitalization, and culminating in 'a severe stuttering problem' (Dahmer, 1994: 217). From around the age of eight until his early twenties, Lionel also suffered, 'periodically' from 'a horrifying sensation of something remembered, but not directly experienced':

> In the grip of that unreal memory, I would wake up suddenly with the frightening sense that I murdered someone ... I would be terrified at what I might have done. I would feel lost, as if I had gone out of control.
>
> (ibid: 213)

Whilst Lionel, like Jeffrey, suffered a 'dread' of social interaction, feelings that might otherwise have manifested themselves as depression found more aggressive outlets. A fascination with fire gave rise to an interest in explosives. This period culminated in nearly burning down a neighbour's garage, an event that gained him a reputation amongst his peers as the school bomber. 'I think that in order to act against my own corrosive and infuriating sense of weakness and inferiority, I began to gravitate toward violence ... In adolescence, I started making bombs' (ibid: 225). By Lionel's late teens, working-out had become a defence against feelings of weakness and inadequacy:

> More than anything during my childhood, I was plagued by the certainty that I was both physically weak and intellectually inferior ... I was almost the stereotype of the weak, skinny kid ... the elementary-school kid who was bullied ... the kid who finally decided that a 'great body' was what girls wanted, and who

then methodically went about the task of creating one, working out three times a day until the 'skinny kid' had been replaced by someone else.

(ibid: 223–4)

But as a parent struggling with his wife's mood swings, Lionel retreated back into the world of work. He did not notice his son's increasing reclusiveness. Jeffrey's silence on the issue of the trauma of his hernia operation was either overlooked or mistaken as 'goodness'. Similarly his son's dread of social interaction was perceived as something he should overcome alone, just as he, Lionel, had done: 'I had been plagued by the same feelings that were plaguing him, but I had learned to cope with them ... I saw no reason why my son could not learn to live with them, too' (ibid: 65–6). Thus, Dahmer's 'imitative' identification with his depressed mother could not be successfully counterbalanced by identifying with his father because his father was also prone to depression. Indeed, it seems likely that Dahmer's unconscious identifications with his father worsened his feelings of inner deadness because that is exactly how Lionel describes *his* inner world. So, not only was Lionel too distracted by work and a depressed wife to rescue his son from his pathological symbiosis with her, any unconscious identification Dahmer made with his father is likely only to have reinforced the feeling of inner deadness. Lionel's later proactive attempts to enliven his 'dead' son were probably too little, too late; but they were probably also undercut by the strength of the unconscious identification. Consciously, Dahmer would have known that he was a disappointment to his high-achieving father; unconsciously, Jeffrey does seem to have been 'only the deeper, darker shadow of himself', as Lionel himself put it (ibid: 185). Cartwright's (2002: 36) words on the relation between 'the absence of a coherent paternal introject' and violence, can also be applied to Dahmer:

> In most cases the paternal object is found to be an intermediary object breaking a pathological symbiosis or fusion between self and the primary object. The paternal object is felt to be less of a threat as it is less contaminated by projections of hate and envy. Therefore it follows that the absence of a coherent paternal introject is often isolated as one of the key problems with violent individuals.

Underlying the young Jeffrey's 'goodness' was his withdrawn solitariness: he was undemanding, 'no trouble'. During his frightening ordeal in hospital, his mother recorded that he was 'so good'. He even said she could go home each night, despite the pain he was in (Masters, 1993: 30). The possibility that his son was more afraid of the damage he was somehow doing to his dreadfully unhappy mother than the operation itself went unnoticed by Jeffrey's father. He 'saw only a quiet little boy' (Dahmer, 1994: 60) and an inconsolably troubled mother. When, as a six-year-old, Jeffrey had to adjust to a new baby brother, he did not appear 'jealous ... in the smallest degree' (Masters, 1993: 34). And when his mother became depressed yet again, when he was ten, he blamed himself and 'repaired' the damage by being extra good:

> Jeff's response [to his mother's depression] was classic. He blamed himself for his mother's illness. He had known for as long as he could remember that she had been depressed following his birth and that he had therefore caused the illness. He had to keep himself to himself, say little and do less, to protect her.
>
> (ibid: 40)

The rigid split that Duncan Cartwright (2002) notes in the defensive organization of his rage-type murderers is thus also observable in Dahmer: in his case between the internalized 'dead' mother, and its terrifying threat of annihilating any sense of life, and his desperate attempt to be good, to cause no trouble, even to blame himself for his mother's 'badness'. If only he could be good enough, his fantasy was that his troubling inner world, to say nothing of a difficult and fractious external reality – a depressed mother and pre-occupied father in a difficult relationship – might be appeased. Masters (1993: 42) also makes this connection between such apparent goodness and Dahmer's 'inner deadness': '[T]he child who does not ask for attention … betrays an inner deadness which can be mistaken for goodness and sweetness of character.' Put differently, we could say the child who does not ask for attention cannot own its own desire, its own neediness. This seemed to be the case with Dahmer whose desire for intimacy was very rarely expressed in his relationships with adult men.

The effort to be good in Dahmer's case was extraordinarily difficult because the nature of his bad objects robbed him of any sense of life and livelihood and 'being good' meant keeping out of the way, not intruding into the lives of his preoccupied parents. Tellingly, Dahmer's efforts to make himself seem good – becoming socially reclusive, apathetic, uncommunicative and the almost complete shutting down of affect – were doomed to failure from the outset because they are not the most desirable of qualities (although he was able sometimes to mimic a form of goodness). The result was that his external world must have come to resemble his internal one, full of 'bad objects', people who saw him as withdrawn, 'odd', a social misfit, not the all-good child he desperately needed to be. This can only have made matters worse, creating a poisonous psychosocial dynamic.

Given the difficulty Dahmer undoubtedly experienced with the defensive strategy of 'being good', his first attempted solution to his painful feelings, it is unsurprising that he was forced to attempt another one. This, what we will call his second attempted solution, involved retreating into a fantasy world. This fantasy solution, which took the form of a repetitive fantasy game, was where he could acknowledge and own his desire:

> In his solitary moments, which were frequent, he had dreamt up a game involving stick men and spirals. The stick men were spindly figures who would be annihilated if they came too close to one another … The spirals were tightly drawn, intensely imagined symbols of descent, whose ultimate destination was a black hole. He called the game 'Infinity Land'. He was about nine years old at the time … Dahmer fantasised about Infinity Land for years, enjoying it by himself, telling nobody.
>
> (ibid: 38)

What this extraordinarily arid and desolate fantasy reveals is an uncanny similarity to the deadness that we have argued lay at the heart of Dahmer's internalized bad objects: the threat of annihilation made manifest. Why was this enjoyable? Because, it brought both his *desire for* and *fear of* intimacy within a concrete, game-like structure that he could control. Thus, where the real world constantly undermined his idealized one, in fantasy at least he could embrace his desires *and* keep his fears at bay by transforming both into a concrete game that he controlled. This notion is also in accord with another intra-psychic factor that Cartwright (2002: 131) found to be typical of his rage-type murderers, namely, their 'impoverished representational abilities that are more vulnerable to collapse in the face of threat'. In other words, the inability to think about, or symbolize, how one is feeling – since to do so would threaten the rigid barrier established to keep painful feelings at bay – not only leaves a person inadequately equipped to imagine how others are feeling, but also makes such a person more likely to act upon, rather than reflect upon, their feelings. Dahmer's inability to reflect upon his painful feelings is replaced with the action of playing a fantasy game. It might also be possible to see his fascination with dead animals, his other main childhood pleasure, in a similar light: a concrete enactment of an unsymbolizable fear of his own inner deadness.

The coveting of body parts and cannibalism that characterized Dahmer's murders echo features of this childhood game. Closeness is desired but also feared. This ambivalence can be transcended, the circle squared, but only in death – within the 'black hole' of 'Infinity Land'. His father captured something of this fatal connection between desire and dread:

> The dread of people leaving him had been at the root of more than one of Jeff's murders. In general, Jeff had simply wanted to 'keep' people permanently, to hold them fixedly within his grasp. He had also wanted to make them feel literally a part of him, a permanent part, utterly inseparable from himself. It was a mania that had begun with fantasies of unmoving bodies, and proceeded to his practice of drugging men in bathhouses, then on to murder, and finally, to cannibalism, by which practice Jeff had hoped to ensure that his victims would never leave him, that they would be part of him forever.
>
> (Dahmer, 1994: 216)

The retreat into fantasy – he only ever shared this fantasy with one other boy – like his first attempted 'solution' of being good, can only have made matters worse for Dahmer in the real world of childhood. His father recognized this and attempted to do something about it by getting his son involved in 'normal' pursuits. Dahmer, ever obedient and too apathetic to resist, went along with his father's wishes, as he would later do by enrolling at university and then joining the army. But his fantasy world was a more enticing option: a 'better' defence.

At puberty, in high school, there is some evidence of a renewed attempt to 'be good' by appeasing his peer group: the attempt to become the class clown (an unusual role for a withdrawn social recluse to adopt) and beginning to drink alcohol might be interpreted in this light. But, given his history of social ineptitude and isolation, it is hard to see how this could have succeeded. In the event, it did not, of course, and Dahmer's fantasy world, now sexualized in the wake of adolescence, became ever stronger. If childhood loneliness is a problem, adolescent loneliness is probably more acute. The importance of peer group and sexual relations, especially their role as markers of identity and status, make the ability to connect with others a key *rite of passage*. As Dahmer's inability to actually connect deteriorated, his reliance on his, now sexualized, fantasy world increased.

But this 'solution' too proved insufficient, which left only the next fateful step: actualizing his fantasies. It is important to remember that Dahmer's first murder happened at a time when his social situation was as bad as it had ever been: his parents had just divorced, going their separate ways and leaving him alone in their previously shared house; he was between school and university, friendless and without any 'normal' diversions and routines. Dahmer preferred men or boys who were physically fit – like his father: 'He had wanted bodies, muscular, male bodies' (ibid: 191); 'Hicks, who was hitchhiking … had taken off his shirt, so that he was naked to the waist, and it was this that had initially attracted Jeff' (ibid: 215). Indeed, Lionel Dahmer alludes to the possibility that Jeff's murders symbolized some form of attack on him. Commenting on a time when Jeff insisted on carving a 'mean face' into a Halloween lantern, Lionel reflected: 'I wonder by what miracle that mean face, symbolic as it is of all that is insanely evil, was not me' (ibid: 228). Unsurprisingly, Dahmer was unable to articulate his motivations. His fantasies were 'like arrows, shooting into my mind from out of the blue' (quoted in Masters, 1993: 64). Described thus, they seem almost as painful and unwelcome as the reality – inner and outer – they attempt to defend against. What 'sated' the fantasies, if only temporarily, was the release granted by masturbation (ibid). The collapse of Dahmer's representational capacities was in evidence in the killings: in his 'loving' response to body parts – caressing and kissing the chest in some cases – and his penchant for listening to bodily sounds by laying his head on the victim's chest or abdomen. Although Dahmer could not remember what happened, he awoke on top of a severely bruised and dead Steven Tuomi with whom he had spent the night, with bruised hands and arms. This would seem to testify to the rage that shadowed his desire. Brian Masters (ibid: 109–10) interprets this as a possible attempt by Dahmer 'to get inside him, to achieve … the ultimate intimacy?'. We can agree, if we remember that Dahmer's desire for intimacy was never free of his fear of it – and that the two had to be split apart, if necessary by the permanence of death, before his desires could be freed from their hateful shadow. This desire freed from rage was also evident in his more aggressive forms of sexual pleasuring – masturbating over the dead body; the use of the viscera to masturbate with; and the use of the severed head as masturbatory stimulant. These practices, evident in many of his killings, seem to have been enacted during a dissociated 'high' where Dahmer was, triumphantly, finally 'in control'.

We know that when reality re-entered Dahmer's consciousness he was petrified. He was also, gradually, plagued by feelings of guilt, so strong that he reverted to his previous 'solution'; and again attempted to 'be good'. This 'solution', especially the two-year period he spent living with his 'sweet' Grandma, worked, albeit with increasing difficulty towards the end and liberally assisted by alcohol to ease the pain, for eight years. But Dahmer's unfulfilled needs could not be assuaged. After this collapse of his defensive organization, the evidence suggests that Dahmer gave up the effort. His attempts to be 'good' by attending work regularly and keeping himself clean and tidy, for example, gradually disintegrated as his fantasy world – of killing and necrophilia – became his real world: his work, his mission, his compulsion, his life. By this time, the defensive organization had all but collapsed and no other 'solutions' were possible. He could only go on killing until he was physically stopped – and the long overdue effort to mentalize his distress, through the long confessional interview and psychiatric examinations, commenced. Afterwards, feeling guilty but free of the obsessional compulsions, 'what remained was the depression, all the greater for being born of belated self-knowledge' (ibid: 220). The extent of Dahmer's inner torment, and the lengths to which he went to defend against it, were such as to ensure that his reorganized defences only let in as much reality as he could bear.

Conclusion

As cases go, this is as sickeningly gruesome as they come. Many people would probably prefer not to know about many of the details we have written about. But, as we have been arguing throughout the book, it is only through attending to the detail of particular cases that we can begin to make the connections between things that may, at first, seem totally unrelated. It is these connections that provide the basis of an understanding. In Dahmer's case, we have tried to make a series of connections among traumatic and troubling early life experiences, his fantasy life, the development of necrophiliac desires, situational contingencies, particularly those involving relational issues, and becoming a killer. These connections implicated past and present, fantasy and reality, inner and outer worlds: they were, in brief, psychosocial. Only by being resolutely psychosocial could we have made these connections. Only by making these connections could we detect an underlying 'logic' – strange, horrific, perverted and tragic – to his tortured life; a logic that, however monstrous his crimes, enabled us to see him, albeit with difficulty, in human terms.

But, this 'logic' was not given in the connections but had to be produced theoretically. That is to say, we noticed what we did and made the connections we did because of our particular psychosocial orientation. Thus, we made less of the hernia operation that was central to Masters' explanation, and more of Dahmer's relationship with his depressed parents. By giving more weight than Masters did to how we imagined Dahmer internalized traumatic events, to their psychic dimension, we were able to make more connections among more areas of his life. More crucially, it enabled us to *explain*, rather than simply note, as Masters does, the connections between Dahmer's inner deadness and the development of his necrophiliac desire. This is not to suggest that our explanation is right in every particular; it is offered in a far more open and tentative spirit than that. But it is to suggest that we were looking with the right theoretical tools, tools we define as psychosocial, tools with the scope, properly handled, to build a serviceable explanation of Jeffrey Dahmer's life and crimes.

To the extent that we have achieved an explanation of a single, all but unique case, we will be better placed to explain other cases of serial killing. As we argued in Chapter 1, the atypical case is 'as useful as any other' in this respect because the whole point of the exercise is the development of theory. If we have managed to produce convincing theoretical links in this case, then they can shed light on other dissimilar cases, if their role in the new case is properly established. By the same token, theoretical links made in rather different cases can help us make sense of this unique case. In this case, we drew on work by Cartwright developed in relation to 'rage type' killers, all of whom fitted a profile that would have excluded Dahmer, to show something of the similarities in the defensive organization of his rage type killers and Dahmer's. In so doing, we help firm up the link and widen the scope of Cartwright's argument. Thus, theoretically driven work can transcend the particular case or the particular profile which first develops it and helps generalize the argument. Cartwright's profiling work is of this order; most, as we showed earlier, unfortunately is not.

8

UNDERSTANDING THE PERPETRATORS
OF RACIAL HARASSMENT

We can now say with confidence that racist violence affects a considerable proportion of the ethnic minority communities on an enduring basis, that serious and mundane incidents are interwoven to create a threatening environment ... What is now required is a shift away from the victimological perspective to an analysis of the characteristics of offenders, the social milieu in which violence is fostered, and the process by which it becomes directed against people from ethnic minorities.

(Bowling and Phillips, 2002: 114)

Summarizing what little has been written about the perpetrators of racist violence, Ben Bowling and Coretta Phillips (2002: Chapter 5) point out that most of what we know is derived from victims' accounts. These reveal that racially motivated offenders are disproportionately male, aged 16 to 25, and often, but not always, living in areas where people from ethnic minorities make up a small but growing, or increasingly visible, proportion of the local population (cf. Hewitt, 1996). Alcohol is often a contributory factor, as are some forms of illicit drug use (see also Messner et al., 2004), but political affiliations to the far Right much less so (see also Karstedt, 1999; cf. Björgo, 1997). In this chapter, we provide an overview of the small collection of recent studies that have further illuminated the characteristics of offenders, before looking at the case of one perpetrator from our own study (Gadd et al., 2005), a man we have re-named 'Greg'. Our overview considers typological, structured action and shame-sensitive approaches. Our case study, however, demonstrates that, while all three of these approaches capture things that are distinctive about the perpetrator population, they fall short of the adequately psychosocial understanding of offenders' subjectivities that is needed to explain the difference between those who are simply prejudiced and those who engage, however occasionally, in acts of violent racism.

Typological approaches

McDevitt, Levin and Bennett's fourfold typology

Until recently those academic studies that addressed the motivation of racist offenders were almost exclusively typological. McDevitt, Levin and Bennett's (2002) fourfold typology is one of the best-known US works about hate crime perpetrators, not least because it builds on a slightly simpler typological approach outlined nine years earlier (Levin and McDevitt, 1993). McDevitt, Levin and Bennett's (2002) typology is based on an analysis of 169 hate crime files compiled by the Boston Police Department in 1991. On the basis of these hate-crime files, McDevitt and colleagues identified four distinct types of hate-crime motivation.

1 Sixty-six per cent of hate crime perpetrators committed their crimes for the excitement or thrill. These so-called 'thrill offences' were predominantly committed by groups of young people who got a 'sadistic high' from seeking out victims in areas where gay people and/or ethnic minorities were heavily concentrated, and who enjoyed bragging about these violent escapades afterwards (ibid: 308).
2 Twenty-five per cent of hate crime perpetrators committed their crimes to defend their turf. These offences occurred, almost by definition, in those areas where offenders lived and were primarily directed towards minority groups who had recently moved into the neighbourhood, and who were accessing community resources.
3 Eight per cent of hate crime perpetrators were retaliating against real and/or perceived degradations and assaults by members of another group. These offences involved vengeful cycles of action and reaction, often after particular assaults had acquired a high-profile in the media.
4 Less than one per cent of perpetrators saw it as their mission in life to rid the world of groups they considered evil or inferior. Members of extremist groups – who made 'hate a career rather than a hobby'– were often, but not always, responsible for 'missionary offences' (ibid: 309).

Even though it was 'widely adopted by law enforcement' (ibid) this typology had a number of shortcomings. First, most hate crimes are not reported to the police, and, even when they are, police records are usually insufficiently detailed to enable even this fourfold coding to be undertaken (ibid: 306). Second, McDevitt and his colleagues assumed that the four types of offending correspond to four different types of offender, but they cite no evidence to support this claim. It is entirely feasible that many missionary offenders get a thrill out of their crimes, consider themselves protectors of their countries, and feel themselves degraded by the actions of particular sexual or minority ethnic groups. Third, there were different levels of participation in hate crime amongst its perpetrators. Some young perpetrators 'did not fully participate' in the hate crimes for which they were arrested, having successfully resisted the momentum of their peer group, whilst others, despite their reservations, had gone 'along with friends' in order to 'save face' (ibid: 313). Fourth, this typological approach (as Levin and McDevitt concede in their book that was also written in 2002) remains unsatisfactorily speculative on the question of why some people commit hate crimes and others do not:

> Hate crimes represent the end point on the continuum of prejudice and bigotry. For economic, social, and psychological reasons, countless individuals feel resentful. They have suffered a drop in self-esteem or status and are eager to place the blame elsewhere ... Yet millions of Americans have suffered a decline in their standard of living and/or their self-esteem but would never commit a criminal act against individuals who are different from them. Perhaps some potential offenders simply do not buy into the culture of hate; others may possess enough self-control that they are able to stop themselves from behaving in a deviant or violent manner ...
>
> (Levin and McDevitt, 2002: 98)

Sibbitt and diverse perpetrators with multiple disadvantages

A more challenging analysis of official records is provided by Rae Sibbitt's (1997) study of the cases of victimization catalogued by the police, housing departments and youth services in two London boroughs. Sibbitt found that the majority of the perpetrators of racial harassment within the boroughs she studied were young men. However, Sibbitt's analysis cautions against the view that those who commit most racially motivated crime are *simply* young thrill-seekers. In many of the cases Sibbitt studied it was evident that the co-presence of a range of criminogenic risk factors, mental-health problems and prejudice had contributed to the behaviour of the perpetrators. In Sibbitt's view, weak and/or abusive families, truancy, alcohol and substance misuse, unemployment, ill-health, stress, poor living conditions, together with the internalization of the various kinds of racist, nationalist and anti-immigrant sentiment espoused by British politicians over a number of years, had all contributed to the strength of racism within perpetrators' communities:

> For perpetrators, potential perpetrators and other individuals within the perpetrator community, expressions of racism often serve the function of distracting their own – and others' – attention away from real, underlying, concerns which they feel impotent to deal with.
>
> (Sibbitt, 1997: viii)

In constructing a typology of perpetrators, Sibbitt tried to show how the convergence of this kind of displacement activity impacts differentially on subsections of London's white working class. Included within Sibbitt's typology were:

- The pensioners who are generally friendly to their black neighbours, but have become fearful as a consequence of young people's criminal activities and perceive their country as being invaded by non-white foreigners.

- The young or middle-aged couple next door who have experienced hardships – unemployment, poor housing, reduced welfare benefits – and have usurped racialized discourses in order to explain their misfortune. This family may join with others in abusing minority or immigrant groups who appear to have got a better deal than they have from the council, the health service, or the police.
- The (multiply disadvantaged) problem family, whose members are paranoid that the authorities are out to get them. 'The children, experiencing abusive and threatening behaviour from their parents, behave abusively towards others' (ibid: 78–9). Because of their antisocial behaviours this sort of family may be gossiped about (disparagingly) by their neighbours, and typecast by other local people and service providers alike. The adults in this sort of family are prone to harassing many of their neighbours, and are 'virulently abusive and intimidating towards ethnic minority neighbours' (ibid: 79).
- Those in mid- to late adolescence who will have accommodated the tension between the racist attitudes of their parents (with whom they have some sympathy) and their friendships with other black youths (some of whom they actively admire because of their style, sporting abilities, etc.). These teenagers may have hung around, after school, with older youths who are particularly racist, and will have joined in with the older boys' violent and racist behaviour, perceiving it as both fun and a source of esteem.
- Younger teenagers – especially those unsupported at home and doing less well at school – may try to improve their self-esteem by picking on a range of others, including people in the street. Ethnic-minority children may prove easy targets for these teenagers, particularly if such children have few friends.
- Finally, younger children may mimic the views of adults and older children within their families, and thus confidently proclaim that non-whites should 'go back to their own country' without necessarily understanding what this means (ibid: 80). These children may intimidate ethnic-minority pupils in their class by refusing to sit next to or play with them.

In sum, Sibbitt provides a multi-layered analysis of racism that captures the way in which some sections of London's white working class have come to perceive themselves as disadvantaged by multiculturalism and unfairly accused of being racist (Back and Keith, 1999; Collins, 2004; Hewitt, 1996). In grasping the interconnections between multiple disadvantages and multiple manifestations of racism Sibbitt's approach is eminently more sophisticated than McDevitt and colleagues' typology. Yet, for all the emphasis on the copious seductions of racism, Sibbitt's perpetrators still appear like rather unthinking victims of circumstance, adopting racist discourses simply because of their age and structural disadvantages. Why some racists keep their views to themselves whilst others physically attack ethnic-minority groups still remains unexplained.

The structured action approach

Messerschmidt and crime as structured action

The notion that crime of all kinds is related to multiply structured patterns of inequality is better theorized within James Messerschmidt's 'structured action' approach to criminology. As we outlined in Chapter 4, in his attempts to explain the maleness of crime Messerschmidt (1993, 1997) has conceptualized crime as a 'resource' that some men draw upon in certain situations to accomplish their masculinities. Three ideas, you may remember, are critical to Messerschmidt's thesis:

1   In Western industrialized societies there are a range of masculinities that coexist within relations of domination and subordination and compete among themselves and in relation to a range of femininities. Where one version of masculinity achieves an obvious dominance it is said to be hegemonic.
2   These gendered social relations are multiply structured by inequalities of power, the prerogatives of the labour market and sexual preference, as well as by class and race. One consequence of this is that white, middle-class, heterosexual men are repeatedly able to occupy the hegemonic position in social relations, whilst working-class, ethnic-minority and gay men are routinely subordinated.
3   Individuals are held 'accountable' for their actions according to the demands of these social relations. In this respect, race, class and gender are not simply given, but have to be situationally accomplished through actions that are judged to be suitably masculine or feminine.

Using this framework Messerschmidt tried to address the question of why it is that economically marginalized young white men, who are thus disadvantaged in class terms but who occupy privileged positions in terms of their race and gender, are most frequently responsible for attacks on ethnic and sexual minorities. Messerschmidt's answer to this question was as follows:

> For some white, working-class boys, their public masculinity is constructed through hostility to, and rejection of, all aspects of groups that may be considered inferior in a racist and heterosexist society … Indeed, the meaning of being a 'white man' has always hinged on the existence of, for example, a subordinated 'black man'. Thus a specific *racial gender* is constructed through the identical practice of racist violence; a social practice that bolsters, within the specific setting of white, working-class youth groups, one's masculine 'whiteness' and, therefore, constitutes race and gender simultaneously. White, working-class, youthful masculinity acquires meaning in this particular context through racist violence.
>
> (Messerschmidt, 1993: 99–100, emphases in original)

Developing this work further, Messerschmidt has also tried to explain why the lynching of African-American men became more commonplace in the US South after the abolition of slavery, and particularly why, during this period, black men who knocked into or looked at white women were sometimes falsely accused of rape and punished accordingly. Messerschmidt's argument is that interracial sexuality symbolized a threat to Southern white men's masculinity, founded as it was, on the ability to control, provide for, and protect the family home. In this context, the

> lynching scenario constructed white women as frail, vulnerable, and wholly dependent for protection on chivalric white men. In this way, lynching and the

mythology of the 'black rapist' reproduced race and gender hierarchies during a time when those very hierarchies were threatened ... Protection of white women reinforced femaleness and thus the notion of 'separate spheres,' while simultaneously constructing racial boundaries between white and African American men ... Lynching, then, was a white male resource for 'doing difference' ... Accordingly, lynching the mythic 'black rapist' not only constructed African American men as subordinate to white men, but simultaneously perpetuated the notion of separate spheres and inequality between white men and white women.

(Messerschmidt, 1997: 35)

Perry and hate crime as a resource for doing difference

Barbara Perry further elaborates the utility of the structured action approach to hate crime. Within Western culture, Perry argues, difference is often constructed in negative relational terms – as 'deficiency' – so that those who deviate from the hegemonic position are constructed as inadequate, inferior, bad, or evil (2002: 48). From Perry's perspective, hate crime happens because of the conventional culture, which is itself derivative of the way ethnic and sexual minorities are structurally subordinated.

Hate crime ... connects the structural meanings and organization of race with the cultural construction of racialized identity. On the one hand, it allows perpetrators to reenact their whiteness, thereby establishing their dominance. On the other hand, it coconstructs the nonwhiteness of the victims, who are perceived to be worthy of violent repression either because they correspond to a demonized identity, or, paradoxically, because they threaten the racialized boundaries that are meant to separate 'us' from 'them'.

(ibid: 58)

Perry claims that the perpetration of hate crime serves multiple objectives. It reinforces the normativeness of white sexuality whilst punishing those who transgress, or who are imagined to have transgressed, the norm. Victims are often harassed for *transcending* normative conceptions of difference – for doing things white men think ethnic minority men are not entitled to do – but they may also be punished for *conforming* to relevant categories of difference, for behaving in ways whites consider to be stereotypical of non-whites. Whilst the process of victimizing others instils a positive sense of identity in those perpetrators who feel marginalized in terms of their class, knowledge of this victimization amongst the victim's community reinstates the injustices of the present institutional arrangements.

Unlike the typological approaches, both Messerschmidt and Perry's theses are sensitive to issues of context and motive, structure and agency. The structured-action approach accounts for the way in which so many racist attacks often appear to be as much about gender, age and sexuality as they are about 'race'. Within the structured-action approach, perpetrators are perceived as not unlike the law-abiding majority, many of whom also ascribe to essentialist conceptions of race. Yet, despite these strengths, structured-action theorists have not managed to free their approach from some of its original shortcomings, as we saw in Chapter 4. Too often within the structured-action approach motive is deduced from what victims or witnesses claim offenders said, or worse still, simply presupposed. For example:

> a Hispanic youth who excels in school is perceived by the majority to be cross-ing established racial boundaries. He is 'discredited' to the extent that he has forgotten his place. Consequently, a white youth who victimizes this 'upstart' will be justified and in fact rewarded for his efforts to reestablish the racialized boundaries between himself and the victim. Both actors have been judged for their actions, with predictable and reconstitutive consequences.
>
> (ibid: 58–9)

Maybe, maybe not. The example seems to be hypothetical one. The hypothesized victim is attributed with no resources with which to resist his 'discrediting'. The racist white youth – of unspecified intellectual ability – is congratulated for his hate crime and is rewarded by unidentified others – presumably not from the victim's community. Yet, in reality things are likely to be more mixed and more contingent. There might be academically successful white youths who identify with their Hispanic peer's success. There might be unsuccessful Hispanic youths who have no time for their more studious colleague. There may well be adults – racists amongst them – who think that all violence is wrong, irrespective of whom it is directed towards. What will determine which of many possible scenarios gets played out will depend on biographical as well as situational and structural factors. In short, the fail-ure to attend to the complexities of subjectivity, understood in relation to a unique personal biography as well as a set of shared social circumstances, continues to con-fer on structured-action theory a deterministic feel (Jefferson, 1997a).

Shame-sensitive approaches

Scheff, unacknowledged shame and bloody revenge

Thomas Scheff (1994) does take the issue of subjectivity more seriously. Scheff's argument is that shame is a 'master emotion' that is insufficiently acknowledged in contemporary Western societies. It is an emotion that Nobert Elias (1978) conceived of as crucially implicated in the civilizing process (through instilling a form of 'modesty' that renders certain forms of intimate knowledge – most notably around sex and reproduction – unspeakable, at least in certain contexts). By shame, Scheff means feelings like humiliation, embarrassment and disgrace, the sensation that our decency has been judged by another and found lacking. For Scheff, shame can be conceptual-ized as the opposite of pride, or otherwise the kind of self-consciousness that arises when we see ourselves negatively 'from the viewpoint of others' (Scheff, 1994: 42).

The significance of the other's (often imagined) viewpoint is that it renders shame a thoroughly 'social emotion' which, like the Freudian superego, is a product of the value humans place on social bonds. In fact, the many sources of data Scheff collates provide considerable support for psychoanalytic thinking – particularly the significance it attaches to denial – even if psychoanalysis has, by and large, neglected shame as a subject of study (a point to which we return in Chapter 11). Through the analysis of domestic and international conflicts, Scheff demonstrates how people often 'deny and disguise' their feelings of shame by attributing their discomfort to 'awkward situations', boldly asserting that they do not care or that they are not bothered, and by distracting themselves from painful feelings through rapid and/or compulsive activity (ibid: 50–1). Painful feelings that have been repressed, however, have a habit of coming back to haunt the individual, who may then internalize them or project them out onto others, where they can be aggressively attacked.

Scheff defines this latter possibility as a 'shame–anger sequence', highlighting how it can give rise to 'self-perpetuating chains of emotional reaction' that 'loop back on themselves' (ibid: 49). Scheff contends that without proper acknowledgement, shame is likely to become embedded in the social relationships of individuals to the extent that they start to feel ashamed of being ashamed, preoccupied with appearing weak, defensive towards those who they think have noticed their shame, and caught up in an 'unending spiralling of emotion in feeling traps' (ibid: 66). Unconsciously motivated reactions to shame may then intensify, manifesting themselves behaviourally as righteous rages or spiteful acts of vengeance, directed either at those perceived to be sitting in judgement or scapegoats who are (mistakenly) perceived to be the real source of the humiliating experience.

By way of illustration, Scheff argues that unacknowledged shame is the key to understanding Hitler's rise to power in the years before World War II. Humiliatingly defeated during World War I, coerced by the international community into accepting sole responsibility for initiating that war, excluded from the League of Nations with their homeland fragmented and their colonies redistributed under the Treaty of Versailles, by the mid-1930s the German people were perceiving themselves – through the eyes of other nations – as completely disrespected. Hitler, however, had his own personal reasons for feeling belittled, his relationship with his own father having been 'charged with violence, ridicule, and contempt' (ibid: 109). As Scheff points out, Hitler's biography is testimony to the intense, maddening shame the dictator felt and the 'lifelong history of intense rage states' to which this repressed shame gave rise (ibid: 113). More significantly, however, the public projection of Hitler's inner conflicts onto communists, Jews, gypsies and homosexuals accomplished a form of emotional catharsis for the masses:

> Hitler's hold on the masses was that, instead of ignoring or condemning their humiliated fury ... he displayed it himself ... His rage and his projection of German shame onto the Jews would have temporarily lessened the pain of the average German by interrupting the chain reaction of overt shame and rage. His own behaviour or beliefs implied, 'You needn't be ashamed of being humiliated

and enraged; it's not your fault.' The secret of charisma may be exactly this: the emotional, not the cognitive content of the message.

(ibid: 118)

The problem with all this – as we pursue in more detail in Chapter 11 – is the unproblematic elision of levels: Hitler's appalling relations with his father producing the repressed shame that is resentfully projected onto a variety of scapegoat groups; the masses respond to this because it echoes their own shame consequent upon the post-World War I treatment of Germany. Not only is this too social an account, in that events in Hitler's childhood produce his shameful inner world just as events in the social world produce the shameful inner world of the German public, it also says nothing about why shame is too painful to acknowledge, why it needs to be repressed – an issue which requires that psychoanalytic ideas be taken seriously and not simply smuggled in as and when it suits.

Ray, Smith and Wastell and shame, rage and racist violence

Perhaps unsurprisingly, given its application to the study of nationalism, Scheff's thesis proved persuasive to Ray, Smith and Wastell in their study of those convicted of racially aggravated offences in Greater Manchester (Ray and Smith, 2001, 2004; Ray et al., 2003, 2004). In Oldham the problem of racist violence was amplified – both in the public consciousness and in reality – by 'a vicious spiral' of social reactions that heightened the visibility of young South Asian males, who were then identified as 'gangs' of racially motivated offenders by the police and media, often after agitation from the British National Party (Ray and Smith, 2004). In reality, most of the violence in Oldham was perpetrated by white, working-class men, from estates where both poverty and racism were rife. Residents in these areas tended to perceive themselves to be under threat from an expanding South Asian population, even though this population was, like them, also deeply affected by the decline of local manufacturing industries.

Ray et al.'s (2004) interviews with those on probation for racially aggravated offences uncovered that most (white) racially motivated offenders were little different from the general population of offenders. They were better characterized as generalist offenders with a propensity for violence than specialist violent racists. Many were from disrupted, unhappy homes and impoverished neighbourhoods, with few educational qualifications, and vaguely known to their victims, often as a result of commercial transactions. Those white offenders who were actually responsible for most racist incidents were typically those sections of Oldham's working class that felt excluded from the cosmopolitan and multicultural lifestyles celebrated in other parts of the Greater Manchester conurbation. Following Scheff, Ray et al. detected unacknowledged shame in the verbal disclosures and body language of around two-thirds of their 36 respondents. The racist offenders they met repeatedly revealed a sense of grievance, victimization, unfairness and powerlessness ... [T]hey saw themselves as weak, disregarded, overlooked, unfairly treated, victimized without being recognized as victims, made to feel small; meanwhile, the other – their Asian victims ... – was experienced as powerful, in control, laughing, successful, 'arrogant'. An act of violence represents an attempt to re-establish control, to escape from shame into a state of pride that is necessarily 'false', because not based in secure social bonds of mutual respect and understanding. It is an act of bloody revenge ...

(2004: 355–6)

Ray and colleagues (2004) argue that the racism evident in Oldham during the late 1990s was akin to German anti-Semitism during World War II. The Jews, like Pakistanis and Bangladeshis in contemporary Oldham, stood accused of having accumulated undeserved wealth, of having been dishonest, lazy, and culturally and religiously exclusive. Echoing sentiments that were widely felt in their neighbourhoods, the white racist offenders Ray et al. interviewed complained about feeling fearful of Asians who 'stick together'; being cheated out of benefits, childcare, housing entitlements and educational opportunities; being wrongfully accused of being racist; and being 'expected to change' because 'they' won't integrate. South Asians – who were constructed as the source of white people's shame – were typically accused of being 'parasitic', 'arrogant' and prone to using their own language to talk about white people behind their backs.

But Ray et al.'s analysis, like Perry's, is not fully substantiated by their data. While they have published many accounts of what offenders think about ethnic minorities, they have published very few, if any, of their interviewees' explanations of their actual offending behaviour. This makes it hard to gauge whether unacknowledged shame is more acute for those who commit acts of racist violence than for those who simply hold racist viewpoints. It also makes it impossible to assess the relevance of the unhappy childhoods and neighbourhood deprivation that characterized their interviewees' backgrounds. The resentful feeling that other people are getting a better deal than you sounds like envy; the fear that others are talking about you is a form of paranoia; accusations about 'parasitic' behaviour sound like disgust; and the desire to see minority groups do 'hard graft' has a sadistic feel to it. Certainly there is evidence of 'brooding' shame in many of the accounts Ray et al. (2004) elicited, but it is questionable whether shame and pride are necessarily and always the 'master' emotions behind racist violence: a point that we can best illuminate through the study of a single case.

Racial violence: the case of 'Greg'

A pen portrait of 'Greg'

Greg was a 16-year-old offender serving a three-month 'action plan' for assaulting his stepbrother's girlfriend (who had assaulted his mum). At the time he was interviewed,

Greg was attempting to sort himself out, i.e. get his drug use under control. Smoking cannabis from the age of nine, taking ecstasy from his early teens and snorting cocaine from around the age of 14 – from a gram every few days to 'snorting seven grams a day' – eventually 'everything just fell to pieces': 'I'd lost most of me mates'; 'I'd fallen out with me mum all the time'; and his girlfriend (of three years) and his best mate both threatened to leave him unless he made changes. The threat of losing his best mate and his girlfriend had initially made matter matters worse: 'I just went dead depressed and that … weren't bothered. Started drinking as well, at night'. But ultimately it was this threat that motivated 'Greg' to 'sort' himself out: 'or me girlfriend and me best mate were going to walk away and leave me. So I said, right, I'll get clean … I done loads of … drug work and victim support, avoiding custody … It's sound now.'

A year prior, when Greg had been banned from their estate, Greg's girlfriend's mum had made her daughter have an abortion. Despite this, Greg's girlfriend – the 'closest thing' to him – had stood by him, helping him 'through a lot'. Unlike other 'money-grabbing' girls who just wanted his 'respect', Greg's girlfriend had looked out for his 'best interests' and did not 'want nothing off' him. If he lost her Greg said he would: 'go back into it … I wouldn't be bothered if I lost me girlfriend. I would do time in jail … I'd either hurt someone … or go back into dealing and I'd end up doing somebody over that way'. Likewise, Greg considered his relationship with his best mate to be indispensable. Not only had the mate taught Greg how to 'nick cars and stuff' and taken on Greg's bullying halfbrother, but he had also taught Greg respect: 'if anyone learned me respect, it was him': always 'just gave me respect' and so 'I give it him back'.

Brought up by his mum and a stepdad who 'scared' Greg that much that he never spoke to him, Greg was only close ('dead close') to Lenny, his stepbrother. Lenny was at least five years Greg's senior, and, Greg claimed, had 'always looked after' him. This brotherly looking-after included introducing Greg to cannabis at the age of nine – giving Greg a chance to 'prove' that he could 'take more than most people' his age – and to burglary and drug-dealing by the time he was 14. Greg's younger stepbrother and stepsister were usually 'okay', but were prone to calling him 'a dickhead', 'mouthy' behaviour that would easily cause Greg to 'kick off'. Greg no longer spoke to one of his two older half brothers. This halfbrother used to beat Greg up when they were younger. When, several years later, this halfbrother was seen to push Greg's mother, Greg took the opportunity to get his revenge, beating up his halfbrother 'with a bar'. Unlike his halfbrothers, Greg had never met his biological dad, but had heard his father was violent to his mum, knew he was 'loaded' and drove a 'Merc'. When offered an opportunity to meet his dad, Greg failed to show up, claiming 'he didn't need the money' at the time and that he was no longer bothered whether his father knew him or not:

> I seen him like … and he didn't even know who I was. So I wasn't really bothered. He was just sat there, so fucking ain't it. I ain't bothered at the end of the day. If he wanted me he would have got in touch with me. So I don't really bother about stuff like that.

Greg's relationship with his mum was somewhat precarious. On the one hand, he felt very protective towards her. His assaults on his stepbrother's girlfriend and on his halfbrother, as we have seen, were both precipitated by their aggressive acts against his mother. This protectiveness (which also extended to his stepsister) was also in evidence in Greg's attack on the property of a Turkish man (described below). On the other hand, Greg only 'sort of' got on with his mother and, at the time of the first interview, preferred life at his 'dead laid back' foster parents' (an arrangement instituted as an alternative to being remanded in custody) because there he had his 'own space', no 'mouthy' siblings to contend with and a daily routine (even though he 'felt like killing meself at first ... Being away from me family cos I got kicked off me estate, cos I couldn't see no-one. Proper did me head in'). Greg criticized his mother for not providing him with 'nice clothes and trainers' when he was younger, even though 'she got loads of money' in her purse. This, Greg claimed, was 'another reason' he went 'stealing'. Nevertheless, in the two-week gap between interview one and interview two, Greg had left his foster home, and had begun living between his mother's home and the home he shared with his girlfriend and Lenny.

The earliest fight he remembered involved a 'lad' in the park punching Greg, and Greg 'just laughing at him', feeling 'nothing': it 'just weren't bothering me' – despite getting a black eye. If these early fights were 'just petty things', his fighting at school – 'kicking off on the headmaster ... I used to try and hit him'; 'throwing chairs at the teachers' – were deemed serious enough for the school to have him examined and then to exclude him. The spell at his primary boarding school that followed Greg's exclusion was 'hard cos never been away from me family', but did have the desired effect for a while. Having been told that being good would get him back to 'normal' school Greg calmed down. But when the school reneged on this promise, denying Greg a place in a normal secondary school, he 'just got worse ... [and] started fighting and that again'. With 'a couple of lads' he knew from his primary-boarding-school years, Greg set about 'running' the secondary school by 'bullying people ... [I]f they didn't do what we told them, I'd hit them'. In response, four lads at his school beat Greg up. Greg was excluded for threatening a series of retaliatory attacks. Stealing, TWOCing ('borrowing' cars without the owners' consent), shoplifting and burglary followed 'just like for a laugh' until Greg realized 'there was money in it': 'making meself loads and loads of money', 'I started doing it every day. Going out at night, robbing cars and that and then started taking pills'. Eventually Greg – still in his early teens – needed £200-a-day to feed his cocaine habit, which is when he started dealing.

As well as this instrumental crime, there was also the fighting. Just as Greg saw it as 'his school', he also regarded the town and the estate as 'his': 'I thought it were my town ... like when I was on the streets and they came running their mouths off, "this is like our side", I say, "No, its all mine, mine and me mates and you got no say in it now".' As well as this inter-estate rivalry, Greg had made a lot of enemies, partly because of rumours spread by his girlfriend's mum and his stepbrother's girlfriend, partly because of his reputation as a fighter and drug-dealer, and partly because of racial animosities. On one occasion, 'enemies' spray-painted his walls with 'racist stuff, like ... Paki-shagger': something Greg found to be stupid and incomprehensible because 'two doors up one of me other mates is black' and 'these Chinese people lived next door to him'.

Greg described a long-running saga of brawls with a particular group of local Asians who thought they 'ran' a school on his estate: 'these are just muppets ... They are having a joke ... Cos if that school's on my turf that's my school'. To make matters worse these Asians were also 'mouthy': 'They say stuff to you, like to your sisters'. The things 'they' would say included, 'Your brother's wank'; 'Tell him he's going to get it'; and 'Tell him I has shagged his mum'. One reprisal for causing offence involved Greg's mate demanding a cigarette from one of two Asian youths who were standing together. When the youths ran off and one started to phone the police, Greg and his mate gave chase, his mate punched the Asian 'and the tip of his nose just fell on the floor' – an attack which whilst 'funny at the time', became worrying to Greg, as he thought about being charged by the police, and which did, in fact, lead to his mate being convicted of racially aggravated assault. By way of revenge, when Greg was walking home alone one night, five Asian teenagers who knew the victim asked Greg for a cigarette, and then beat him up. Greg explained, however, that he was, 'not racist against Asians cos I got Asian mates in Leicester ... I used to ... sell skunk to them ... They aren't racist ... They are just dead sound lads.' Greg also spoke positively about black people, whom he and Lenny got on 'dead well' with, at least when it came to dealing and using illicit drugs.

On the other hand, 'asylum seekers', an increasing number of whom he believed to be descending on his city, Greg did not like: 'they don't think twice of pulling out a blade'. When asked to talk about his relationships with asylum seekers, Greg explained that he had recently smashed up the car of a Turkish man, before throwing a bottle through the man's window. The origins of the attack were that Greg had taken exception to the Turkish man following one of his stepbrothers for weeks – apparently because the Turkish man believed Greg's stepbrother to have stolen things from his car – and finally chased his brother 'while me little stepsister was with him'. Involving his little stepsister in this way was decisive for Greg: 'I weren't really bothered about him chasing me brother cos he's old enough to look after himself. It was just with me little sister, so I got pissed off about it. And that's when I went up that Sunday night.' What triggered Greg's bottle-throwing, however, was the realization that the Turkish man had a white girlfriend, a woman who had previously dated one of Greg's stepbrothers:

> I just thought, the cheeky twat. Taking my white woman and that ... not my woman, but my race. So I threw a bottle at her for being dirty. I was buzzing at the time. [Int: 'Have you ever felt like that before?'] Yes, every time I see a white woman with an Asian bloke or a Turk. I don't mind about black men, they can have as many white women as they want. It's just Asians, Turks, Albanians, whatever you want to call them. It's just I don't like seeing them with white women.

When the Turkish man came 'running out with a bar', Greg and his best mate tried to flee the scene, but Greg's mother – who was also in attendance – was hit on the head. Greg then started fighting the man, the police turned up and Greg ran off. Seeing his mother hit 'wounded' Greg: 'not like ... bruises. It got in me head, just messed with me ... I was going to kill him if I got hold of him'; murderous sentiments he was still feeling: 'If it were up to me he'd be lying in his coffin now.' At home with his mum after her discharge from hospital, Greg was clearly disturbed by the consequences of his behaviour:

> It was bad that night that was, cos I had to look after me mum ... no-one at all in the house, just me and me mum. Don't even know where the kids or no-one was. So I just couldn't sleep just in case me mum fucking [pause] needed me or something.

How well might different approaches analyse this case?

Types and typologies

Re-reading Greg's story through the typological approaches we considered earlier on in this chapter we learn that Greg was not an atypical offender. Like most of the perpetrators of racial harassment he was young, male, already involved in crime, and experiencing problems with alcoholism and drug addiction. Whilst his mate's attack on an Asian man was largely thrill-seeking – 'funny at the time' – it was one of many assaults exchanged in a long-running dispute over 'turf' and hence 'defensive'. This particular assault also gave rise to a retaliatory attack in which Greg was himself beaten up by friends of the victimized Asian man. Although he was not interested in the far Right – at one point insinuating that the local skinheads who had caused disorder in Stoke either had more 'bottle' than him or were 'stupid' – Greg's preoccupation with which men white women could and could not sleep with, did have a missionary feel: 'every time' Greg saw a white woman with 'an Asian bloke or a Turk' he was enraged, sometimes quite viscerally 'buzzing', as he put it. In other words, Greg traversed all four of McDevitt et al.'s types, thus rendering them redundant as a means of comprehending his relationship to racially motivated violence.

Turning to Sibbitt's profile, Greg was almost certainly a member of a 'problem family', broken by divorce and domestic violence. Greg's father – a perpetrator of domestic violence – was conspicuous by his absence whilst his mother was prone to fighting in the street with his stepbrother's girlfriend and complicit in her son's antisocial behaviour – as the tale of the Turkish man's harassment reveals. As Sibbitt puts it: 'The children, experiencing abusive and threatening behaviour from their parents' often do 'behave abusively towards others' (1997: 79). One of Greg's older halfbrothers was a bully, his stepbrother a drug-dealer and the younger stepsiblings were, at least, well-versed in the use of abusive language. Greg himself had been identified by the courts as an antisocial youth, excluded from school and banned from his estate. The best mate who taught him respect, it transpired, was an accomplished car thief and violent racist. Like Sibbitt's adolescents and like his stepbrother, Greg actively admired other black men, or at least those whom he imagined to share his interests in drugs and fighting. It was 'just Asians' – or at least the local ones – together with 'Turks' and

'Albanians', or 'whatever' the interviewer wanted 'to call them', whom Greg sought to put in their place. But, as we shall see, the particular pattern of Greg's violence is beyond the explanatory scope of even Sibbitt's complex typology.

Doing difference, accomplishing masculinity
Much of this would be predicted by structured action theory. A troubled boy, with relatively few legitimate resources for accomplishing his masculinity, the adolescent Greg proved himself by competing in the illicit market place; protecting the women in his family from the threats posed by outsiders; and through fighting and asserting his difference from a range of minority ethnic groups. Constructed as childish, intellectually deficient and incompetent 'muppets', local Asian men were harassed by Greg both for lacking the streetwiseness he imagined himself to possess and for making the kinds of sexually derogatory remarks he considered to be typical of their kind. His masculinity challenged by these remarks, Greg reasserted a form of 'racial gender' – as Messerschmidt and Perry would conceptualize it – by attacking a dangerous 'asylum seeker', a Turkish man, whom he believed posed a threat to his younger sister. White women who willingly went with men deemed 'other' by Greg, were, in his worldview, also deserving of punishment for being 'dirty' – the normativeness of white heterosexuality being used to subordinate both white women and ethnic minority men. Indeed, Greg's threefold ethnic coding system – black, white, Asian/asylum seeker/other – was not radically different to that assumed in many of the ethnic coding systems deployed by the British government, juxtaposing, as they usually do, colour and region of family origin (Phoenix and Owen, 1996).

In these respects, Messerschmidt and Perry are right. Marginalized, white working-class, youthful men, like Greg, often perpetrate violence to accomplish their masculinity, to subordinate women and ethnic and sexual minorities alike. Yet, the detail of Greg's account suggests that the psychosocial dimensions of race and gender were not as uncomplicated as the structured action approach assumes. Greg did not see himself as a 'racist' because he got on well with Asians in Leicester and because he had black friends. The drug-dealing Leicester Asians, in Greg's worldview, were like him, streetwise entrepreneurs, 'sound lads', unlike the 'muppets' in Stoke, who were not only 'racists' themselves, but illegitimately tried to claim 'his' territory as their own. Because his stepbrother's black friends allowed him (perhaps as a lonely and somewhat friendless) nine-year-old to join them in their chill-out sessions, Greg also had respect for black men, who, because of their comparable streetwiseness, he said could have as many of 'his' white women as they wanted. Rather, Greg's real problem was with 'asylum seekers', a term widely used by politicians to denote the inferred 'bogusness' of many of those seeking refugee status in Britain, and sometimes conflated with the terrorist threat assumed to be posed by 'Islamic fundamentalism' (Fekete, 2004). In the tabloid media, as well as the discourses of the far Right, the threat posed by Islamic fundamentalism is vicariously attributed to Britain's settled Asian population, and sometimes sensationalized as the 'problem' of 'Asian gangs' whose predatory sexuality is assumed to pose a danger to (white) women and children (Webster, 2003). In contemporary anti-immigration discourses, as for Greg, racism is re-expressed through more socially acceptable concerns: the fear of crime; competition for scarce resources; and the threat posed to family values. In effect, the term 'asylum seekers', like the configuration 'Asians, Turks, Albanians, whatever', refers to a population so ill-defined that it can be easily mythologized as the ideal receptacle into which the various anxieties felt by Greg, his mother, stepbrother, best mate, along with many people living in his locality, could be projected. Given the significance of this projective dimension and the subtleties of his position vis-à-vis race, it is therefore questionable whether Greg's behaviour can be understood only in terms of the workings of 'structures of domination' as the structured action approach sometimes implies.

Unacknowledged shame, rage and bloody revenge

The case material presented earlier suggests that Greg's contradictory investments in racism were rooted, at least in part, in his own emotional needs. Consistent with Scheff's thesis, we know that Greg had started to see himself negatively through the eyes of others – his best mate, his girlfriend, and to some extent his mother – and that acknowledging the astuteness of their criticisms had been a key part in his decision to desist from cocaine consumption. It seems plausible that the pride Greg took in his control over his school, his estate and his town were in stark contrast to the unacknowledged shame of his partly self-instigated exclusion from his home, his family and his natural peer-group, and there are several places in his life-story where there is evidence that unacknowledged feelings were implicated in the volatility of his behaviour:

- At home Greg was falling out with his mum 'all the time', whilst at school and on his estate he was constantly 'making loads of enemies ... fighting all the time', behaviour that resonates with Scheff's notion of being caught in a 'feeling trap'.
- Similarly, when he was sent to live with foster parents, Greg 'felt like killing' himself, his exclusion from all that really mattered to him 'proper' doing his 'head in'.
- The local Asian boys made sexual slurs about Greg and his mum, slurs that Greg could dismiss as the infantile behaviour of 'muppets'. However, when his younger brother and sister started endorsing these insults – calling Greg a 'dickhead' – Greg would 'kick off' either at his siblings, or in revenge attacks on Asian men mounted with the assistance of his best mate.
- Tellingly, it was the disrespect displayed by the Turkish man for the vulnerability of Greg's 'little sister' that 'pissed off' Greg: an example of the significance of imagining one – or one's family – has been perceived negatively through the eyes of others. How could the Turkish man imagine his innocent younger sister to be deserving of such threatening behaviour? What kind of family did he think they were?
- Greg interpreted the white women's relationship with the Turkish man as evidence of her dirtiness ('I threw a bottle at her for being dirty'). In Greg's view this dirtiness denoted a source of shame for his 'race', and maybe even his family, given the woman's previous association with one of his brothers.
- Perhaps the most shaming incident of all for Greg was the realization that he had exposed his mother to the repercussions of his harassment of the Turkish man. Seeing his mother hit 'wounded' Greg psychologically, sending him into a murderous rage, from which (at the time of the interview) he had yet to recover.

A psychosocial approach: dependency, vulnerability and hardness

The shame thesis thus provides an account of Greg's motivation that is lacking from the structured action and typological approaches, and, in so doing, begs us to consider the difference between what racially motivated offenders say about their behaviour and the feelings they are unable to acknowledge. Sibbitt suggests as much when she argues that perpetrators' 'expressions of racism often serve the function of distracting ... away from real, underlying, concerns which they feel impotent to deal with' (1997: viii). Yet, whether these underlying concerns are simply about shame in Greg's account of himself is open to question. When he was not recounting his fights with his siblings, his battle of wills with school teachers, and armed conflicts with those who wanted to steal his reputation and drug business, Greg was reflecting on what he really wanted to do: return home to his family, neighbourhood and to 'normal' school. Whilst there is – as we have illustrated – evidence of unacknowledged shame in Greg's account, it seems to be his vulnerability that is most frequently denied. Whilst the social performance of this denial was in many senses typically masculine, it also had specifically biographical roots in Greg's childhood banishment from the people and institutions upon whom he was most dependent. As we shall illustrate, this dependency was also exceptionally difficult for Greg to acknowledge.

Psychoanalysis teaches us to expect the opposite when people make bold, especially omnipotent assertions. The stubbornness of the developing infant, for example, can be a form of omnipotence that denotes 'feelings of triumph and contempt which conceal the pain associated with the inevitable loss of the mother as well as the phantasy of total control over her' (Minsky, 1998: 41). Read psychoanalytically, Greg's insistence on his abilities and 'possessions' can be interpreted as evidence of his inner feelings of powerlessness. Perhaps playing the boy who could consume more cannabis than most; the powerful bully who ran the school; and later, the drug-dealing hard man who owned the town (including schools he had never attended) helped Greg keep out of his consciousness his impotence to change his circumstances. There is further evidence of this kind of defensiveness in what Greg said about his biological father's inability to recognize him. 'And he didn't even know who I was'; 'so fucking ain't it'; not 'bothered' repeated three times; 'if he wanted me he would have got in touch with me': Greg's (understandable) response to rejection was to reject the rejecter and thus avoid the possibility of further rejection and the consequent pain that would entail.

However, neither the complexity of the emotions being avoided here, nor the capacity for emotional pain to resurface in times of anxiety, should be underestimated. Unable to speak to his fearsome stepfather, Greg might have imagined his real father – despite the rumours about his violence – to be a desirable source of identification, especially given his 'loaded' status. As for Greg's mother, her status as a victim of domestic violence probably made her a difficult source of identification for a young man struggling with his identity and himself a victim of bullying. In her role as 'carer' Greg's mother constantly disappointed: she failed to protect him from his older stepbrother's bullying and seemed unable to contain his waywardness and violence. She could neither prevent Greg's expulsion from school nor his stepbrother from introducing him to drugs at a very young age. Greg even blamed her for his entry into crime because she would not provide him with 'nice clothes and trainers'. By identifying with the masculine role of the hard man Greg could be protective towards her and his stepsister, and by becoming the successful drug-dealer ('making meself loads and loads of money'), he could provide for himself, in the areas where his parents had – in his view – been lacking.

To this end, Greg's investment in the identity of the local hard man, as well as being necessary to defend his illicit business, can be interpreted as a defence against his unresolved feelings of dependency. Greg's sense of vulnerability could be safely denied by projecting it onto the women he protected and the local Asians whom he was willing and able to fight. However, once this hard man image started to falter – as it did when he was himself beaten up, and, perhaps most humiliatingly of all, when he failed to protect his mother from the wrath of the Turkish man he had harassed – Greg's vulnerability resurfaced, inducing feelings of panic, isolation, nervous irritability and insomnia. Alone and disturbed by the consequences of his own behaviour, Greg, might have felt better had his mum or the absent younger kids 'fucking needed' him, enabling him to reclaim his position as their protector. But what 16-year-old boy having witnessed such a brutal attack on his mother, and having discovered his own impotence to intervene against a 'real' (rather than a mythologized) bar-wielding 'asylum seeker' would not need some comfort himself? Greg's hesitant sexual expletive, like that used in reference to his father not knowing him ('so fucking ain't it'), hints at his unacknowledged dependency, hidden below a public persona that constantly pretended not to be 'bothered'. In this context, it is perhaps unsurprising that Greg's girlfriend had something of the little mother about her: 'she's closest thing to me ... She's helped me through a lot ... she's just an ordinary girl to me ... just looks out for my best interests ... she don't want nothing off me'. Nor is it surprising that Greg claimed to be similarly not bothered – 'I just went dead depressed and that ... weren't bothered ...' – about his dependency on drugs; a dependency that arose as he denied his reliance on family members who had repeatedly indicated that they did not need him.

Conclusion

Herein lies part of the answer to the question as to why it is that some resentful individuals buy into the culture of hate and sometimes, but not always, lack the self-control needed to stop themselves enacting this hate. The deep-rooted problems of identity Greg experienced stemmed from a series of damaging events in his early life. These deep-rooted problems produced a young man who characteristically acted out his hostilities. The target groups for his animosities were various and certainly not confined to popularly racialized groups. What determined which groups did or did not become an object of hatred for Greg was whether they became defined as part of 'his' world or as a threat to that world. This distinction was the result of contingent, biographical factors, (including his best friend's shared investment in fantasized racial threats) and the way in which the shifting social contours of contemporary manifestations of racism attribute such threats to a multitude of minority ethnic groups.

Although the structured-action approach helps us to grasp something of the gendered dynamics of Greg's racism, and the shame-sensitive approach draws our attention to the unacknowledged emotions that motivate violent behaviour, an adequately psychosocial understanding of Greg would not be possible without sensitivity to his denied dependency. This underscored his defensive insistence not to be bothered about his parents' ambivalence towards him, the impact of his drug use on his physical and psychological well-being, and the consequences of his violence to ethnic minorities and white people alike. Hence, the complexity of Greg's case should make us wary of those approaches that suggest that violent racists conform to particular types that are relatively unchanging across the life course and fixed in their ways of thinking.

In Greg's account there were hopeful signs of change, motivated by a fear of the consequences of not doing so: principally, losing the love of those – mother, girlfriend, best friend – who had stood by him. But Greg's inner fears and hostilities remained. His move to his criminally accomplished stepbrother's house and his continued respect for a best mate who shared his racialized resentments suggest that Greg's involvement in crime and violence, including his attacks on ethnic minorities, would not be so easily relinquished. Likewise, the fragile hold his relationship with his girlfriend had on his emotional stability – 'if I lost her that's when I'd go back into it … I wouldn't be bothered if I lost me girlfriend. I would do time in jail' – suggest that issues around gender relations, masculinity and heterosexuality, with all their racializing potential, were highly likely to resurface in Greg's life, despite his professed progress with the drug, victim support and 'avoiding custody' work he was pursuing with his youth workers. For the study of violent racism then, Greg's case illustrates that what is needed most is not more studies of the characteristics of offenders, but more adequately theorized understandings of the emotional and social benefits that accrue to perpetrators of racism and violence, and a greater willingness on the part of criminologists to grapple with the complex, often contradictory, aspects of offenders' subjectivities.

9

RE-READING 'THE JACK-ROLLER' AS A DEFENDED SUBJECT

The Jack-Roller (Shaw, 1930) is widely regarded as a criminological classic. First published in 1930, it was republished as a paperback in 1966, 'an edition that had sold over 23,000 copies by the 1980s', according to Snodgrass (1982a: 3) who went on to conduct a follow-up study, *The Jack-Roller at Seventy*. Why all the interest in a book centred on 'a delinquent boy's own story', that of 'Stanley', the 'jack-roller' (someone who robs drunks) of the book's title? Who was he and what can this single case contribute to an understanding of criminal offending? The fact is that, despite the books by Shaw and by Snodgrass and numerous articles addressing the topic, these questions remain inadequately answered. Part of what follows will explore why this is so, focussed in particular on three issues, namely, the uncritical acceptance of Stanley's account 'as told'; the tendency to read Stanley as a 'social type', i.e. as an example of the powerful influences of social and cultural factors; and the failure to integrate Stanley's psychological characteristics with his socio-cultural background. Although various commentators have addressed some of these points, none has done so in the systematic fashion we intend, that is, animated by our psychoanalytically informed psychosocial re-reading of 'Stanley'. This re-reading of Stanley as a defended subject constitutes the main body of this chapter.

'A delinquent boy's own story'

Clifford Shaw thought this aspect of his approach – the boy's own life-story, as told or written, in his own words – important enough to make it the book's subtitle. Although the first three chapters constitute Shaw's introduction of the case and the last one Burgess' 'Discussion' of it, 142 pages of Stanley's own words to 57 pages of academic commentary leave little doubt as to the importance attached to the former. So, what was it about Stanley's own words that Shaw and Burgess considered especially revealing, and should they, as Shaw and Burgess assumed, be taken at face value?

Stanley's initial interview took place when he was 16 years old and produced 'a list of his behavior difficulties, delinquencies and commitments', which were then 'arranged in chronological order and returned to him to be used as a guide in writing his "own story"' (ibid: 23). Specifically, 'he was instructed to give a detailed description of each event, the situation in which it occurred, and his personal reactions to the experience' (ibid). This produced the original six-page document printed as Appendix II to Shaw's book. Over the next six years, and punctuated by a spell in the Chicago House of Correction, Stanley was encouraged to elaborate on his first document, the end result being the 142-page document, 'Stanley's own story' (ibid: 45–183). The whole process was very directive. Stanley's own words they may be (albeit tidied up for publication), but the story's subject matter – what it was that was to be 'guided', 'instructed' or 'elaborated' – was defined by Shaw and his colleagues. We regard these questions and interventions as 'leading', in this case, encouraging Stanley to ruminate about 'Why and how I became a criminal', to quote the heading chosen for his original document.

In other words, Stanley's original response to the instruction 'to give a detailed *description* of each event, etc.' (our emphasis) is to offer an *interpretation* in which the idea of a 'germ of criminality', mentioned four times in six pages (ibid: 201, 202, 203, 205), becomes the linking leitmotif. This was used to link the injustices of a home life that propelled him onto the streets, the development of a criminal mind-set through association with 'the old [criminal] gang', the lack of will-power that 'easy' pickings induces, and the pull of the criminal lifestyle when confronting the difficulties, as an ex-con, of going straight. But nowhere does Shaw reflect upon the question of whether the idea of a 'germ of criminality' would have figured so prominently, or at all, in Stanley's life-story, if he, Shaw, had not been so obviously interested in the question – nor the implications of this for understanding Stanley as a person, and not just his criminality. Short makes a similar methodological point: '[W]hile the narrative is relatively free of constraints as to content, the editor's questions and identity as a criminologist perhaps oriented Stanley to focus on and interpret his personal problems and behaviors' (Short, 1982: 137). One consequence of this narrowing of focus, for Short, was to reduce the story's value even as a personal chronicle: 'his narrative is not as revealing of personal experience as we might wish' (ibid: 136).

Although Shaw saw Stanley's own words as the key to his inner world of 'feelings of inferiority and superiority, his fears and worries, his ideals and philosophy of life, his antagonisms and mental conflicts, his prejudices and rationalizations' (Shaw, 1930: 4), there is no evidence of him questioning a single word of Stanley's. The same can be said of the 'Discussion' by Burgess for whom Stanley's style is 'vivid and dramatic' but essentially truthful (1930: 187). Burgess claims to know this partly because of the cross-checking that was done with official records, and partly because of the way Stanley's testimony is written: '[T]he best guaranty, perhaps, of the reliability of a document is the degree of spontaneity, freedom, and release which a person enjoys in writing or in telling his own story' (ibid: 188). The problem is that whether used by Stanley to describe an event or a feeling or by Burgess to describe Stanley's personality, there is never a hint of difficulty, disjunction, surprise or contradiction. Indeed, Burgess goes so far as to conclude that Stanley's account 'shows more unity and consistency with increasing detail. It stands up under the test of internal coherence' (ibid: 189). He even refers to Stanley's own words as 'objective data' (ibid: 187) – data that he, as we shall see, was over-eager to generalize from.

'Why this case is typical' (Burgess, 1930: 184)

> The case of Stanley is, and is not, typical of juvenile delinquency in Chicago. No single case could be representative of all the many variations of personality, of the permutations of situations and the diversity of experiences of the hundreds of boys who year by year have entered the Cook County Juvenile Court.
>
> (Burgess, 1930: 184)

With this somewhat quixotic opening, Burgess begins his 'Discussion'. But after this nod in the direction of Stanley's uniqueness, 'why this case is typical' becomes the focus of attention. Typical here means 'in the sense that it has aspects that are common to a statistically high proportion of cases' (ibid), thus demonstrating the dominance, then and now, of the idea of statistical generalizability as the 'proper' model for the social sciences. Thus, because Stanley was from a 'broken home'; lived in a 'high-crime' area; became delinquent at a very young age; had been institutionalized often; and had been a 'runaway' (an experience commonly associated with 'jack-rolling' in Chicago) – a set of experiences he shared with a large proportion of juvenile delinquents – he was deemed to be socially typical: 'Judged by these external characteristics the experiences of Stanley may be assumed to be roughly similar to those of a large proportion of other juvenile delinquents' (ibid: 185).

The next stage in the argument is, for us, as revealing as it is problematic. If Stanley is a typical case, the argument continues, 'then an intensive study of this case and of other cases may enable the student of human behavior to probe beneath the surface of delinquent acts and to take a firm grasp upon the underlying motives of conduct' (ibid). The theoretical flaw in this argument is the idea that external, social circumstances can offer a way into internal motives merely by 'intensive study'. Methodologically, it demonstrates a misunderstanding of what single cases are designed to do. These two flaws are linked because the role of the single case, as we argued in Chapter 1, is not typicality but to assist theory building. The implicit question with each case tested is, you may recall: 'does the new case confirm the theory?' If the answer only partially confirms the case the unexplained parts of the case then act as a stimulus to the refinement or development of the theory.

But Burgess was also interested in the 'not typical' or individual part of Stanley's case: in other words, his personality. Adopting the then current idea of personality types, Burgess described Stanley as a 'Self-defender' (or 'egocentric') personality type (other types being, 'Chronicler', 'Confessant' and 'Self-analyst') (ibid: 190, 192). Such 'types' were thought to be relatively fixed, i.e. laid down early in life by a mixture of constitutional endowment and childhood experiences and 'subject to only minor modifications in youth and manhood' (ibid: 191). What was thought to be changeable, according to Burgess, was 'social type' – a term that refers to 'attitudes, values and philosophy of life derived from copies presented by society' (ibid: 193). In other words, depending on our social location, society provides us with various 'roles' – 'professional runaway', 'a delinquent' and 'a criminal' in the case of Stanley (ibid: 194). These are subject to change, as we change our social location, throughout our lives.

In this way, then, the theoretical importance of Stanley's uniqueness to an understanding of criminality was removed: first reduced to a personality 'type', and then frozen in childhood. Personality thus becomes subordinated to culture, the single case to a typical case, and the inner world to a reflection of external circumstances. What matters theoretically from now on is the transmission of cultural norms and values through various 'social' – including 'criminal' – types. Thus, although Stanley's egocentric personality – 'overorganized … rigidly set … finds difficulty in making the usual normal adjustments to other personalities or to changing situations' (ibid: 193) – contributed to Stanley's take up of the criminal role, it was the transplantation of Stanley to a new social situation that was seen, by Burgess and Shaw, as the key to his redemption, not the need to work on his personality.

To return to our initial question of why Stanley's actual words were treated so uncritically, we have now a stark answer: from Burgess' perspective, the case of Stanley was essentially an illustration of the social factors 'common to the actual experiences of thousands of youthful bandits and gangsters' (ibid: 190). Despite much talk of personality and inner world issues, psychological characteristics were clearly subordinated (if not effectively reduced) to socio-cultural ones when it came to theorizing crime causation. This brings us to our third critical focus, namely, the failure to integrate the psychic and social dimensions of Stanley's case in a non-reductive fashion.

From socio-cultural to psychological readings of Stanley

If Shaw and Burgess saw Stanley as an illustrative social 'type', thus demonstrating the importance of the cultural transmission theory of delinquency, later commentators tended to suggest the reverse, emphasizing Stanley's atypicality. One reason for this shift has to do with the availability, courtesy of Snodgrass' follow-up study, of Stanley's autobiographical update. Consisting of written and interview material from the vantage point of an old man whose life had almost run its course, this sequel meant commentators were in a position to evaluate Stanley's whole life, rather than, as had been the case for Shaw and Burgess, just part of it. In the first of the three analyses by 'prominent criminologists' that follow Stanley's updated autobiography (Snodgrass, 1982a: 121–65), Geis made the case for reversing conventional wisdom on the significance of *The Jack-Roller*:

> To my mind the appeal of *The Jack-Roller* must be credited not to its sociological insights and contributions but to the extraordinary nature of Stanley himself. The protagonist is truly Dostoyevskian in his complexity and in his

appalling ability to act in ways that seem stunningly self-destructive and self-defeating by almost anyone's standards.

(1982: 123)

Geis even went so far as to describe *The Jack-Roller*'s contribution to sociology as 'relatively lightweight' (ibid: 124). Unsurprisingly, in the light of this re-reading, he reversed Burgess' stress on the importance of social situations determining behaviour, arguing 'that Stanley was destined to get into many kinds of difficulties regardless of his surroundings and status' (ibid), a point he illustrated by suggesting that Stanley's lifelong difficulties with women were 'rather predictable' (ibid: 127). Geis' idea that *'Stanley's story is interesting precisely because it is atypical'* (ibid: 132) is used to suggest that Shaw's commitment to the idea that Stanley was representative probably explains the 'self-limiting' nature of 'the life-history technique' as he deployed it, as well as why 'eighty-five case histories ... remain in the Shaw-McKay archives [with] ... no clamour to see them into print' (ibid).

Kobrin covers similar theoretical ground. Situating the work of the Chicago School in relation to symbolic interactionism and the importance of a person's own definition of a situation for understanding their subsequent behaviour, Kobrin aligns Shaw's work with this 'subjectivist' tradition, citing G. H. Mead, W. I. Thomas and Max Weber. According to Kobrin:

> [I]t was precisely this component of subjectivity, of the actor's perception and interpretation of the meaning of his experience, that Shaw had reference to in speaking of the aspect of delinquent behavior that 'eluded quantitative studies'. In his view, it was this element in its patterned form over time that had to be taken into account in a theory of delinquency.

(1982: 155)

What this implied was that 'a theory of crime and delinquency includes [sic] a social-psychological component within a framework of structural determinants' (ibid). Strain, labelling and social-control theories have all failed to integrate, 'at least in systematically developed form' (ibid), social psychology and structure, a failure they shared with Shaw's own cultural transmission theory. This resulted in the absence of 'a general theory that embraces the structural as well as the social-psychological factors implicated in crime and delinquency' (ibid; see also Geis, 1982: 130). This was needed because 'only with such a theory can we begin to understand why substantial numbers of lower class, male, minority group youth do not become persistently delinquent, and why somewhat reduced numbers of male youth in structurally favored populations do' (Kobrin, 1982: 156).

Re-reading Stanley psychosocially

Our contention is that the analytical integration that both Kobrin and Geis called for cannot be achieved without taking seriously the nature of the inner world. For us, an integrated reading 'that embraces the structural as well as the social-psychological factors' entails a properly psychosocial reading of Stanley; this is our final task. Before attempting this, let us, briefly, remind ourselves of what is known of Stanley's life through Shaw (1930) and Snodgrass (1982a).

Stanley: a pen portrait

Stanley was the second son of Polish immigrants, born in 1907 to his father's second wife and into a family enlarged by five children from his father's first marriage. Soon after his younger sister was born, when Stanley was four, his mother died of tuberculosis. Stanley's father quickly remarried a widow with seven children from two previous marriages. Of the 15 children, only the six youngest, including Stanley, lived at home according to Snodgrass (1982a: 5) (although Stanley's accounts suggest alternative figures of 13 (Shaw, 1930: 200) or ten (ibid: 48)). Stanley claimed to hate his stepmother for her unfair treatment of him and his natural siblings, and from the age of six ran away from home regularly and started getting into trouble. Stanley's father was a hard-drinking labourer who was abusive to his wife.

The neighbourhood in which Stanley was born and raised was a notoriously deprived area of Chicago – the 'Back of the Yards' – where successive generations of immigrants settled because of the housing's proximity to the manufacturing district. Rates of delinquency were high among the children who lived there, and even higher among young men (aged between 17–21) of the neighbourhood. Between 1924–6 the Back of the Yards had the worst arrest rate in the whole of Chicago for 17–21-year-olds. On account of considerable changes in the area's immigrant population (from predominantly Irish, Czechoslovakian and German in 1900 to largely Polish, Russian and Lithuanian by 1920), the area was thought to suffer 'considerable disorganization and confusion of moral standards', as Shaw (ibid: 35) put it. In addition, there was the problem of conflicts between foreign-born parents and native-born children. In 1920, slightly over half the Polish community in Stanley's neighbourhood were foreign-born, including both Stanley's father and stepmother.

Stanley's running away from home, for days or weeks at a time, quickly became chronic. Usually, he would be picked up by the police, for truanting, begging or for petty stealing, and then returned home, sometimes after a short placement in a detention home. Most times he was found in the company of older companions. His first arrest, for example, aged eight, involved two older companions, including his stepbrother, William. By the time he was nine, and after many court appearances, Stanley was deemed beyond parental control and was, first, assigned a probation officer and then, when the arrests and running away continued, committed to the Chicago Parental School, a correctional institution for difficult boys. Paroled after six months to live at home, the running away continued and, after another arrest for truanting and stealing, Stanley was committed to St Charles School for Boys for 15 months. Picked up by the police twice in one month after his release, he was returned to St Charles for ten months and then paroled to live on a farm in Illinois. After three months he ran away to West Madison Street – a deprived, transient, crime-ridden, inner-city Chicago street, home to 'homeless men … [T]he bootlegger … the dope peddler … the professional gambler … and the "jack-roller" … peddlers, beggars, cripples, and old, broken men' (Anderson, 1923, quoted in ibid: 38) – and, despite an arrest for vagrancy, managed to live there for five months before a further arrest led to 17 more months in St Charles. Paroled at the age of 14 to his stepmother, his father having died in the meantime, he ran away again to live on West Madison Street. Aged 15, Stanley was charged with the more serious crimes of burglary and 'jack-rolling' and sentenced to a year in the State Reformatory. Eight months after his release, he was arrested again on West Madison Street for identical offences and received, now nearly 17, another twelve-month sentence. Stanley served this in the Chicago House of Correction. Just before this last sentence, he gave his first interview to Shaw.

From chronic runaway beyond parental control as a child, Stanley appeared to have become an incorrigible criminal beyond institutional control as a teenager when Shaw first interviewed him. Despite the new gaol term, Shaw maintained contact after Stanley's release a year later and 'put into effect a five-year rehabilitation program that involved foster home placements, a change of neighbourhoods, employment, and individual interviews' (Snodgrass, 1982a: 6). The programme also involved, at least in the first two years of treatment, weekly contact with Shaw. All this appeared to 'work' and by the end of the first book, Stanley was, apparently, a reformed character having gone five years without offending. He had found a job (as a door-to-door salesman) that he liked (after a woeful employment record of over 30 miscellaneous, unskilled jobs that had lasted from two days to four months, often ending with Stanley getting the sack, quitting or simply running away), and had settled down into marriage and fatherhood. He was then 22 years old.

A year after the book's publication, Stanley had lost his job as a result of the economic depression. Feeling psychologically depressed at the prospect of looking after his two boys in a poor tenement he loathed whilst his wife became the breadwinner, he was persuaded by his 'gambling cronies' (ibid: 35) to get involved in an ill-fated armed 'hold-up'. This led to another twelve months in gaol, a sentence that might have been longer but for the intervention of Shaw and his provision of a persuasive attorney. Stanley remained depressed in prison, worrying about his family, and suffered poor health, including the onset of painful stomach ulcers that were to prove debilitating for many years. Upon release, his wife continued to be the breadwinner and Stanley remained the unhappy, sometimes angry and resentful, unemployed man around the house, finding 'some escape in … card playing in joints throughout the city' (ibid: 40). When he did manage to get a job selling again, his worsening ulcer meant time off work and reduced earnings, which meant his wife had to continue working. Eventually he did manage to persuade his wife to give up working, but this only lasted a short while. A short period in Republican politics ended with a fight, and the ulcer condition forced him to take up his brother's offer of taxi driving. Eventually, in 1942, his 'gnawing hell of an ulcer' (ibid: 43) led to a perforated duodenum and a period in hospital. This also meant that Stanley failed the draft – Pearl Harbor had recently brought the US into World War II – a rejection he felt keenly.

During the next period – 'the middle years [which] are often regarded as critical' (ibid: 47) – everything started to unravel. His marriage broke down on account of his wife's affair. He was twice committed to a State mental hospital, probably at his wife's request, the first time after threatening her with a knife. He was given 'a series of electric shock treatments' (ibid: 50) which left him with a 'burned-out' memory (ibid: 51) and only a hazy, conjectural recollection of these years. He escaped both times from the mental hospital and found work, variously, as washer-up, bar tender, poker dealer (until a gambling clampdown) and taxi driver (until his past caught up with him in the form of a revoked licence). He found solace and companionship in gambling (to which he later admitted being addicted) and the company of women from the local dance ballroom. He managed some kind of reconciliation with this wife and, through her, some limited contact with his sons. He met and 'grew quite fond of' (ibid: 63) a call girl. She 'contributed to' what he came to regard as 'one of the happiest periods' of his life (ibid), but this ended when an unexplained dismissal from his bartender job saw him take a new job 'converting gas stoves' (ibid) out of town. When this proved beyond his technical competence, Stanley left and returned to Chicago.

By his mid-forties Stanley was relatively settled. He lived in a familiar hotel in Chicago. He worked successfully as a salesman once more, in a job that lasted for five years. He was visited by his wife, who kept him informed about his sons, by then young men. His health, however, was not good and his 'stomach attacks … seemed to grow more severe more often' (ibid: 66). This resulted in time off work and hence lost earnings. This period came to an end after a row with his sales manager (who up to this point had also been a friend). This row resulted from Stanley's feeling that he was being taken advantage of, and led to him leaving the job. An offer to buy and work a farm with an old friend Bill, a fellow escapee from the State mental hospital, fell through when Bill brought a woman friend along with him and Stanley decided to engineer an argument so that they would break up. Another job as a salesman in Detroit fell through after a row with his interfering sales manager. A visit to his mother-in-law stirred up his old hatred for his wife when his mother-in-law insinuated that his wife had had him committed in order to see another man. This 'true explanation for my institutionalization' left Stanley in a 'deep fury' (ibid: 67). A new job in sales followed, but his worsening stomach condition affected his earnings and so enforced a move from his much-loved hotel to a 'modest apartment' (ibid: 68) near to his work. After Christmas at his brother's, Stanley's condition forced him to re-enter hospital where 'a good portion' (ibid: 69) of his stomach was removed. After his discharge from hospital, his son took him to relocate in the warmer climes of Miami. But, while settling in and on the morning he was due to start a new job, Stanley was arrested for vagrancy and gaoled when he could not afford the fine imposed. Stanley's wife sent the money to secure his release, after which he was 'escorted to the bus station' (ibid: 70) and placed on a bus that took him out of town.

Life seemed to continue in this vein, i.e. sales work punctuated by bed-rest for his still not improving stomach condition. Stanley's relationship with his woman friend Kitty ended when she 'mounted a vigorous marriage effort' (ibid: 71) – he having by this point in time been divorced by his wife – and he baulked at Kitty's idea that she would support him financially through his illness. Then Stanley's stomach condition was, in his view, miraculously cured by an operation. The death of the wife of his friend George led to an offer, from George, to pay for them to resettle in California. This they did, although George died soon after. Thereafter, with Stanley now in his fifties and prematurely aged as a result of his long-term health problems, he settled into a quiet life of card-playing, reading and seeking 'feminine companions' (ibid: 72) at local dances. This non-working-life was funded by disability payments for his 'weakened' heart, the result of 'a gall bladder operation in the early 1960s' (ibid: 73), money from Social Security and 'windfalls from my proclivity at games of chance' (ibid). Although he resisted the matrimonial overtures of 'a few' of his 'feminine companions' (ibid: 72), boredom and his 'needs for intimacy' (ibid: 73) did result in an 18-month marriage. But this ended in separation after Stanley and his new part-ner's 'incompatibility ... became intolerable' (ibid).

At 70, Stanley chose to end his story by emphasizing his 'feelings of peace and tranquillity' (ibid: 75) and counting his blessings. These he listed as: a family 'pleas-antly devoid of behavior problems' (ibid: 74); a 'host of many acquaintances ... [that gave him] a certain richness ... to spice [his] daily routine' (ibid); 'comparatively good health, considering my age' (ibid); a new-found 'mellowness ... [quite] lacking in the past' (ibid); 'a rather dim memory' of the past (ibid); and the pleasurable, levelling discoveries of reading, such as his reassuring realization that he and Balzac both suf-fered cruel mothers. Although he still saw himself as 'a casualty of social conditions', he could also accept 'that a great deal of blame for [his] ... suffering can be attributed to failures on ... [his] part, exclusive of other influences' (ibid). Past wounds 'have healed appreciably and all animosity has been replaced by a philosophy of under-standing' (ibid: 75).

Re-reading Stanley's defensiveness

The unconscious, identification, containment and reformation

There would seem to be widespread agreement about the defensive tone of the ado-lescent Stanley's original account of his young life. Shaw hypothesized that Stanley's '[A]ttitudes of persecution and suspicion originated in the antagonistic family rela-tionship ... [particularly] the stepmother's attitude of partiality toward her own children and her discrimination against Stanley and his brother and sister' (Shaw, 1930: 50, n. 4). Ernest Burgess, as we have already noted, characterized Stanley as a self-pitying and self-rationalizing individual, a 'self-defender' whose 'personality type', like that of many individuals in 'adverse circumstances', was rigidly egocentric. It thus offered, Burgess suggested, a form of psychological protection (or defence) 'against an unfriendly even hostile social world' (1930: 191).

The problem with this notion of Stanley's defensiveness, as we argued earlier, is the idea that it was a fixed, unalterable, part of his personality, with the corollary that it was only a change in his social circumstances – and hence his exposure to different social norms and customs – that could hope to change him from criminal to law-abiding 'social type'. This produced too psychological a reading of personality and too social a reading of the possibilities of changing someone. It also produced an unnoticed contradiction. If Stanley was the rigidly egocentric type who 'finds difficulty in making the usual normal adjustments to other personalities or to *changing situations'* (ibid: 193, our emphasis), how could he also be susceptible to changes in social circumstances? Noticing this contradiction would seem to be implicit in the commentary on Stanley's updated story by Geis (1982), where he suggested that it was Stanley's psychological continuity – his succession of stories of 'self-destructive and self-defeating' behaviour – that seemed more significant than his apparent reformation. But, rather than address this as a contradiction, Geis simply restated it from the other side: Stanley's 'outlook' was bound to get him 'into many kinds of difficulties' regardless of social circumstances, a conclusion that overlooked, as Kobrin persuasively put it, 'the fact [that] whatever other forms of unconventional activity he engaged in, it did not include either serious or persistent law violation' (1982: 156).

How then to understand Stanley's defensiveness in a way that resolves, rather than dissolves, this contradiction? The final commentary, by Snodgrass himself in the follow-up book, provides a starting point. Although he called the chapter 'A note on Stanley's psychology', it actually offered a way of thinking psychosocially about Stanley's defensiveness. Like Geis, Snodgrass noted the persistence of behavioural patterns – 'regardless of the social environment' (1982b: 170) – throughout Stanley's life. By *'pattern'*, Snodgrass meant 'that there is a structure or form to his actions that appears time after time' (ibid: 167). Stanley, 'as an older adult' (ibid), also recognized this, revealing this side of his character in various disclosures. Reflecting on when he met Clifford Shaw, Stanley explained: 'I had spent over half my twelve years in institutions and was very much *on the defensive'* (Snodgrass, 1982a: 3, our emphasis). Commenting on his first year of treatment, Stanley confessed to Snodgrass: 'I was often unduly sensitive, carrying a chip on my shoulder, particularly if I fancied myself being imposed upon. I reacted aggressively at critical times, which resulted in dismissal' (ibid: 27). Much later in his story, Stanley reiterated:

> When the behavior of others affects me personally I have a rigid code of my own; I simply do not allow anyone to take advantage of me, and there is no compromise. My attitude is such that any violation of my welfare in any way is resisted at the slightest provocation.
>
> (ibid: 66)

Snodgrass suggested that Stanley's insight into this behavioural pattern matched his own, even allowing Stanley the last word on the subject in an extended final quotation, 'because it allows Stanley to act as the ultimate authority on the personal meaning of his conduct' (Snodgrass, 1982b: 171–2). This democratic gesture was certainly in line with the Chicago School's commitment to the veracity of the told story, but it was somewhat at odds with the notion of defensiveness that animated Snodgrass' own analysis. Where Stanley talked of his strong reactions being a response to 'anything I feel is unfair' (ibid), including something as apparently innocuous as losing at cards, and explained it, to the extent that he could, in terms of a response to being 'pushed around before I was five–six–seven years old' (ibid) and the effect of that on his 'personal makeup', Snodgrass' explanation was subtly, but importantly, different. What Snodgrass argued, using examples from different periods of Stanley's early life – 'earliest recollection, delinquencies, and relationship with Shaw' (ibid: 170) – was that the pattern showed Stanley reacting *in a way that was the exact opposite of how he was feeling*: 'in order to avoid feelings of inferiority he repeatedly reacts by attempting to impress his superiority on others' (ibid). In other words, where Stanley (and Shaw and Burgess) interpreted his strong reactions as rational, if misguided, responses to the perceived injustices of various external events, a consequence of his egocentric personality type built up as a defence against the many 'hard knocks' he experienced in childhood, Snodgrass interpreted these same reactions as attempts to avoid painful inner feelings (of inferiority).

Herein lies an important difference between the ego-psychology deployed by Burgess (and, implicitly by Shaw) and the psychoanalytically informed psychology of Snodgrass: in the latter, things are not always as they appear; the inner world is not a direct reflection of the outer world. Crucial to this difference is the role of the unconscious. This requires that we attend to what is said, but symptomatically: we listen to the words but try to 'hear' what lies behind them; what they obscure as well as what they reveal; the unsaid as well as the said. This is what Snodgrass did. He tracked down Stanley's feelings of inferiority by noticing Stanley's talk about superiority in 'the first story about himself at the youngest age': 'All in all, I was a rather conceited little boy who thought himself superior to the other boys of his age; and I didn't miss impressing that little thing upon their minds' (ibid: 167). Rather than dismiss this as idle boasting or accept it simply as a truthful account of how the young Stanley was feeling, Snodgrass took it seriously because of its patterned nature, but then noticed the (unspoken) neediness behind the words: 'Stanley acts superior to avoid feeling inferior' (ibid: 168). Snodgrass was able to do this because, implicitly anyway, he questioned the words of the young Stanley: why would a young boy *need* to impress his superiority on his male peers? It is not something everyone does and, in many respects, is counter-intuitive because so patently self-defeating: impressing one's superiority on others quickly makes enemies, not friends, as Stanley's penchant for falling out with others, even those who were his friends, constantly revealed. Whatever social cachet the feeling of superiority might bring was immediately negated by the resulting social isolation: loss of friends, jobs, etc. But, the repeated (patterned) nature of the behaviour shows it must have been satisfying some need. Tracking this patterning enabled Snodgrass to conclude that the manifest behaviour was a defence against the pain of feeling the opposite. This was not, as we saw earlier, something of which Stanley was conscious. Although Snodgrass did not use the term, we will: it was an *unconscious* defence against the anxiety (and the associated feelings of painful vulnerability) that Stanley's recurrent feelings of inferiority promoted.

We can use the third of Snodgrass' examples, namely, Stanley's relationship with Shaw, to show the importance of the psychological level to Stanley's transformation. In doing so, we will also show how Snodgrass' commentary can be read psychosocially. Having posited Stanley's 'need for attention and admiration by others he considers superior [the older boys he looked up to], in order to feel superior himself' (ibid: 167) as the motivation for his early delinquencies, Snodgrass used a similar argument to explain the huge impact Shaw made on the young Stanley. In other words, Shaw, intuitively and fairly unselfconsciously it seems, enabled Stanley, so often beset by incipient feelings of inferiority, to feel wanted ('Mr Shaw greeted me warmly and pleasantly'), important ('He was very happy that I had come'; 'I got to telling about my experiences, and they showed great interest') and 'much more respectable' (once he had put on the 'new set of clothes' Shaw provided) (all quotes from Snodgrass, 1982b: 168). Shaw never once, it seemed, made Stanley feel inferior (he 'never upbraided me or told me that I was in the wrong' (Shaw, 1930: 171)), but was consistently concerned and available, especially during the early years of Stanley's treatment; and Stanley rewarded Shaw with lifelong devotion and sufficient personal change to be able to move on from a life of crime and, as Snodgrass carefully phrased it, 'to become better able to care for himself emotionally and physically and begin to develop as an individual' (1982b: 169). Psychoanalytically, it is possible to see this as a good example of 'containment' on Shaw's part: of being able, consistently, to 'hold' and detoxify Stanley's bad feelings about himself. In other words, Shaw was able to let the split off parts of Stanley's psyche live in his own for long enough for them to 'undergo modification ... [and] then be safely reintrojected' (Bion, 1959: 103, cited in Hinshelwood, 1991: 130).

This experience of containment enabled Stanley to *identify with* Shaw, fostering a desire within Stanley to be like his biographer and mentor. It is in this sense that Stanley perceived Shaw as a father figure, since his own father was too absent or collusive with his hated stepmother to have been a desirable figure with whom to identify. Stanley's constant looking up to older 'superior' boys for approval could be seen in a similar light. Given his obvious lack of suitable parental figures, he sought out – where he could – figures with whom he could identify. This is one of the main ways in which 'personality' develops: through the 'taking in' and becoming akin to those we desire to be like. The young Stanley's chosen alternatives to his unsuitable parental figures were his older stepbrother William and Wiliam's friend, Tony, 'close companions that I looked up to with childish admiration and awe' (Shaw, 1930: 50), who introduced Stanley to stealing and with whom he 'learned to smile and to laugh again' (ibid: 52). Another was 'Pat Maloney ... seven years my senior, a big husky Irish lad and a "master bandit" ... [who] the young guys, me included, looked up to' and whose attention and taking a liking to Stanley caused his 'feelings of pride [to swell] to the breaking point' (ibid: 57–8).

When he met up with Shaw after his year in the 'House of Corruption' (ibid: 167), Stanley was ready for a change. At that time, he felt 'humiliated', he was financially destitute, he was in poor shape physically ('broken and ... weak'), and mentally he was 'confused and uncertain' (ibid: 167–8). Luckily, Shaw provided the loving care that enabled Stanley to laugh, smile and feel pride, to feel good about himself, and hence negated the need for the unsuitable love objects that had been all that Stanley, hitherto, could find. Now, and here is the psychosocial rub, Snodgrass recognized the importance of Shaw 'as a principal agent in Stanley's development' (Snodgrass, 1982b: 169), but continued to regard the psychological as independent of the social: '[T]he basic pattern [acting superior to compensate for feeling inferior] appears to be maintained regardless of the social environment in which Stanley is placed' (ibid: 170). Burgess (1930) and Shaw (1930), as we know, both downplayed Shaw's role in Stanley's development, favouring the idea that Stanley's changed social circumstances – different foster home, new neighbourhood, and new job – were the key to understanding his reformation. However, an earlier change in social circumstances – when Stanley was being fostered by a wealthy couple – the childless company vice-president and his wife – who apparently intended to adopt Stanley and make him their sole heir – did not work and he ran away to have 'fun' (Shaw, 1930: 89). What was the difference between these two social transplantations, the fostering that did not work and the one that did? Although it would be reductive to put it down to just one factor, we would like to suggest, by way of a hypothesis if you like, that not only was Stanley readier for the change by the time of the second fostering, but his new foster family and her family were better able, like Shaw, to contain Stanley's persistent feelings of inferiority.

In both cases of being fostered Stanley talked of the difficulty, as a delinquent street urchin, of adjusting to a world of wealth, civility and refinement: of constantly feeling ill at ease, out of place, not good enough. Each time, he missed his old pals and neighbourhood and, even in the successful fostering, he would constantly return to his old haunts after work. During this period, he lost several jobs, even those he liked, in familiar fashion (fighting for his rights not to feel inferior) but Mrs Smith continued to stand by him. She counselled and encouraged him, but did not judge him: 'Mrs Smith became greatly concerned about me [after Stanley had quit another job], and talked to me in her usual kind and sympathetic way. She encouraged me … I knew full well the wisdom of her advice, and I wanted to make good and gain her approval' (ibid: 181). By contrast, in the earlier unsuccessful fostering, the vice-president and his wife 'didn't have much life' but 'had lots of company of snobbish people, and they looked down on me' (ibid: 87). The vice-president's wife, his new foster mother, could not help judging him: 'I couldn't do the things just right [a reference to table manners], and my foster-mother looked at my blunders through the corner of her eye' (ibid: 88). It may have helped that Mrs Smith had children, unlike the childless vice-president's wife. It certainly helped in the case of the successful fostering that all of them, mother, two daughters and son 'treated me as their equal' (ibid: 172). In sum, our hypothesis is that the crucial factor mediating Stanley's relationship to a new social situation was the degree to which his recurrent feelings of inadequacy and inferiority could be successfully contained. Shaw managed it, as did Mrs Smith. Unfortunately, his other foster mother failed on this count; as did numerous work colleagues, hence the continuation of the pattern of falling-out/fighting/dismissal for apparently trivial reasons. This psychosocial reading of

Stanley's reformation, then, is able to accommodate both his successes and the recurrent failures; to see them as necessarily contingent, not fixed, responses to social circumstances.

Paranoia, ambivalence and unhappiness

Approaching the question of Stanley's defensiveness from another angle, we want to focus on what was, to us, a key area of Stanley's experience, one that was more significant than his limited involvement in criminality. This was his fairly persistent if not lifelong feelings of inferiority, inadequacy and unhappiness. Although he claimed to have found some contentment in his twilight years (a claim which, having a certain end-of-life settling-accounts feel to it, does not strike us as being the whole truth), that did not expunge what for us was most noteworthy about Stanley, namely, the fact that he had a very difficult life, was constantly fighting painful feelings of inadequacy or coping with the equally painful aftermath of his 'self-defeating' responses to these feelings, and suffered, intermittently if not chronically, from depression. A purely social reading of these experiences might stress the fact that his move from the chaotic excitement and tolerance of the crime-ridden ghetto to the humdrum routines of working and family life conducted under a more judgemental suburban gaze was never going to be easy for a bright but uneducated and largely unqualified young man with a criminal record. Stanley did indeed often talk of the lure of his old way of life when the going got tough (and, of course, his addiction to gambling meant he did stay in touch with one element of his old way of life). But accepting such a reading ignores, as Stanley never did, the early origins of his unhappiness: the loss of his real mother and her replacement by a 'cruel' and 'unjust' stepmother.

Once again, we need to start with Stanley's words:

> As far back as I can remember, my life was filled with sorrow and misery. The cause was my stepmother, who nagged me, beat me, insulted me, and drove me out of my own home. My mother died when I was four years old, so I never knew a real mother's affection.
>
> (Shaw, 1930: 47)

However, we want also to go behind (and beyond) them. Imagine the scene. Four-year-old Stanley, recently usurped from his special place in his mother's affections by the arrival of his baby sister, then loses his mother. How long Stanley's mother had been ill is unclear, but it is probably safe to assume that her illness impacted on the care she was able to provide to Stanley and his siblings for some time before her death. When Stanley's mother died she left Stanley's father with three children – two boys, of whom Stanley was the second, and a younger girl. There were also other children from Stanley's father's first marriage in the family home, although some of the older ones (being 16, 17 and 18 at that time) may have lived elsewhere (see above for the various estimates of how many children were living at home at this time).

Back in the 1920s little was known about the impact of bereavement on children. The work of John Bowlby (1980) has since shown that many children who lose their mothers in infancy are at greater risk of depression in adolescence and later life. Stanley, as we know, suffered from depression throughout his life, including suicidal thoughts during his teens. Yet, 'maternal deprivation', or more specifically 'maternal loss', does not necessarily lead to mental-health problems in adolescence. Whether or not children who lose a parent or alternative primary carer suffer depression depends critically, as Michael Rutter explains, on 'the course taken by mourning after the loss in childhood' (1981: 194). Most critical of all, 'the pattern taken by family relationships before and after the loss is thought to be influential'. We need to imagine, therefore, the pattern of family relationships pertaining in Stanley's household after his mother's death.

Within a year Stanley's father remarried, and the bereft Stanley now had to cope with a new stepmother and seven more step siblings (to add to the five from his father's first marriage). '[T]rouble [soon] started' (Shaw, 1930: 200). Unsurprisingly, perhaps, given the inevitable fights for attention and food, Stanley did not like his stepmother's seven children: 'and a bad lot they were' (ibid). But it was the new stepmother he particularly hated and his original essay is full of expressions of contempt for her. For example: 'The stepmother done with us just what she pleased. We were well abused, and continuously ... Well, she beat us at every meal ... because we would get mad when she served her children first and made us wait' (ibid); 'She nagged me, beat me, insulted me, drove my sisters and brothers and me out of the home ... She will repay some day, if not in this world, in the next' (ibid: 203). Given the miserable, extremely unhappy situation that the young Stanley found himself in, did his 'quiet' and 'industrious' father (ibid: 40) step into the breach to help Stanley come to terms with the loss of his mother and adapt to his new, much enlarged family? Not at all, according to Stanley. All his father wanted was 'regular meals, a bed to sleep in, and his daily can of beer and whiskey' (ibid: 48). Stanley and his siblings were 'just "kids", who had to be provided for', and 'there his parental duties ended. Never did he show any love or kindness' (ibid: 48–9). Stanley's somewhat harsh assessment that his father tolerated his many 'kids' in the hope that one day they would be 'financial assets' (ibid: 49) was perhaps a young man's fancy; but it was indicative of how unsupported Stanley felt. The pressures on Stanley's father as provider could only have increased after his acquisition of a new wife and seven more children to feed. But Stanley's indictment of him was about him failing to stand up to his wife for beating Stanley: 'My father gave me no comfort. He spent his time at work, at the saloon, and in bed. Never did he pet or cheer me' (ibid: 49). Stanley also rationalized his father's non-interference in the beatings in terms of a fear of having to bring up his children alone: he 'couldn't interfere, because if he did the stepmother would threaten to leave' (ibid). Either way, both readings testify to just how emotionally unavailable Stanley felt his father was.

But this was not the full extent of Stanley's father's failure. Although Stanley makes little of it, perhaps because he so hated his stepmother, official records indicated that Stanley's father was repeatedly violent to his stepmother, beating her, 'every time' he got drunk with 'anything he gets hold of' (ibid: 42). This happened, Stanley's eight-year-old sister noted, even when his wife 'did not say a word to him' (ibid: 43) and could be one of the reasons why Stanley's stepmother was hostile to Stanley and his siblings. Just two years into the marriage, the stepmother tried to have Stanley's father prosecuted for 'excessive drinking and cruelty' (ibid: 41). In a letter written to Stanley while he was in St Charles, Stanley's sister explained that on one occasion their father had cracked his wife's rib and threatened to kill her. This violence in the home, even if directed at his hated stepmother, must have been frightening for Stanley. In fact Stanley talks of the first beating by his stepmother as 'the first time that I ever knew fear' (ibid: 49).

Whether this kind of familial background was typical of those born in the Back of the Yards in the early twentieth century, as Burgess implied, is hard to say. What is certain is that such a heart-rendingly difficult start – traumatic, fearful, unloving, violent – will have effects, as we outlined in Chapter 4. There we considered how Melanie Klein (1988a and b) conceived the way a baby's early anxieties – partly constitutional and partly arising from the relation to the mother – promote feelings of love and hate and how distressingly 'bad' feelings need to be split off from good ones (in order to protect the latter) and projected, in phantasy, onto other objects. The unconscious defences against anxiety of splitting and projection, which Klein thought was characteristic of the early months of a baby's life (although by no means confined to it), are associated with the 'paranoid-schizoid position'. Once the baby learns to cope with the ambivalent feelings resulting from perceiving the mother as the source of both love and hate, Klein talked of the baby entering the 'depressive position'. But, this was not an automatic process but a developmental achievement: how well we are nurtured will affect both our level of general anxiety and our characteristic ways of defending against it. In other words, some will have greater difficulty than others in operating consistently from the depressive position.

In Stanley's case, whether or not he achieved the depressive position with his natural mother is impossible to say. However, denigrating his stepmother in the way that he did (and to a lesser extent his father), allied with his tendency to idealize certain older boys, constitutes evidence of him operating from a paranoid-schizoid position. In doing so, the intolerable anxieties brought on by the traumas of losing his mother so young and finding himself in a hostile, unjust and unsupportive family setting, could be held at bay. His real mother (or others to whom he looked for succour) could become an idealized good object and his 'wicked' stepmother (and to a lesser extent his father) could become the receptacles for all his bad feelings. But, this projective fantasy of the wicked stepmother was not the whole story as there were signs that Stanley was capable of operating from a more depressive position in relation to her. Thus, as well as how awful she was, we also learn that throughout Stanley's adolescence his stepmother made repeated attempts to show him some affection and nearly always welcomed him back when he was released from custody. For example, for the first two days after Stanley (aged ten) was paroled from the 'Baby Bandhouse', the stepmother treated Stanley 'like a prince' (Shaw, 1930: 63), if only for 'two days' (ibid). She also sent him a suit so he would be smartly dressed upon his release from the St Charles School (aged eleven) (ibid: 79). A few pages later in Stanley's story, he revealed that his stepmother thought him 'a good boy' (ibid: 83) when he was working. If the stepmother had, as he claimed, started Stanley on the downward path, she sometimes tried quite hard to get him off it, it seems; and Stanley occasionally recognized this.

Indeed, if one examines all of Stanley's disclosures about his stepmother it is possible to detect a degree of ambivalence, buried beneath his more dramatic expressions of outright contempt. For example, whilst Stanley slept rough to be free of his stepmother, and once 'told the police his parents were dead' (ibid: 26), he also considered going back to live with her (ibid: 81). Despite her inability to speak English, he could detect through her 'toothless smile' when she 'was glad to see me at home again' (ibid: 82). Stanley 'tried to love' his stepmother even though he 'could not stand her caresses' during her (rare) 'sympathetic moods', nor her attempts to get Stanley 'to kiss her' (ibid: 50). At these moments, Stanley struggled to overcome his 'fear and hatred' (ibid) and tried to 'avoid her', at which point she became, once again, the wicked stepmother: 'she would get angry and beat me' (ibid). In his early twenties Stanley conceded, in conversation with Shaw, that his criticisms of his stepmother might have been overstated: 'I don't believe that I exaggerated the faults of my stepmother, but if I did, I certainly didn't exaggerate my feelings toward her' (ibid: 55, n. 8). Much later on, aged 70, and with the life-changing experience of his association with Shaw behind him to say nothing of the chastening experience of a lifetime of 'hard knocks' and his impending mortality, Stanley was able to express some recognition for the hardships endured by his stepmother, explaining that while he did not 'condone' her treatment of him, he knew that she had taken on a 'burden of responsibility' for which a 'plus point should be added to her account ... [S]he assumed a task that required courage and fortitude' (cited in Snodgrass, 1982a: 79).

Abuse, sexuality and jack-rolling

Surprisingly, given the book's title, neither Shaw nor Burgess, nor indeed any of the commentators who have examined the case since, have expended much energy on asking why Stanley got into jack-rolling, beyond the predictable idea, based in the theory of cultural transmission, that he learned 'the technique' from 'close contact with adult criminal groups' around West Madison Street where jack-rolling was 'a more or less traditional aspect of the social life' (Shaw, 1930: 165). Because both Shaw and Burgess 'read' Stanley as socially typical there is little more to be said. Since jack-rolling was simply the adult version of petty theft in areas where Stanley spent a lot of time, it was a culturally predictable outcome: a natural extension of the petty 'crimes of necessity' he was involved in as an infant, a reading that matches Stanley's own account.

However, this 'cultural transmission' reading ignores the fact that when Stanley revealed what he was in gaol for to older, 'hardened' criminals, having just been sent down for his first jack-rolling offence, they were singularly unimpressed. 'Bill', for example, was, apparently, 'disgusted' with Stanley because jack-rolling was 'not a white man's job' and should be left to the 'niggers' (ibid: 101). This upbraiding left Stanley 'too scared to say anything' (ibid). On his transfer to Pontiac, 'Billy' (not the same man as Bill), 'a notorious criminal character in Chicago' (ibid: 105n4), 'chided' him 'for petty stealing' (ibid: 106), as did everybody else, it seems: 'Even the guards have contempt for the petty thief. They were considered ignorant and cowardly. Nobody had respect for you if you were in for petty stealing' (ibid: 109). The result was that he 'never really made any friends in Pontiac', was pitied for his youthfulness and worldly inexperience 'and humiliated to the extreme by being looked down on for petty thieving' (ibid). Stanley felt so upset by all this that he resolved 'never [to] be a petty thief again' (ibid). But he did continue jack-rolling. Despite the contradiction between word and deed, Stanley's explanation for his jack-rolling was accepted unquestioningly, rather than regarded as a possible rationalization. This more critical take on jack-rolling (which is threaded throughout Stanley's account) was simply ignored. Statistically common to the West Madison Street area jack-rolling may have been, but its association with ignorance, cowardice and 'niggers' made its choice as a crime of necessity rather more problematic than Shaw and Burgess implied.

Jack-rolling was a term that covered a variety of forms of stealing from another: simply taking from someone too drunk to resist; 'strong arming' or deploying violence to accomplish the robbery; enticing a homosexual to a room with the promise of sex and then depriving him, violently or otherwise, of his property. Stanley's account mentions involvement, always with others, in all three kinds. For brevity's sake, we will focus on the most problematic of these, namely, the jack-rolling, through enticement and violence, of homosexual men. We do this because, invariably, Stanley was the enticer and this involved, on occasions, having sex, or as he more euphemistically put it, 'relationships' (Snodgrass, 1982a: 107) with the victim. In a society that saw sex between men as 'perverse', the choice of becoming, however occasionally, a sort of male prostitute, albeit in the commission of a property crime, cannot simply be explained in terms of cultural transmission. Rather, we will need to explore Stanley's relationship to his sexuality and to violence.

As always, we start with Stanley's own accounts of his sexuality. When asked directly by Snodgrass whether he had ever had a sexual friendship with a man, Stanley proffered probably his frankest disclosure about the contexts in which he encountered those men whom he and his friends jack-rolled and what it meant to him:

> Oh, when I was a kid on Madison Street there were 'fruits'. I had relationships with them. I didn't like it, I didn't like it at all. We used to exploit them, you know. It was sickening to me. I couldn't stand it … When it comes to men, its unnatural.
>
> (ibid)

The idea that Stanley found sex with men 'sickening' was constant. Talking about his life 'on the road' making him 'a constant victim of sex perverts', he said, although he 'yielded to them a few times … the act was nauseating to me' (Shaw, 1930: 89).

Elsewhere in the text, the 'sexual pervert' became a 'moral pervert' (ibid: 128). Stanley appeared in no doubt about where he stood in relation to homosexuality. Moreover, his accounts were also littered with references to his heterosexuality (e.g. ibid: 85, 89, 118): like his friend 'Buddy', Stanley 'was crazy about girls' (ibid: 121). But, if homosexuality was so abhorrent to him, why did he not stick to 'strong arm-ing' the drunks, of whom there seemed to be a plentiful supply around West Madison Street, and burglary (Stanley's other 'crime of necessity')? Part of an answer might be found in Stanley's apparent attractiveness to homosexuals: 'As I'd walk along Madison Street there'd always be some man to stop me and coax me into having sex relations with him' (ibid: 85); 'We would let them approach one of us, usually me, because I was so little and they like little fellows' (ibid: 97). This would suggest that Stanley and his accomplices were simply exploiting their resources to maximize returns. But this explanation is too rationalistic: Stanley had still to overcome his extreme distaste for the activity. Maybe he was willing to sacrifice himself for the 'greater good' of the gang or simply to ingratiate himself with his fellows-in-crime? Certainly there is plenty of evidence of Stanley wanting to please and impress, espe-cially those who were older, bigger, tougher than him (and most of those he came into contact with were all those things). But there is also plenty of evidence that when he felt threatened he fought or argued back or simply ran away. Performing a 'sickening' homosexual act would seem to be threatening. For someone whose small size, timidity and frailty – labels he consistently applied to himself – cannot have made his relationship with conventional notions of masculinity very easy, the threat would have been even greater.

It would seem then that Stanley's own words about his sexuality are not the whole story. But, then, whose are? As before, we will need to delve behind them, to see what they obscure as well as what they appear to reveal. An obvious starting point is to piece together what we can about Stanley's sexual development from his accounts. Two things stand out from these: his early initiation into sex and the issue of abuse. According to his own account, at the age of six Tony's two sisters introduced him to sex, Tony being a close friend of Stanley's older stepbrother William. The sisters apparently 'had sex relations openly with all the boys in the neighbourhood' and 'would talk … about sex things' to Stanley and 'touch … [his] body.' Although Stanley was 'too young to know what it all meant', he 'soon learned and developed many sex habits, like masturbation and playing with girls' (ibid: 51). In the official record, the report Dr Healy compiled when Stanley was nearly eight, Stanley appeared to have implicated William and Tony more directly: 'These … boys [William and Tony] long ago taught him bad sex habits. Says that these older boys do bad things to him in the public baths; that they look at the girls there and say bad things about them. These boys got him into this bad habit (masturbation), which he has done much' (quoted in ibid: 25). In either event, but for the fact that these older boys were themselves only ten years of age at the time (the sisters' ages were not given but we can probably assume they were children too), we would certainly regard this sort of introduction to sex as sexual abuse. Be that as it may, this early commin-gling of desire and exploitation, whatever we call it, would certainly have coloured

Stanley's relationship to his sexuality. His incarcerations, which started when he was very young (before he was ten), tell a similar story. Writing about his first time in St Charles School for boys, Stanley said he was 'frail' and 'little' and 'couldn't defend myself against the bullies that lorded it over me' (ibid: 71). These same bullies, we had already been told, 'would attack the younger boys in the dormitories and force them to have relations' (ibid: 69). The previous sentence spells out the nature of these 'relations': 'sex perversions in the form of masturbation and sodomy' (ibid). Earlier on the same page Stanley recounted being transferred 'with five of the youngest boys' to 'the worst cottage in the whole joint' (ibid). In the light of all this, it seems inconceivable that Stanley was not sexually abused or raped during his time in St Charles.

Putting all this together, we can safely say that, whatever Stanley's conscious relationship to his sexuality, this particular combination of elements (precocious, abusive, mostly involving males) will have had strong effects on the formation of Stanley's sexual desire. We are also now in a position to offer a reading of Stanley's sexuality which embraces both his heterosexuality and the apparently contradictory attraction of offering sex to men in the course of jack-rolling them. Given Stanley's sexual history, a conscious embrace of a virile heterosexuality would be one way of dealing with the 'perversions' of his past in which, however abusive the setting, he would feel implicated because his desire, at some level, would be engaged. In other words, Stanley's tendency to look up to older boys, to want their attention and to be liked by them would probably have entered even the abusive relations. However, such abusiveness, being painful, emasculating and a reminder of his powerlessness, must have promoted feelings of anger, however masked these might need to have been during the years of helplessness when to give vent to them would have been unsafe. Jack-rolling (with a partner or gang) would appear to provide the perfect 'solution' to all these apparent contradictions: homosexual desire could be deployed in a heterosexual cause – beating up and robbing the 'fruits'; at the same time, revenge for the years of abuse – the transformation from victim to victimizer – could help assuage the deep anger.

Some sense of these contradictory feelings – desire mixed with anger and glossed with discursive justification – comes across in Stanley's description of possibly his first jack-rolling of a homosexual. First, the desire:

> This ... day a fellow stopped me and asked for a match ... He was about eight years my senior, and *big and husky* ... he promised to get a job for me at his shop. He invited me to have supper with him up in his room ... He was a *kind guy, with a smile and a winning way*, so I went up to have supper on his invitation. We ate, and then he edged up close to me and put his arm around me and told me how much I appealed to his passions. He put his hand on my leg and *caressed me gently*, while he *talked softly to me*.
>
> (ibid: 85, our emphases)

As our emphases highlight, this is not a hostile memory, but one remembered with a certain fondness. However, once Stanley's buddy arrived to 'help put the strong arm on this man', anger took over: 'we sprang into the fellow with a fury' (ibid). Once his 'buddy' had 'dealt him a heavy blow', and they 'found thirteen dollars in his pocket' (ibid), the homophobic rationalizations were trotted out:

> Since he had tried to ensnare me I figured I was justified in relieving him of his thirteen bucks. Besides [and just for good measure], was he not a low degenerate, and [to eliminate any possible remaining sympathy] wouldn't he use the money only to harm himself further?

> (ibid: 85–6)

Expressed in terms of identification, Stanley's response to the painful helplessness of his earlier abuse by older boys and men was to transform himself from the passive recipient of other men's sexual advances into a physically dominant aggressor: from victim to victimizer through identification with the aggressor. Expressed in terms of defensive splitting and the paranoid-schizoid position, Stanley was a vulnerable child, easily groomed by older males who exploited his vulnerability for their own selfish sexual gratification. But Stanley, like so many abused children, entered these 'relationships' freely, or otherwise – to borrow from the Freudian terminology of the time – was 'seduced' (Mollon, 2000). Part of the disgust Stanley felt towards homosexual men was an expression of his disgust with himself for his 'perverse' desire for the affections of the 'fruits' he jack-rolled, split off and projected onto them, and justified using a conventional, aggressively heterosexual, homophobic discourse.

Conclusion

An interpretative exercise of this kind is basically an attempt to shed new light on puzzling or problematic features of the selected case. Starting with contradictions within, and among, existing commentaries on the case, we attempted to show ways in which these might be resolved. This entailed giving sustained critical attention to certain puzzling aspects of Stanley's case, forcing ourselves to interrogate what others seem to have rather too readily taken for granted. Our attention alighted first on the incuriosity towards Stanley's actual words displayed by both Shaw and Burgess, a failing that stemmed, ultimately, from the sociological reductionism informing their work: because Stanley's personality was a fixed entity, his social world determined his social type, and thus his learning, and unlearning, of criminality. We noted that the reverse happened with later commentators. In their accounts, Stanley became the victim of a psychological reductionism, his social typicality replaced by a totally idiosyncratic atypicality. The apparent gain in psychological complexity was achieved at the expense of a social decontextualization: Stanley's behaviour was then interpreted as a product of his inner world, his personality, and thus beyond the shaping of social circumstances. Although nobody seemed to know how to build on it, there was a recognition that what Shaw was attempting was to integrate the sociological and the psychological, but without the theoretical interest to do so. Advancing that theoretical task, using the case of Stanley, was what we then set out to do: to show how particular aspects of his behaviour – however apparently contradictory or self-defeating – might be understood as responses that met, simultaneously, the 'demands' of unconscious needs and of social circumstances.

Focussed generally on something that all commentators seemed to agree on, namely, Stanley's defensiveness, we used our psychoanalytically informed psychosocial approach to show how, if this was read in terms of Stanley unconsciously defending against anxiety, it could help explain both his conscious need to act as if superior in situations that made him feel inadequate and how this need could be successfully 'contained' in other social situations, most dramatically when he met someone like Shaw with whom he could also identify. Read thus, his 'reformation' was not simply a product of changed social circumstances nor of Shaw's intervention, but a complex product of both combined: in other words, a psychosocial achievement. But, this 'reformation' was never an absolute, once-and-for-all achievement but had constantly to be struggled for in a lifetime's battle with the legacy of a traumatic, fearful and loveless childhood. This legacy, we argued, included a tendency to split off bad, unwanted feelings and project them onto others where they could be safely hated. This defensive splitting, characteristic of what Klein called the paranoid-schizoid position, seemed evident throughout his life, both in his relations with his hated stepmother, and in his constant falling out with people, including friends, over apparently trivial matters. Part of his reformation included an improved ability to recognize the good and bad in even his hated objects (e.g. his stepmother), and to live with the resulting ambivalence: what Klein called operating from the depressive position. Once again, the question of which position was dominant at any given time needed to be understood psychosocially: that is, it depended on the degree to which the social situation triggered feelings of anxiety and prompted defensive splitting or ameliorated them and thus enabled living with ambivalence to predominate. Finally, we used Stanley's early and abusive introduction to sex to unravel the contradictory psychosocial admixture of unconscious homosexual desire and rage with a conscious discourse of nausea and (a socially sanctioned) heterosexuality that we argued lay behind the unhealthy seductions of his brief foray into jack-rolling.

10

DOMESTIC ABUSE, DENIAL AND
COGNITIVE-BEHAVIOURAL INTERVENTIONS

> The two counselors who ran the group ... worked hard to make 'control' a central issue. Each new member would be asked to describe to the group what he had done to a woman, a request that was generally met with sullen reluctance, vague references to 'the incident,' and invariably the disclaimer 'I was out of control.' The counselors would then expend much energy showing him how he had, in fact, been in control the entire time. He had chosen his fists, not a knife; he had hit her in the stomach, not the face; he had stopped before landing a permanently injurious blow, and so forth ... I cannot conceive of a circumstance that would exonerate such violence. By making the abusive spouse take responsibility for his actions, the counselors were pursuing a worthy goal. But the logic behind the violence still remained elusive.
>
> (Faludi, 1999: 8)

In this chapter we are interested in the apparently simple question of why some men are violent to their partners when other men are not. Our aim is to produce an understanding of violent men that avoids pathologizing and hence neither overstates the differences between perpetrators and other, 'normal' men, nor assumes that there are no differences to be explained. In our view, this political objective has been compromised as research and intervention work has become preoccupied with challenging offenders' cognitive distortions. We deploy a combination of psychoanalytic concepts – denial, 'acting out' and containment – to illustrate how many of the feelings experienced by violent men are themselves a product of the tensions between their own psychological sense of powerlessness and more widely endorsed expectations about masculinity and femininity. Our argument is that while there are many biographical and situational contingencies that collude to make it harder for some men to contain their feelings of anger, fear, and vulnerability, a psychosocial understanding of masculine subjectivity aims to illuminate why some contingencies, in the context of a particular biography, prove to be more salient than others. Domestic violence, we argue, often occurs when perpetrators are unable to contain threatening anxieties. Read psychosocially, their violence can be conceptualized as a form of 'acting out', an unconscious defence against anxieties that are too troubling to admit to conscious awareness.

Feminist victimology and the problem of male power

Since the 1970s feminist work inside and outside of criminology has exposed the pervasiveness of men's domestic abuse of women and children, the failure of the criminal-justice system to provide support, justice and protection to victims and survivors of this abuse, and the wider culture of sexism and gender discrimination that supports, and even exacerbates, abusive practices (Hester et al., 1995; Kelly, 1988; Lees, 1997; Stanko, 1990). The enormity of the task accomplished by these feminist scholars and activists can be too easily underestimated today. Without feminist scholarship and activism there would be few, if any, of the services now available for survivors of domestic and sexual abuse; much wider public acceptance of the kinds of myths that blame rape victims for their own victimization; little attention paid to the systematic abuse and torture of women in times of war; limited awareness of the international trades in people-trafficking; and much ignorance of the role masculinity has played in perpetuating domestic and international conflicts.

Set within these broad contexts, our particular gripe with the way in which some strands of feminism have conceptualized the subjectivities of violent men can seem like something of a side issue. However, as we shall argue, the question of how to conceptualize the subjectivities of men who are violent to female partners is critical because interventions (albeit small in number) in this area, which are currently premised upon an inadequate notion of masculine subjectivity, largely fail to deliver. In the long run, such failures can only undermine the credibility of the feminist project. The American feminist and journalist Susan Faludi, quoted above, puts her finger on the key problem, namely, the essentialist, expressive equation of male violence with masculinity.

Since the 1980s many sociologists of sex and gender have preferred the notion that there are a number of competing masculinities, some of which are inherently violent, but most of which are complicit with, but subordinated to, a hegemonic position that owes its authority to global capitalism and Western military–industrial complexes (Carrigan et al., 1985; Connell, 1995). While the new literature on masculinities breaks with much of the structural determinism that characterized early feminism, Connell's claim that most men accrue a 'patriarchal dividend' from the minority's domestic violence suggests that this break is less than absolute (Connell, 2000: 53; Hood-Williams, 2001). In any case, the essentialist legacy of feminist victimology has proved hard to shake off within the criminological literature that is more exclusively focussed on domestic violence, including criminological work on masculinities (Messerschmidt, 2000). Within many of the key texts that deal exclusively with men's violence towards women and children the notion that violence is a defining male characteristic fundamental to men's power over women in a patriarchal society continues to be uncritically reproduced (Dixon, 1998; Milner, 2004). Leading domestic-violence researchers, Dobash et al., for example, argue that:

> Men expect and demand domestic service throughout the day and night … Men who are violent toward their partner do not believe a woman has the right to argue, negotiate, or debate, and such behavior is deemed both a nuisance and a threat to their authority. Violence is commonly used to silence debate, to reassert male authority, and to deny women a voice …
>
> (2000: 26–7)

Likewise, Audrey Mullender argues:

> The real problem is that *all* men are encouraged to be aggressive, competitive, unemotional, sexual and powerful in order to define their masculinity and their difference from women … Both masculinity and male sexuality are rendered synonymous with power and hence are socially constructed to be oppressive … Despite important class differences and race differences between them, virtually all men can use violence to subdue women and keep them subordinate …
>
> (1998: 63, emphasis in original)

Put more cryptically, Jeff Hearn claims: 'Men remain violent to women through social power and control, which in some cases, is combined with physical size and strength, reinforced by social power and control that reduces intervention against them and that violence' (1998: viii). All three of these quotes suggest that men's violence is best explained as an instrumental response to threats to male authority within value systems founded upon patriarchal power. Our position is subtly but importantly different. We take the position that the argument that domestic violence is *primarily* about most men's social power rides roughshod over the complexity of the evidence and, crucially, misses that which is less manifest, namely, men's dependency. It thus fails to engage with the problem in a way that is likely to resonate with men's experiences of masculinity. Let us elaborate.

Attitudes towards and experiences of domestic violence

Survey research has shown men's and women's attitudes towards domestic violence and sexual assault to be remarkably similar (Ward, 1995). For example, a recent survey of over 1000 British adults' attitudes found that 87 per cent of men and 90 per cent of women said they would end their relationship if exposed to repeated violence, and that 76 per cent of men and 79 per cent of women would end their relationship if forced to have sex by their partner (BBC, 2003). In this same survey, only 28 per cent of men and 25 per cent of women agreed with the argument that 'Domestic violence is not acceptable unless one person has nagged the other', and only 30 per cent of men and 31 per cent of women agreed with the statement, 'Domestic violence is not acceptable except if one partner has been unfaithful'. If there were demographic reasons for agreeing and disagreeing with these statements, 'sex' would not appear to be a particularly important one.

Second, while the bulk of the evidence suggests that the burden of domestic and sexual assault falls most frequently on women who live with male partners, both forms of victimization can be and are perpetrated against heterosexual men and gay and lesbian people. The 2001 British Crime Survey estimated that around 45 per cent of women and 26 per cent of men aged between 16 and 59 had experienced abuse, threats or force from a partner, sexual victimization or stalking at least once in their lifetimes (Walby and Allen, 2004). Although such statistics tend to conceal the tendency for domestic abuse against women to be a repeat offence, to cause injury and to incite fear, there are men who experience serious and repeated forms of domestic abuse from female and from male partners and there are abusive relationships in which it is difficult – if not, misleading – to identify one individual as 'the perpetrator' and the other as 'the victim' (Gadd et al., 2003). This problematic has been highlighted by studies of domestic abuse in same-sex couples, amongst whom rates of victimization appear to be broadly similar to those for opposite-sex couples (Milner, 2004: 89). The implication of all this data is that while domestic violence has much to do with sex and gender, the causes of domestic violence are not to be found in the single idea of heterosexual men reasserting their social power.

This brings us, finally, to the question of what exactly is meant by men's social power. Mullender has it that '[b]oth masculinity and male sexuality are rendered synonymous with power' (1998: 63), whilst Hearn claims, '[m]en remain violent to women through social power and control' (1998: viii). Yet the relationship between men's experiences of power and their violent behaviour is an under-researched question. There is some evidence that exclusively psychological forms of abuse are more common amongst higher socio-economic groups, and that this is particularly likely to be the case in heterosexual couples where the female partner is more highly educated than the male partner (Schumacher, Smith and Heyman, 2001). This suggests that differences of status and/or intellectual ability within relationships contribute to men's abusiveness. Those domestic abusers known to practitioners tend to be poorer than average and more likely than the general population to have unstable lifestyles, low verbal intelligence, and a history of criminal behaviour (Gilchrist et al., 2003). British Crime Survey data suggests that this pattern is not just a product of the criminal-justice system's tendency to criminalize the poor. Those perpetrators with criminal records for other offences generally commit the most severe forms of domestic violence (Walby and Allen, 2004).

Furthermore, psychological studies of US perpetrators demonstrate that witnessing and/or experiencing domestic violence as a child, depression, substance abuse, alcohol dependency, low school attainment and insecure attachment styles are all risk factors found more predominantly in the male-domestic-violence-perpetrator population than in samples of non-abusing men (Barnish, 2004). Of course, none of these factors are causative and, in some cases, like alcoholism and depression, these risk factors can also be consequences of relationships that have ended violently. Many men exposed to similar risk factors do not become domestic abusers, and most of the men who are domestic abusers do not experience all of these problems (Mullender, 1996). Nevertheless, collectively the evidence suggests that those men whose violence is severe and repetitive enough to come to the attention of criminal-justice practitioners are typically troubled by their own behaviour and unhappy about other aspects of their lives (Milner, 2004; Morran, 1999). As the following extracts from Mary Barnish's extensive review of the psychological literature reveals, violent men may experience more intense emotions, feel more insecure and act in more volatile ways than men who are not routinely violent, although the differences are ones of degree not quality.

> [A]busive men generally exhibit more negative communication, offensive negative behaviours, belligerence, contempt, overt hostility and less positive communication in interactions with their partners than other men ... They also make more demands on their partners and show less competence in resolving relationship tensions ... The psychological profiles of men who assault their partners characterise them variously as alienated, distrustful of others, overly concerned about their masculine image, impulsive, narcissistic, angry, hostile, emotionally dependent, and insecure.
>
> (Barnish, 2004: 44–5)

Taken overall, this array of evidence suggests that domestic abusers are not always men. When they are, their social profile reveals they are not generally the most successful or socially powerful of men and, psychologically, they are troubled, insecure and angry. This should have problematized the simple equation men = masculinity = social power = violence. Unfortunately, this has not been the case. The promotion of cognitive behavioural treatment has tended to reproduce this equation, albeit in a more technocratic form.

The ascendancy of cognitive behavioural programmes

Nearly all treatment interventions aimed at perpetrators of domestic violence in the UK are cognitive behavioural in focus – that is, addressed principally to the (conscious) thought patterns assumed to inform offenders' violent actions – and are increasingly 'taught' in standardized formats from groupwork manuals (Scourfield and Dobash, 1999). This is primarily because of the political impact of feminist activism in Britain and the concessions practitioner groups have made, not necessarily of their own volition, to the New Labour government's 'evidence-led' policy agenda. The history of such interventions began relatively recently with the importation of the 'Duluth model' to Scotland during the late 1980s and (currently) ends with the reluctance of the Home Office to make available the findings of its evaluations of the 'Pathfinder' Programmes that were commissioned to enable policymakers to establish the best way forward, commissioned in the year 2000 (Gadd, 2004b; Raynor, 2004).

Best known for its 'power and control wheel', the ethos of Duluth assumes a connection between sexual inequality, physical violence and the many different techniques of control used by men against women. These include: 'threatening to leave', 'making her feel guilty about the children', 'treating her like a servant', and more generally 'making her feel bad about herself'. Men who come to understand and accept the wheel would be those who also learn new ways of thinking about themselves and their partners, and thus come to embrace the alternative 'equality wheel', signifying, as it does, connections among 'nonviolence', 'responsible parenting', 'mutually agreeing on a fair distribution of work' and 'respect' (to name but a few of its components). The key attractions of the Duluth Domestic Abuse Intervention Programme (DDAIP) for those at the CHANGE project in Stirling and the Lothian Domestic Violence Probation Project (LDVPP) were threefold:

1   it combined an intervention for perpetrators with a support service for female victims;
2   the focus of the work with perpetrators was specifically about challenging men's use of 'power and control' in a whole range of circumstances (not just violent incidents);
3   there was a package of exercises and procedures that could be readily borrowed from Duluth and implemented in Scotland.

The confrontational package of intervention work appealed both to sentencers and feminist activists alike, while the promise of 're-educating' perpetrators to make better choices appealed to the reformist aspirations of those social workers who were uneasy about their responsibility to punish offenders (Morran, 1996). At this time, however, there was little evidence to suggest that such interventions were effective in reducing programme attendees' abusive and controlling behaviours, or in changing the attitudes of the wider male population.

The US research base showed then, and continues to show now, that group-work programmes for domestic abusers modelled on the Duluth intervention have, at best, a modest impact on the minority of offenders who complete the course. And, even the achievement of this level of impact is contingent on other factors, including: skilled and enthusiastic practitioners who can ensure programme sessions are responsive to particular men's needs; additional services and/or counselling for men with more complex problems; and partner-support services adequately resourced and responsive to the concerns of women and children (Healey et al., 1998; Jones et al., 2004). Despite these qualifiers, Dobash et al. (2000: 48) regard the Duluth project as 'one of the most successful community-based projects for violent men in the world'. Indeed, their evaluation of the CHANGE and LDVPP programmes did find evidence to support the claim that interventions modelled on the Duluth approach are generally more successful than 'other criminal justice interventions' in reducing the incidence of violent and controlling behaviour of men convicted of domestic violence offences (Dobash et al., 1996).

However, further scrutiny of this evaluation research has cast doubt on the effectiveness of the interventions. While only 7 per cent of those men participating in the programmes initiated five or more violent incidents during the follow-up period compared to 37 per cent of men sanctioned in other ways, the number of valid responses received was too small to make 'cause and effect claims' (Mullender, 2000).

Moreover, during the period of evaluation the CHANGE and LDVPP programme groups dealt only with a sub-sample of violent men selected because their problems were, in some respects, not as complex as other men known to exhibit similar behaviours. The men who attended the programmes were less likely to be unemployed and unmarried than the men subjected to other criminal justice sanctions (Dobash et al., 2000: 109) and very few of those men considered by the courts to present such a danger that they should have been incarcerated, or to have serious drug and alcohol problems, were allowed to attend the programmes (Morran, 1996). Finally, while Dobash et al. have made much of the CHANGE programme's capacity to challenge violent men's 'faulty thinking', their research illuminated that the justifications for violence could have been products of both the style of intervention used and the confrontational method of interviewing preferred by the research team (ibid: 54–60; Cavanagh and Lewis, 1996). The fact that the programme facilitators of CHANGE and LDVPP adopted more person-centred modes of working after the evaluation concluded, together with the apparent success of more narrative-based approaches to assessment and intervention, lend further support to this hypothesis (MacRae and Andrew, 2000; Milner and Jessop, 2003; Morran, 1999).

With these provisos in mind, some of the most experienced British practitioners of domestic-violence intervention work have warned against prematurely standardizing interventions into a format prescribed by the Duluth model (Bell, 2000; Blacklock, 1999). Nevertheless, in 2000 the British government announced that two different probation services had been given Pathfinder status to develop pro-feminist psycho-educational/cognitive behavioural programmes for domestic-violence perpetrators in England and Wales (Home Office, 2000). One consequence of this decision was that funding for alternative ways of working with violent men was withheld, pending the results of the evaluations. Paradoxically, two Duluth-styled 'Integrated Domestic Abuse Programmes' were given 'accredited' status even though five years after the launch of the Pathfinders the results of the evaluations were still not publicly available. There are hints in the academic literature (Eadie and Knight, 2002; Raynor, 2004) and the Home Office's own process evaluations (Bilby and Hatcher, 2004; Hollin et al., 2002) that the reasons for this have to do with the failure of the Pathfinders to produce positive results and, worse still, that it is impossible to tell whether the lack of positive results was a product of the styles of intervention, or implementation problems arising out of under-resourcing, inadequate training, and/or morale problems induced by the imposition of a new managerialist agenda on the National Probation Service. In practice, these problems have sometimes led those working with violent men to abandon the partner-support work with women – typically regarded as critical to effective practice with men (Burton et al., 1998; Blacklock, 1999). Tellingly, some of those administering the Home Office's Integrated Domestic Abuse Programmes have suggested that their work would be more effective if perpetrators were first subject to an additional intervention that helped them 'deal with their denial' (Bilby and Hatcher, 2004: 10).

While we would not refute that there is a cognitive component to domestic abuse, nor that cognitive-behavioural therapies can help some people some of the time (Roth and

Fonagy, 1996), to suggest that a cognitive-behavioural intervention is the best solution to a problem with many emotional antecedents – dependency, psychopathology, negative early experiences, to mention the ones Bilby and Hatcher (2004: 10) found 'across the sample' of men they studied – is somewhat odd. Moreover, within the context of punishment, the message that offenders are characterized by their cognitive distortions can easily be experienced as prejudicial. When this happens it is not uncommon for the men sentenced to such programmes to seek out strategies of resistance, for example turning up late or drunk, absenting themselves, playing language games, positioning themselves as the protectors of female group facilitators, picking on other group attendees whose behaviour appears to be even less socially acceptable than their own, or querying the masculinity of male facilitators (Cayouette, 1999; Godenzi, 1994; Morran and Wilson, 1999; Potts, 1996). Kathryn Fox's observational study of a cognitive self-change programme administered in Vermont illustrates this point most evocatively (Fox, 1999). When programme participants began to experience the intervention as oppressive, some resisted by co-opting the cognitive rhetoric for their own purposes. For example, some participants came to accept the programme's definition of them as 'victimizers' not 'victims' as wholly consistent with the model of self-sufficient masculinity to which they aspired and justification enough for 'choosing' to retaliate physically against those they perceived to be bullying them. Others were able to see through the non-judgemental façade assumed by the facilitators, realizing that they had to learn to 'talk the talk' of cognitive change in order to become eligible for parole, while privately concealing their bitterness at the group facilitators' condescending tendency to dismiss their explanations for violence as denials of responsibility grounded in cognitive distortions.

Three case studies

How, then, should we understand the role of denial in the perpetration of domestic violence? And can the shortcomings of the cognitive perspective be transcended? To see how our psychosocial understanding of masculinity can better address the issue, we will examine the case studies of three men, interviewed by one of us for a project about the life-histories of men who perpetrate domestic abuse (Gadd, 2000). All three of these men were interviewed using the Free Association Narrative Interview Method (Hollway and Jefferson, 2000) we described in Chapter 5 and more detailed accounts of their lives are published elsewhere (Gadd, 2000, 2002, 2004b). All three of the men described violence towards their partners that was typically 'explosive' in form, more akin to rage than sadistic manipulation, and barely comprehensible to them in terms of its motivational origins.

A pen portrait of Gary

Gary was a 26-year-old unemployed man of slim build. His childhood appeared to have been a confusing and lonely one. Gary's parents separated when he was four years old, and thereafter he was told to refer to his mother as his 'aunt'. In his early teens Gary suspected that his paternal grandfather was sexually abusing his sister, but he had failed to report his suspicions, despite having been taught about sexual abuse at school. After the abuse was discovered and a criminal conviction secured, Gary's father and step-mother later invoked Gary's desire to see his grandfather again as a reason for welcoming their daughter's abuser back into the family. Around this time, Gary's stepmother became increasingly physically abusive towards Gary and his sister. Gary tried to tell his father about his stepmother's behaviour, but his father responded with disbelief, head-butted Gary, and informed social services that he no longer wanted Gary to live with them.

Gary had a history of self-harming and depression that he attributed to the guilt he felt about not reporting the abuse to which his sister had been exposed. Gary also had a history, dating back to his late teens, of abusing alcohol and painkillers although he explained that he usually only turned to substance abuse to suppress his own feelings of self-hate after he had been abusive to his girlfriend, Rebecca. Gary explained that much of what had happened between him and Rebecca was 'all like mixed' in his memory: 'like one big blur like of shouting and screaming and being abusive'. He could not actually remember strangling Rebecca, but had no reason to doubt the truthfulness of her complaints. Gary's violence had become 'worse and worse, until … a lot of the time, [it] didn't need … anything to trigger it off'. His violence happened most typically when Rebecca was 'panicking' about not being ready to take her son to the nursery.

> Every week she would get in a right panic … running about like mad, saying, 'I'm not gonna … be ready in time'. So I was trying to help her … She [was] … just panicking and panicking. I said, 'Look. Just calm down. I can't like. We're not going to get anything sorted out if you don't calm down' … And she'd think I was having a go at her … And eventually, I'd just … be like shouting … 'Don't! Just calm down. Please calm down' … And she'd say, 'Well you are just picking on me' … And no matter how much I'd say, 'I'm not doing' she wouldn't seem to believe me … I'd just get really like wound up … Just like completely lose it and go completely over the top. Like breaking things and chucking things and punching holes in stuff and hurting Rebecca.

Not knowing 'how to stop' himself, Gary was 'despairing that much' that he came to consider suicide his only option. After his suicide attempt, it was Rebecca that got Gary to hospital and persuaded him to accept some psychiatric help. Gary reflected: 'Despite what I've done. Despite how much I've upset her … Despite how much I've hurt her she's always been like … She's … always trying to help me. And I'm really like grateful for that.'

A pen portrait of Mark

Mark was a 33-year-old man of stocky build, an industrious salesman and a committed rugby player. With the exception of his 'aggressiveness', Mark felt that everything was perfect in his life: 'Great jobs … a lot of money … the old little cottage in the country'. Mark depicted his wife, Maria, as 'a delicate little thing' who 'needs looking after' – her vulnerability enabling him to be 'the boss' in their relationship. Yet, despite this protective proclivity, Mark had been violent to Maria for nearly all of the ten years they had been together. At the time of the interviews, Mark was driving around 400 miles each week to see a counsellor whom he hoped would help him overcome his violence.

Mark explained how when he 'first started becoming quite verbally aggressive and nasty … it didn't really need a reason or anything to set it off'. By way of explanation Mark initially invoked Maria's recurring tendency to 'get upset' as provocation for his violence, but subsequently corrected himself, explaining that it was his 'inability to cope with her upset', especially after a drink, that 'seemed to be the catalyst for things'. Matters were made worse when they 'were slagging off one or another's family', particularly if Maria accused Mark of being like his father. Mark likened this accusation to 'somebody punching me in the face'. Mark's father, a soldier, had also been a wife-beater, and hence much of Mark's childhood had been spent in boarding schools, his mother preferring her sons not to see the abuse to which she was subjected.

Mark explained how when Maria accused him of being like his father he would feel the need to 'fight' his way out that 'corner':

> I could of quite easily killed her with the rage I felt and the damage I wanted to do. And I always felt like it was a release to grab her round the neck … It was like I could be in control of my hands whereas I knew if I punched her, with the size I am and the size she is, I could cause her. [sic] I knew that. And deep down I always wanted to when I was in that rage.

In the aftermath of his violence, Mark often 'felt it necessary to make love … as a way of being closer' to Maria.

> She'd never like resist, like push me away … But, it would be like holding her and just feeling, 'Yeah, she's there'. But she doesn't want to be. I'd know that. But it was just like a comfort to me.

That Maria had been thinking of leaving Mark 'frightened the life' out of him, in spite of his claim that he had 'always been frightened of that commitment'. At the time of the interview, Maria was pregnant and Mark described them both as 'very made up … over the moon', but also complained about Maria's 'negativeness': 'Everything is going to happen to her like'. Maria was worried about the possibility that her baby might have Down's syndrome, as well as the danger that Mark's violence might pose to the child. Mark added that one upshot of Maria's 'negativeness' was that it enabled him to be 'positive and reinforcing'.

A pen portrait of Paul

Paul was a 33-year-old man, with a severe physical disability caused by injuries that were incurred when he had hung himself – from the swing in a children's play area – not long after he had discovered that his then girlfriend, the mother of his first child, had been unfaithful. Paul walked with a stick, wore a body brace to hold his spine in place, and a glove to enable his left-hand to grip. Paul had been a heroin addict since his mid-teens, a friend having introduced him to the drug the day after he completed his first prison sentence for burglary. Paul's childhood had been a brutalizing one; much of it spent in between his father's house and the 'battered wives' refuges his mother fled to when his father beat up her and her children. Paul's father, who was later 'diagnosed insane', had served two custodial sentences for the injuries he had caused the young Paul. At the time he was interviewed, Paul was attending a probation programme for perpetrators, his probation officer having seen Paul 'filling in' a man Paul claimed had made 'a pass' at his ex-wife, Karen (with whom he had two further children).

Karen and Paul's relationship had begun ten years prior to this incident. Karen had befriended Paul after his attempted suicide, subsequently visiting him in prison and supporting him throughout his sentence. At the time of his release from prison, Paul's drugs worker had urged Paul to terminate his relationship with Karen and commit himself instead to a drug-rehabilitation programme. Realizing that Karen had been his 'backbone' and his 'strength', Paul was not willing to let her go 'to pieces' because of the recommendations of an organization that, until then, had had little to do with him.

Paul and Karen married within a year of his release from prison, but while Karen eventually overcame her own heroin addiction, Paul never really succeeded in getting his drug use under control and, in the process, contracted hepatitis C. Paul explained that the severe back pain he suffered caused him to get 'angry quick' and that heroin was one of the few drugs that took the edge of his pain. However, over the years, Karen and their two children had endured much poverty and upset as a result of Paul's habit, inability to work and various returns to prison.

Paul and Karen separated. Afterwards most of Paul's day-to-day existence entailed avoiding or engaging in (often extreme) physical violence with the various men to whom he owed small amounts of money. Because he lived in a flat with no furnishings or heating, Karen continued to let Paul wash and eat at her house before he took their two children to school in the mornings, but she was no longer willing to tolerate his domestic violence.

Paul recognized that his violence towards Karen was wrong, illegitimate and his 'fault'. He knew that Karen was 'totally right' when she explained that she is: 'not there to be punched and battered in front of, away from, or for the sake of her children … Why should she have to go and work with black eyes and things like that?' Paul could not remember much of the violence he had perpetrated against Karen, and therefore relied on her account of his behaviour. Nevertheless, Paul had come to realize that his domestic abuse had escalated 'from only a slap' and 'using the kids against her and things like that', to 'two severe beatings where he 'severely kicked Karen up and down the house … blasting her, full blast with … [his] fist, in the chest … [with] every word' and insult he shouted at her. Paul said he would 'fight to the end of the Earth' to get back with Karen, and was hoping that, having received some 'anger management', things might 'get back to normal'. As Paul was well aware though, his violence was not simply caused by his inability to manage his anger, rather it was also about his incapacity to accept Karen's (well-justified) criticisms of him.

> ... [S]he'd pushed me and pushed and pushed me and pushed me. Coz I'd be like, 'Look. Leave it. I don't want to argue. I don't want to know. I. Don't. Want. To. Know'. But she'd be in me face ... She was in the right ... telling me how much of an idiot I am wasting my life. And I'm losing me kids. I'm losing everything ... So I'm like, 'Look. What has it got to do with you?', sort of thing. 'Anyway. You don't want to know me'. And then I'm back on the victim part ... 'You don't love me anymore', and all this crap. I'd say, 'Well, get off me back, will you?' And she's still in my face. 'Will you please ... Fuck off! Get away'.

On those occasions when he had consumed a mixture of (stolen) prescription drugs and alcohol Paul tended to respond to these criticisms with physical violence. What Paul said he wanted was for Karen to tell him 'that everything will be all right', but, as he himself conceded, there were many things 'severely wrong' with him; things that his doctor had told him were no longer curable.

A psychosocial reading of the three cases

There is much in these three men's accounts that resonates with the experiences that female victims of domestic violence have reported to feminist researchers: the escalation of seemingly inconsequential controlling behaviours into extreme forms of physical and/or sexual violence; the promises of change and the turn to treatment to salvage relationships that are almost beyond repair; the threat of violence lingering over even the most trivial of disagreements; the fear of further violence reducing the female victim's capacity to reason with her male partner. Domestic violence instils inequalities of power in conjugal relationships that are extremely difficult to rectify once one partner becomes afraid of the other. At the same time, there is often nothing self-evidently extraordinary about the relationships in which domestic abuse happens.

The dynamics of many contemporary conjugal relationships are determined by the striving of both partners for relationships in which trust, intimacy and commitment are reciprocal (Giddens, 1991). Like many other relationships, Gary's, Mark's and Paul's all fell short of this ideal, but there is plenty of evidence that this was an ideal to which they aspired. Their aspirations, however, operated in a world where gender differentiated discourses predominate: where the traditional social expectations are for men to be strong, active, independent figures of authority – protector providers (Gilmore, 1990) – and women to be weaker, more passive, dependent and subordinate. It is these discursive justifications for patriarchal authority that both underpin and legitimate the idea that maleness is essentially about power and control; and there is certainly evidence of the influence of these justifications in the narratives of

Gary, Mark and Paul. Witness how Gary's attempts to stop Rebecca 'panicking' positioned him as the calm, rational organizer and her as in need of protection from her own irrational fears; how Mark perceived Maria as a 'delicate little thing' who needed him to look after and reassure her; how Paul, despite his disability, was willing to ward off any man whom he perceived to be harassing his ex-wife, insisting that he would 'fight to the end of the Earth' to get back with Karen. This poses the question: what is it about these men and their relationships that is different from relationships that manage, despite the omnipresence of gender differentiated discourses and the unequal power relations these support, to avoid the violence that characterized Gary's, Mark's and Paul's relationships?

Denial, dependency, containment and acting out

All three of these cases illustrate the workings of denial. For us, this refers to the unarticulated desire to be free of the kind of disturbing knowledge that we know to be true but cannot accept and hence keep at the perimeters of our conscious awareness; what Christopher Bollas defined as the 'need to be innocent of a troubling recognition' (Bollas, 1992: 167). It is this aspect of denial and the way it is implicated in the perpetration of domestic violence that will enable us to get behind the excuses and rationalizations men make for assaulting their partners to expose the unhappiness they mask. By linking psychological distress with social power we will be reading our cases psychosocially. In Gary's case, the idea that he was 'picking on' Rebecca was the 'troubling recognition' that he felt compelled to deny repeatedly, ultimately resorting to 'shouting, screaming and being abusive' to make her accept that he was not – a response that was self-evidently counter-productive, since it confirmed her assessment. In Mark's case, it was the comparison with his father that was so unbearably painful that it felt like a 'punch in the face' and thus enraged him. Like Gary, Mark would sometimes resort to strangulation, silencing Maria by putting his hands round her throat, a controlled loss of self-control that he experienced as an emotional 'release'. In Paul's case, the idea that he had been 'an idiot' and was 'wasting' his life, was something he found too disturbing to let into his conscious mind, even though a part of him knew Karen 'was in the right'.

If the spur for the violence in all three cases was these men's refusal to recognize themselves in their partners' blunter evaluations, we still need to ask why they were so sensitive to their partners' reality checks since Mark did seem to be rather like his father and Paul was in many respects his own worst enemy and, in that sense, was being an 'idiot' and 'wasting his life'. In the case of Gary and Rebecca, both seemed unable to cope with the 'panicking' of the other, hence their shared notion that the other was out of control. In all three cases the issue of dependency was crucial. For what is also evident in these men's accounts is that they were all petrified of losing their partners: the thought of losing Maria 'frightened the life' out of Mark; even the smallest disagreement seemed to cause Gary to panic; and Paul interpreted his arguments with Karen as signs that she did not love him anymore. In situations in which these men actually had much to gain by remaining in control, the reminder – by someone upon whom they were deeply dependent – of something so troubling that it had to be denied at all costs placed them in an emotional space that was too painful to tolerate. This may be why all three of these men claimed not to remember fully the extremity of the violence they had perpetrated. Psychoanalytic studies of violent men in clinical settings have revealed that explosive violence of this kind is often a consequence of the release of unarticulated (or inarticulable) affect (Cartwright, 2002; Hyatt-Williams, 1998). What happens when such men erupt in rage is that psychic pains that cannot be consciously tolerated are evacuated out of the perpetrator's mind by making another physically suffer them. Expressed in the language of clinical psychoanalysis: 'In the absence of adequate reflective capacity, the pre-reflective and physical self may come to substitute for mental functions – the body may reflect experiences instead of the mind and thus be imbued with thought and feeling' (Fonagy et al., 1993, quoted in Cartwright, 2002: 40). As we explained in Chapter 2, those who adopt an orthodox Freudian approach to such matters would describe this process as a form of 'acting out', the body performing the psychic affect that the mind is unable to process. Kleinians tend, instead, to refer to this process as a failure of containment, emphasizing the role intersubjectivity can play in process- ing troubling emotions. Hanna Segal's summary of Bion's theory of the 'container and the contained' captures these intersubjective dynamics well:

> When an infant has an intolerable anxiety, he deals with it by projecting it into the mother. The mother's response is to acknowledge the anxiety and do what- ever is necessary to relieve the infant's distress. The infant's perception is that he has projected something intolerable into his object, but the object was capable of containing and dealing with it. He can then reintroject not only his original anxiety but an anxiety modified by having been contained. He also introjects an object capable of containing and dealing with anxiety. The containment of anx- iety by an external object capable of understanding is a beginning of mental stability.
>
> (Segal, 1975, pp. 134–5, quoted in Hinshelwood, 1991: 248)

What matters then, in determining how adequate an individual's reflective capacity becomes, is the experience of another person, often a parent, sometimes a partner, willing and able to contain their bad feelings. To develop this reflective capacity, children need primary carers who can represent frightening experiences back to them in less disturbing and more manageable forms.

There is evidence in Gary's, Mark's and Paul's biographies to suggest their child- hoods lacked this experience of containment and, furthermore, that their fathers bore much of the responsibility for both the excess of fear these three men experi- enced as boys and for their mothers' inabilities to rectify matters. Think of how con- fusing it must have been for the infant Gary to accept that his mother was no longer his mum but his 'aunt'. Note also the resonance of Gary's current preoccupation with not being believed and the muddling responses of his father to Gary's revelations regarding the physical violence he experienced at the hands of his stepmother and the sexual abuse his sister experienced from their grandfather (Gadd, 2000). Imagine how the adolescent Mark's psychological development would have been disturbed by his conscious knowledge of his father's violence and his inability to discuss with either of his parents the abuse his mother was experiencing, having been exiled to boarding school in order to protect him from the knowledge of what his parents were really like (Gadd, 2002). Contemplate how Paul perceived his world as a child: his father being imprisoned because of the severity of the violence he perpetrated on his sons; and his mother often in hiding to escape further abuse (Gadd, 2004b). Was there a connection between these experiences and the acute feelings of worthlessness that seemed to lie behind Paul's suicide attempt and his unshakeable dependence on illicit pain relief?

While they were all very different men we think it is plausible to assume that what Gary, Mark and Paul had in common were childhoods in which the unconscious emotional learning involved in tolerating early anxieties felt inadequate. This rendered them emotionally vulnerable when faced with reminders of these early anxieties. Denial offered a 'solution' of sorts, providing their bad feelings could be lodged somewhere; split off and projected onto a despised other. Gender differentiated discourses generally assist such splitting; and all can remain relatively harmonious where both parties accept their gendered positioning. But when bad feelings are not contained, and are instead offered up as a reality check by the very loved one upon whom one depends to contain them, then rage at this failure – combined with, in these men's cases, unconscious identification with their aggressive fathers – becomes temporarily uncontrollable. Unsurprisingly, the men's violence probably reduced their partners' capacities to contain, as they themselves had then to contend with the threats to their own physical and psychological well-being. This then seems to have set in motion a vicious psychosocial dynamic involving an escalation in the men's violence: as the women's anxieties about the fear of further violence delimited their capacities to contain the men's hostile projections, this contributed to the spiralling sense of persecution evident in the men's accounts of themselves. In social terms, the substance of the accusations and counter-accusations that contributed to this escalating sense of persecution were unremarkable and everyday, i.e. 'normal'. Money, childcare, and extended kin were what these couples argued about. But for these particular men these disputes were of far greater symbolic significance, impinging on their evaluations of themselves as good fathers and husbands in a way that threw into question their fragile feelings of integrity moulded by their own experiences of parents who, emotionally speaking, were rarely 'good enough' at containing their children's anxieties and often contributed to the feelings of confusion and terror that these children must at times have felt. Questions of social power and the need to be in control certainly figured in all three cases. But, without attention to what needed constantly to be denied (because too painful to think about) and the dependency such denials masked, we have no way of making sense of how apparently trivial remarks and insults could incite such rageful violence.

Conclusion

However inexcusable these men's violent behaviours were, their relationships were in many other respects socially 'normal'. As we saw earlier, this argument, which is also endorsed in many feminist analyses of domestic violence, often leads to the conclusion that violent men's denials are self-serving. From this perspective, men who say they cannot remember their violence do so because it is in their interests to forget, to underplay the amount of harm caused, and to contest allegations of malicious intent. However, if we make the assumption that people are inherently defensive, then the notion that denial is a consciously self-interested phenomenon looks less plausible.

Our argument has been that in a socially unequal world in which contemporary discourses of masculinity and femininity encourage the splitting of gender differences, men and women in intimate relationships are both faced with the tricky task of negotiating relationships based on mutuality, love and reciprocity. Some relationships will conform to gender differentiated stereotypes – he the protector/provider, she the subordinate wife; others will contravene or reverse the stereotypes; and still others may achieve their own version of an equal relationship, conforming to or breaking with gendered stereotypes as befits their own psychosocial profiles. Under 'good enough' conditions all such relationships can prove acceptable or satisfying to their participants, whatever others might make of them. However, relationship dynamics can become hostile and produce violent, bullying behaviours when certain, biographically specific forms of anxiety enter the equation. Domestic abuse is often about one partner with many unresolved anxieties resulting from early care experiences saddling the other with his or her own vulnerabilities through the process of splitting and projection. Prevailing discourses about femininity tend to both idealize (Madonna) and denigrate (whore) women in ways that are consistent with the process of psychic splitting. Gary's, Mark's and Paul's stories are illustrative, in their own unique ways, of this process: their partners were sometimes 'Madonnas', when they successfully contained their anxieties, at other times 'whores', when they failed to do so. In their performances of masculinity Gary, Mark and Paul, despite the obvious social differences between them, were predictably 'normal' men. It was primarily in their particular vulnerabilities, a result of traumas that left them ill-equipped to deal with the troubling recognitions that tend to come to the fore in adult intimate relationships, that these men could be said to be different.

In essence, the problem of men's violence is both more sociological and more psychodynamic than the emergent 'pro-feminist cognitive behavioural' paradigm suggests. The problem is more sociological in the sense that it is embedded in a set of widely endorsed expectations about gender, intimacy and romance that enable men to position themselves as emotionally needless and independent. The problem is more psychodynamic because, to the extent that violent men can be characterized by their 'faulty cognitions', these cognitions are likely to be defences that protect them from confronting the feelings that underpin their aggression and the shame and embarrassment that they would incur should they be identified as perpetrators of domestic violence. It is the fragility of these defences in the case of abusive men that also helps explain why it is that such men are often so afraid of losing relationships with partners they have abused; quite simply, the anxiety masked by denial renders them extremely dependent once they have found a loved object capable of containing these distressing feelings. The loss of these partners also means the loss of a safe container, which is why the failure of their partners to collude in their denials is so devastating. These failures constitute temporary losses of the containing, loved object, and the resulting anxiety can only be tolerated by transforming it into rage. This is why perpetrators are rarely just 'in denial' about what they have done in the sense of pretending they haven't been violent or that it was really the fault of their partners. Denial is about the inability to think through the troubling recognitions that underpin sudden outbursts of rage. It is for this reason that interventions that fail to enable an acknowledgement that domestic violence is a sign of masculine weakness and dependency and is a behaviour of which many men are ashamed, often generate more resistance amongst client groups than they are able to overcome. Indeed, in failing properly to acknowledge the role denial plays in the aetiology of aggression, perpetrator programmes are in danger of colluding with the very desire for omnipotent control over other people's thoughts and expectations that is so often implicated in men's violence towards their partners and children.

11

RESTORATIVE JUSTICE, REINTEGRATIVE SHAMING AND INTERSUBJECTIVITY

There is now a whole library of books and articles on restorative justice. This development is of very recent origin, perhaps the last decade-and-a-half. Given our particular interest in the topic, we do not intend to overview that material here. For those interested, McLaughlin et al. (2003: 2) offer a comprehensive overview of the movement's 'origins ... founding definitions and principles ... institutionalisation ... claims to efficacy and relevance [and] ... significance as a mode of governance'. Somewhat more simply, Daly chooses to discuss the movement in terms of 'the four myths that feature in advocates' stories and claims', namely, that '(1) Restorative justice is the opposite of retributive justice. (2) ... uses indigenous justice practices ... (3) ... is a "care" (or feminine) response ... [and] (4) ... can be expected to produce major changes in people' (2002: 56). We shall have occasion later to return to Daly's counter-narrative, what she calls 'the real story' of restorative justice. For now, however, we wish to highlight only one idea, namely, that restorative or reparative justice can be accomplished through *shaming* the offender.

Whether restorative justice constitutes a novel or merely a rediscovered form of punishment may be a moot point. What is indisputable, and an important part of our argument, is that the subject presumed by such an approach is all too simplistic. Introducing the emotionally based dimension of shame would seem to herald a more sophisticated view of the subject than most criminology presumes. But, unfortunately, this did not happen. Because emotions remain under the sway of reason within the reintegrative shaming literature, both offenders and victims are construed, ultimately, as rational unitary subjects. The emotional dynamic binding them to their communities is thus assumed capable of being (rationally) regulated or controlled, for example, through carefully facilitated restorative justice conferences. It is as if the classicist attempt to administer, in Ignatieff's (1978) memorable phrase, 'A just measure of pain', is being reinvoked as 'a just measure of shame'. This not only misunderstands the nature of shame which, as we shall argue, may begin to account for the rather mixed evaluations shame-based conferences have sometimes received, but also fails to take seriously the problematic nature of public shaming that follows if we posit a properly psychosocial understanding of shame. We are not the first to point to the idea that public shaming is potentially problematic (for example, see Maxwell and Morris, 2002; Retzinger and Scheff, 1996; Van Stokkom, 2002). But, we may be the first to do so by identifying the centrality of a psychosocial approach to an understanding of shame.

Braithwaite and *Crime, Shame and Reintegration*

However diverse its origins, there is little disagreement about the importance of John Braithwaite: 'arguably the intellectual leader of the restorative justice movement and also a highly influential policy consultant across the world' (McLaughlin et al., 2003: 13). The book that launched the whole enterprise was his *Crime, Shame and Reintegration*, published in 1989. For all its engaging modesty, this remains, 18 years on, a very ambitious book offering, as it does, nothing less than an integrated, holistic theory of 'predatory crime', a term Braithwaite (1989: 14) confines to 'crimes involving victimization of one party by another'. It is integrated because it manages to incorporate what is known about control, opportunity, subcultural, learning and labelling theory in a harmonious synthesis with his core notion of reintegrative shaming; it is holistic because it works both as a social and individual level explanation of crime, explaining both high- and low-crime societies and which individuals are more likely to offend. This makes it, in a certain sense, psychosocial. The key to the entire theory is the reintegrative shaming of offenders. This, it is claimed, can help reduce crime without stigmatizing offenders. Given the subsequent phenomenal growth of interest in the idea, it is remarkable that the theory's core concept, 'reintegrative shaming', what it meant and how it worked, was so under-theorized.

As a social explanation of crime, Braithwaite's starting point was comparative. Where those on the political Left tended to locate the causes of crime in the disjunction between Westerners' expectations and the cold realities of living with capitalism, Braithwaite noted that Japan, despite its rapid industrialization and democratization, retained incredibly low crime rates. Where Britain and America, for example, were witnessing (at the time of writing) ever-rising crime rates (ibid: 49–50), the Japanese did not appear to have a crime problem and spent very little on their penal apparatus. Braithwaite hypothesized that the critical difference between Japan and the West was cultural. Where the West had embraced a culture of individualism, the Japanese recognized and valued their community-based culture. The shame of law violation was more commonly borne by the entire community in Japan and not just by individual offenders. An offender's teachers and mentors, family members and peers could all feel ashamed by the deviant actions of one their own. Where Westerners resented the intrusion of the state into 'private' family matters, the Japanese had, Braithwaite claimed, embedded the police within their customs and family-life solidarities. Where Western governments assumed that strictness of enforcement was the key to crime control, the Japanese embraced repentance and apology as the route to forgiveness and loving reintegration of the wrong-doer.

This comparison with Japan led Braithwaite to hypothesise that: 'Societies with low crime rates are those that shame potently and judiciously; individuals who resort to crime are those insulated from shame over wrongdoing' (ibid: 1). Compounding the problem was the highly disintegrative nature of punishment as it operates in the West. Perpetrators of crime are punished not by their communities but by state actors whom they neither know nor care about. The effect of this kind of state punishment is to further estrange offenders from their families and communities – to stigmatize them – so that they become increasingly dependent on others who are similarly excluded from social approval and companionship. To make matters worse, criminology with its 'rather passive conception of the criminal' tends to overlook the critical points at which those at risk of being outcast could be persuaded to 'attend to the moral claims of the criminal law' (ibid: 9). What criminologists needed to realize, Braithwaite argued, is that:

> Crime is best controlled when members of the community are the primary controllers through active participation in shaming offenders, and, having shamed them, through concerted participation in ways of reintegrating the offender back into the community of law-abiding citizens ... Low crime societies are societies where ... tolerance of deviance has definite limits, where communities prefer to handle their own crime problems rather than hand them over to professionals ... [T]he rule of law will amount to a meaningless set of formal sanctioning proceedings which will be perceived as arbitrary unless there is community involvement in moralizing about helping with the crime problem.
>
> (ibid: 8)

As an explanation of why individuals turn to crime, Braithwaite's notion that criminology operates with a 'rather passive' notion of the criminal offers a clue as to his rather different conception of offenders:

> The theory of re-integrative shaming adopts an active conception of the criminal. The criminal is seen as making choices – to commit crime, to join a subculture, to adopt a deviant self-concept, to reintegrate herself, to respond to others' gestures of reintegration – against a background of societal pressures mediated by shaming.
>
> (ibid: 9)

This means that although shaming is 'a tool to allure and inveigle ... to coax and caress compliance, to reason and remonstrate', the offender is 'ultimately free to reject these attempts to persuade him through social disapproval' (ibid). Unlike 'repressive social control' which relies upon 'coerced compliance', 'shaming is a route to freely chosen compliance' (ibid: 10). Despite background 'pressures', this is an oddly archaic 'free will' version of subjectivity, even if one that has been reincarnated as the rational unitary subject of rational choice theory (Cornish and Clarke, 1986).

The psychosocial nature of the theory is secured, apparently, by the relationship between interdependency and communitarianism. 'Individuals', we are told, 'are more susceptible to shaming when they are enmeshed in multiple relationships of interdependency; societies shame more effectively when they are communitarian' (Braithwaite, 1989: 14). However, the definition of 'communitarian societies' as places where 'individuals are densely enmeshed in interdependencies which have special qualities of mutual help and trust' (ibid: 100) seems merely to transpose the individualistic notion of interdependency to the social level. This makes it essentially a social (and tautologous) theory or, at best, a social psychological one: a reading that squares with Braithwaite's assertion that 'interdependency is approximately equivalent to the social bonding, attachment and commitment of control theory' (ibid). As we saw in Chapter 2, control theory gives no independent efficacy to the psychic level because only the family relations promoting or failing to promote attachment are deemed of interest. Effectively, the inner world comes to reflect the (social) pattern of child rearing but does not contribute to how social processes are perceived in the first place.

This oversocial emphasis affects all Braithwaite's key concepts. But it is self-evident in his definition of 'shaming': 'all *social* processes of expressed disapproval which have the intention or effect of invoking remorse in the person being shamed and/or condemnation by others who become aware of the shaming' (ibid, emphasis in original). The qualifier 'reintegrative' also references social processes, in this case 'words or gestures of forgiveness or ceremonies to decertify the offender as dangerous'. These, it is hoped, will provoke internal change (remorse) and hence reintegration 'back into the community of law-abiding or respectable citizens' (ibid: 100–1). In what follows, our intention is to show the inadequacies of such a simplistic conception of shame in several stages. First, by demonstrating the theoretical consensus on the topic across the disciplines of psychology and sociology. Second, by showing how taking seriously the inner-world dimension without losing the social dimension (i.e. reading the literature psychosocially) offers a way of transcending dichotomous (either social or psychological) readings of shame. Third, by showing how this psychosocial reading is able to make explanatory sense of some of the more critical evaluations of restorative justice conferences. Finally, using a case study, to show how a psychosocial approach is able to grasp the deep-rooted nature of shame – within individual biographies and across relationships of interdependency – and consequently how difficult and unpredictably harmful it can be to invoke shame deliberately and publicly.

A cross-disciplinary consensus on theorizing about shame

Braithwaite is not entirely unaware of the dangers of shaming: at one point he admits that '[s]haming is a dangerous game' (ibid: 12); later, that '[r]eintegrative shaming … can be cruel, even vicious' (ibid: 101). But, in *Crime, Shame and Reintegration* this did not detain him long. The idea that shame can be a dangerous emotion to handle is often acknowledged; but, without exploring the nature of shame more fully than Braithwaite does, it is difficult to explain precisely why this should be the case. One of the difficulties in talking about shame is that both psychoanalysts and sociologists have tended either to ignore or misrecognize the emotion. In the case of psycho-analysis, Scheff (2000: 85) places the blame squarely at Freud's door suggesting that shame initially had a central role in psychoanalytic thinking about the hidden affects underlying hysteria but that the development of drive theory made anxiety and guilt, not shame, central. Thereafter (at least until the work of Helen Lewis, to which we turn below), psychoanalytic contributions to the study of shame took place outside of Freudian orthodoxy and tended to go 'unnamed and/or undefined' (ibid: 86). In the case of sociology, Scheff (ibid: 98) argues that Elias' seminal study of the role of shame in the civilizing process (first published in 1939 but not avail-able in English until 1978) also provides an important clue to its fitful and partial treatment, namely, the fact that 'shame is increasing in modern societies, but at the same time awareness of shame is decreasing'. This makes studying shame a very difficult business, especially when, according to Lewis (1971), much shame goes unacknowledged.

However, there has been something of a resurgence of interest in the topic lately. And, despite everything, there does seem to be some cross-disciplinary consensus emerging on the topic. We shall therefore start with these points of agreement in our journey towards a psychosocial understanding. In the first place, shame is seen as part of a 'family' of negative emotions. Here, for example, is Scheff defining the term, having overviewed both psychoanalytic and sociological contributions:

> By shame I mean a large family of emotions that includes many cognates and variants, most notably embarrassment, humiliation, and related feelings such as shyness that involve reactions to rejection or feelings of failure or inadequacy.
>
> (2000: 96–7)

By disciplinary contrast, here is Nathanson, a psychologist who, like Scheff, has made the study of shame central to his life's work; and to whose perceptive insights we will have cause to return. Although he believes shame to be one of the innate affects, Nathanson nonetheless remains very open to psychoanalysis:

> I suggest that we follow the lead of the psychoanalyst Leon Wurmser, who speaks of the shame experience as a family of emotions. These are uncomfort-able feelings, ranging from the mildest twinge of embarrassment to the searing pain of mortification … We will use the word shame to indicate the family of negative emotions associated with incompetence, failure, or inadequacy.
>
> (1992: 19–20)

A second point of agreement is shame's difference from guilt: where shame involves the whole person, guilt is seen as specific to 'acts done or not done'. Scheff draws on the sociologist Helen Lynd to make the point: 'She [Lynd] notes that guilt is usually extremely specific and therefore close to the surface; it involves acts done or not done. Guilt is about what one did, shame is about the self, what one *is*' (2000: 92, emphasis in original). Nathanson, from his very different perspective, made an almost identical point several years earlier:

> Often shame is confused with guilt, a related but quite different discomfort. Whereas shame is about the *quality* of our person or self, guilt is the painful emotion triggered when we become aware that we have acted in a way to bring harm to another person or to violate some important code. Guilt is about *action* and laws.

> (1992: 19, emphases in original)

It is this notion of the all-encompassing nature of shame, implicating our whole selves not just specific actions, that would seem to account for the depth of hurt that shame can elicit. Tomkins, a psychologist in the same 'affects' tradition as Nathanson and to whom the latter was deeply indebted, expresses this as powerfully as anyone: 'While terror and distress hurt, they are wounds from outside which penetrate the smooth surface of the ego; but shame is felt as an inner torment, a sickness of the soul' (1963: 118, quoted in ibid: 146). Less evocatively, but perhaps more precisely, Nathanson draws again on Wurmser to emphasize the critical point: 'Like most writers on shame, Wurmser agrees that the emotion usually follows a moment of exposure, and that this uncovering reveals aspects of the self of a peculiarly sensitive, intimate and vulnerable nature' (ibid: 144). As well as this consensus about the conceptual difference between shame and guilt, there is also, somewhat paradoxically, agreement that in practice the feelings are not always so clearly distinguishable. The sociologist, Van Stokkom, for example, agrees with the conceptual distinction between guilt and shame just discussed – 'A person who feels guilt acknowledges that he or she made a specific error ... [W]hen a person feels shame, it involves the entire being' (2002: 341) – but, using the results of an empirical study of Australian drink-drivers' feelings post-arrest (Harris, 2001), Van Stokkom concluded 'that in the context of criminal offending the distinction between shame and guilt may not be as important as has been suggested for a long time' (2002: 351). Nathanson (1992: 137) agrees: 'people differ both in their descriptions and their apparent experience of shame'.

Given the large family of negative emotions that shame covers, from the 'mildest twinge of embarrassment to the searing pain of mortification', it is not surprising that distinctions between guilt and shame are sometimes easier to make in theory than practice. However, there is another reason for this, namely, the fact that the emotion of shame is often simply unrecognized as such. Once again, psychologists and sociologists can agree on this; and both credit the psychologist and psychoanalyst Helen Lewis with this insight:

> [T]he shame mechanism is triggered often in situations that we do not recognize as embarrassing, painful circumstances when our attention is drawn from whatever had attracted us and we are momentarily ill at ease. The psychologist Helen Block Lewis called this 'bypassed shame'.

> (ibid: 145)

Scheff takes as central to his definition and understanding of shame the empirical work of Lewis, based on the systematic 'analysis of verbatim transcripts of hundreds of psychotherapy sessions' (Scheff, 2000: 94). Despite the 'high frequency of shame markers in all the sessions' (ibid), shame was 'almost never referred to' by therapist or patient (ibid). This led her to distinguish between '*overt, undifferentiated*' shame (when 'the patient seemed to be suffering psychological pain, but failed to identify it as shame') and '*bypassed*' shame (when 'the patient seemed not to be in pain' but engaged in 'rapid, obsessional speech on topics … somewhat removed from the dialogue') (ibid).

Towards a psychosocial understanding of shame

As we have seen, both Nathanson and Scheff draw on the work of Lewis. Ultimately, however, they draw different conclusions from it. Scheff, the sociologist, suggests that what all the 'large family of [shame] emotions' have in common is 'that they involve the feeling of a *threat to the social bond*' (ibid: 97, emphases in original). In other words, it is the fear of 'social disconnection, being adrift from understanding and being understood by the other' (ibid: 93), an observation that Scheff takes from Lewis, that makes 'shame … the most social of the basic emotions' (ibid: 97). It is the failure of 'most psychoanalytic writing' on shame to include 'the social matrix' (ibid: 85) that renders it problematic, according to Scheff. So far, so predictable. Nathanson, the psychologist, on the other hand, finds Lewis' linkage of 'shame to separation' too social 'and for this reason her work must now be considered inadequate to explain all the phenomenology of shame' (1992: 218). Instead, Nathanson prefers Wurmser's psychoanalytic work on the 'core' of shame: 'Leon Wurmser, surely the most gifted psychoanalytic writer ever to plumb the depths of the shame experience, has often remarked that at the core of shame is the feeling that we are both unloved and unlovable' (ibid: 220). Here, then, we get a glimpse of an important difference between psychological and sociological understandings of shame. How do these two understandings differ? How does shame as 'social disconnection' differ from the idea of shame as feeling 'unloved and unlovable'? One social reading would simply elide the two notions: the idea of shame as 'social disconnection' would simply subsume the idea of shame as feeling 'unloved and unlovable'. Crudely, our feelings (of being unloved/unlovable) stem from our (social) experiences (of being unloved). These, ultimately, determine how socially connected we feel. In other words, our inner-world feelings reflect our outer-world experiences. A purely psychological reading would reverse this error: (un)lovability would be read independently of social considerations, a function of (un)healthy psychological development. But, it is possible to read these two views of shame as connected, without reducing them to the social, and also to think of their distinctiveness, without severing their connectedness. To do so involves partially severing the link between feelings and experience: to see feelings as having a developmental, hence biographically unique, dimension, but also as complexly, not simply, linked to social experiences. This is a case we have been making throughout this book. The clues to such a reading are everywhere in the literature – from the differential shame-proneness of individuals to the idea that much shame is not recognized as such.

Scheff's work can be read in such a psychosocial fashion. For example, in his reading of Lewis' work, Scheff acknowledges her argument that in addition to shame occurring 'in response to threats to the bond from the other … it can also occur in response to actions in the "inner theatre", in the interior monologue in which we see ourselves from the point of view of others' (2000: 95). Shorn of its references to Cooley (1922) and Mead ([1934] 1967), the idea of shame being also a response to inner world issues opens the world to a psychosocial interpretation. Combined with other ideas drawn from Lewis – for example, 'A patient [mistakenly] interprets an expression by the therapist as hostile, rejecting, or critical, and responds with shame or embarrassment' (Scheff, 2000: 95) – it is hard not to infer the importance of an inner world that is not just the sum of outer world experiences but is actively engaged with interpreting these in conjunction with a biographically unique set of inner world fantasies (rather than the therapist's overt intentions). How else explain why one person's mild embarrassment is another's painful mortification: 'there are many people who are unusually sensitive to embarrassment, who seem always poised at the edge of shame' (Nathanson, 1992: 143). And, we have all met people who are, apparently – i.e. as we perceive them, if not, in truth – 'shameless'.

But, perhaps the strongest indicator of the need for a psychosocial understanding of shame can be found in Lewis' key concepts of 'overt, undifferentiated' and 'bypassed' shame. These are taken up strongly by Scheff, albeit reduced to the single concept of 'unacknowledged' shame, but nowhere are they explained. Why should shame have such difficulty in being recognized as such; what accounts for it sometimes, if rarely, being specifically acknowledged, at other times acknowledged in an 'undifferentiated' fashion, and at other times being completely unacknowledged or 'bypassed'? These would seem to be important questions for anyone seriously interested in the concept of shame as Scheff demonstrably is.

In keeping with our cross-disciplinary investigation of the topic, let us approach this question via the writings of Nathanson. His compendious overview of the field led him to develop the idea of 'the compass of shame', a set of four basic possible reactions to shame:

> Each time something triggers an episode of shame we tend to act in a very predictable fashion. There are four basic patterns of behaviour that govern our reactions to this complex emotion: these I have grouped as 'the compass of shame'. It is the four poles of the compass that house all the scripts that we know as shameful withdrawal, masochistic submission, narcissistic avoidance of shame, and the rage of wounded pride. For each of us, this group of reaction patterns has a great deal to do with the nature of our personality.
>
> (Nathanson, 1992: 30)

Although Lewis operated with a smaller typology of responses, there are clearly overlaps: if 'withdrawal' constitutes some kind of acknowledgement of shame, 'submission', 'avoidance' and 'rage' are at least compatible with the idea of 'bypassed' shame. But Nathanson's typology of responses are also more revealing than the simple notions of 'undifferentiated' or 'bypassed' shame. Indeed, they would seem to invite psycho-analytically inspired readings since they so closely resemble various unconscious defences against anxiety: 'masochistic submission' recalls the defence of 'identification with the aggressor'; 'narcissistic avoidance' that of 'denial'; and the 'rage of wounded pride' that of 'displacement' (Hinshelwood, 1991). In other words, three of Nathanson's typical reactions to shame can be construed as unconscious defences against the anxiety that we know shame is capable of inducing. Herein, then, lies a simple answer to why shame is so often 'bypassed': because it is an attack not just on what we have done but on who we are and, because it can be excruciatingly painful and humiliating, we unconsciously defend ourselves against its capacity to make us feel 'naked, defeated, alienated, lacking in dignity or worth' (Tomkins, 1963: 118, quoted in Nathanson, 1992: 146). Simple though this notion appears, we have travelled a long way from Braithwaite's idea that shame can be used, simply, to promote remorse as the prelude to reintegration.

Why (some) restorative-justice conferences fail

It is not our intention here to review the literature on evaluating restorative-justice conferences, nor to suggest that conferences inevitably fail. Rather, we want to look at a few evaluations that have exposed the emotional dynamics that underpin restorative-justice conferences and, in so doing, have problematized the nature of reintegrative shaming. With the benefit of our discussion of the nature of shame, we suggest why there is a disjunction between the theory of shaming, as outlined by Braithwaite, and the experiences of many restorative-justice participants.

Kathleen Daly's 'real story' of restorative justice

Kathleen Daly has been researching restorative-justice conferences in Australia for many years. Her analysis of the story of restorative justice in terms of what she calls 'four myths' is based on her own South Australia Juvenile Justice (SAJJ) Research and Conferencing Project. It is the 'real story' behind her fourth myth ('Restorative justice can be expected to produce major changes in people' (Daly, 2002: 56)) that concerns us here. Having shown that books on restorative justice routinely show examples – actual or composite – demonstrating positive outcomes of conferences in which kindness, understanding, repair and goodwill all figure, what Daly asks is: how typical are such outcomes? In what follows, we try to offer brief psychosocial explanations of some of her findings. She starts with the issue of 'misunderstandings':

> Whereas very high proportions of victims and offenders (80 to 95 percent) said that the process was fair ... 'restorativeness' was evident in 30 to 50

percent of conferences (depending on the item), and solidly in no more than about one-third. Thus ... where conferences are used *routinely*, fairness can more easily be achieved than restorativeness. As but one example, from the interviews we learned that from the victims' perspectives, less than 30 percent of offenders were perceived as making genuine apologies, but from the offenders' perspectives, close to 60 percent said their apology was genuine.

(ibid: 70, emphasis in original)

Leaving aside the more than 40 per cent of offenders whose apologies were (presumably) insincere (or not made at all) and assuming both sides were telling their version of the 'truth', what does it mean when a 'genuine' apology is 'read' as insincere? This question points to the different interests of the respective parties – victims and offenders – in the shaming process: where victims want full, public acknowledgement of their hurt, all we have learned about shaming and feelings of self-worth suggests that offenders will typically do everything in their power to maintain a sense of their own dignity. They will try to fend off (in the various ways that Nathanson outlines) or defend against, in our terms, the indignity of shame: 'shaming another in public is like shedding blood', according to Baba Matzia (quoted in Nathanson, 1992: 149). So, from our psychosocial perspective, an 'ashamed' apology is likely to sound very different to victims than it feels to offenders.

Daly also found that

Young people appear to be as, if not more, interested in *repairing their own reputations* than in repairing the harm done to victims. Among the most important things that the victims hoped would occur at the conference was for the offender to hear how the offence affected them, but half the offenders told us that the victim's story had no effect or only a little effect on them.

(Daly, 2002: 70, emphases in original)

Given these predictable mismatches between (unrealistic) victim expectations and (understandable) reluctance on the part of offenders to allow (metaphorically speaking) their 'blood to be shed in public', it is unsurprising that around 50 per cent of conferences got 'a mixed, fair or poor rating' by observers scoring how positively conferences managed to end in terms of reparation and goodwill. When feeling embarrassed, inadequate and vulnerable (ashamed), hanging onto some semblance of self-worth is more important for most of us than the feelings of another, especially since identifying with those feelings will make you feel more ashamed. When the feelings of threat to the self seem acute, we find it particularly difficult to 'hear' or take responsibility for another's pain, and become defensive (Benjamin, 1998; Gadd, 2006). This is one reason why restorative justice conferences appear only to work for some of the participants some of the time. It is probably also why even those conferences that appear to have no *observable* effect arouse a range of emotional reactions from both victims and offenders.

Retzinger and Scheff's critique of conferences as 'shaming machines'

Retzinger and Scheff observed a number of Australian conferences in the 1990s and published their findings in 1996. According to Braithwaite, responding generally to criticisms of restorative justice that it 'can be a "shaming machine" that worsens the stigmatisation of offenders' (2002: 140), the nub of their critique invoked the idea of victim defensiveness causing problems:

> The point about moral indignation that is crucial for conferences is that when it is repetitive and out of control, it is a defensive movement in two steps: denial of one's own shame, followed by projection of blame onto the offender. Moral indignation interferes with the identification between participants that is necessary if the conference is to generate symbolic reparation.
>
> (Retzinger and Scheff, 1996 quoted in ibid)

This is a revealing quotation for a number of reasons. First, despite Scheff's views on the asocial nature of psychoanalytic writings on shame, this evaluation depends on core psychoanalytic concepts – denial, projection, identification – to make its case. More importantly, however, is the (unusual) focus on the shame of the victim. Although, 'rationally', the victim usually has nothing of which to be ashamed, we know that victims can feel shame (Why me? Could I have done more to avoid the situation? Did I put up appropriate resistance? Why did I walk home rather than take a taxi?) in the aftermath of crime. Women's stories of being victims of rape strongly bear this out, as does Fanon's classic text on the effects of colonial subjugation (Fanon, 1968). The victim's response will be the same as any ashamed person; usually some kind of defensive manoeuvre to avoid the pain. It does not take much imagination to anticipate the offender's defensive response to such projections of blame. However, having alerted us to the problem of one ashamed person confronting another (in a public setting), Retzinger and Scheff then spell out the conditions for successful 'symbolic reparation', namely, 'identification between participants'. In contrast to the realism that has preceded it, this resolution reads very idealistically. Unfortunately, it was this idealism that Braithwaite picked up on in his response. Referring back to an earlier article he wrote with Stephen Mugford (Braithwaite and Mugford, 1994), Braithwaite repeated 'that the best protection against the vices of moral lecturing and sarcasm is to do a good job of inviting a large number of caring supporters for both victims and offenders' (2002: 141). Predictably perhaps, 'training of facilitators to intervene against moral lecturing and ... [the promotion of] respectful discussion' were also advocated as remedies (ibid).

Maxwell and Morris on shame, guilt and remorse

Other commentators, however, are less idealistic. For example, in an article that is both theoretically founded in the shame/guilt literature and based in empirical research on young offenders in New Zealand, Maxwell and Morris explore the dangers of shaming, its effects in reducing self-esteem and its unpredictability as an outcome. This leads them to make a crucial point, one that in many respects cuts across the victim focus of restorative justice:

> It has to be the individual being disapproved of/shamed and not the disapprover/shamer who will determine whether or not the disapproval/shaming is actually reintegrative: the disapprover/shamer cannot determine its effect on the offender ... The benchmark for actions must be their impact, not their intent.
>
> (Maxwell and Morris, 2002: 278)

In more general terms 'shame and its associated emotions are felt variably depending on both social and cultural context and the individual's personality' (ibid: 275). This focus on the (potentially dangerous) unpredictability of shaming processes is very much in line with our psychosocial understanding. Maxwell and Morris' empirical findings, based on re-interviewing 'a sample of young offenders and their parents who had been involved in family group conferences' (ibid) after a six-year interval, strongly reinforce the point. Those that had stayed free of reconvictions were those that felt good about themselves and relationships, had a job, and felt remorseful but *not* ashamed. On the other hand: '[A]mong the most important variables in the discriminant analyses to explain reconviction were "feeling ashamed at the conference", "not being remorseful", not getting a job or training after the conference, and not having close friends' (ibid: 280). After a detailed consideration of the rival claims of shame and guilt theorists, Van Stokkom (2002) reached a similar conclusion about the importance of remorse:

> Remorse can be described as a feeling of compunction, or deep regret. According to Gabriele Taylor remorse is, unlike guilt, an other-regarding emotion rather than a self-regarding emotion ... Remorse opens 'the way to redemption': it does not imply acceptance of what has been done as is the case with regret; one wants to undo the wrongdoing. Guilt and remorse share the sense that repayment is due. But the person feeling remorse will regard the repair work as an end in itself, whereas the person feeling guilty will see reparation rather as a means towards self-rehabilitation (Taylor, 1985, 1996).
>
> (Van Stokkom, 2002: 350)

This notion of other-regarding repair work is a less idealistic representation of the emotional labour involved in attempts to establish some form of sustainable identification between aggrieved parties. However, there is much intellectual labour needed in order to be able to offer a properly theorized account of how this might work. Moreover, it is less clear how this could work for those – and this probably includes a fair number of victims and offenders – already living shame-filled lives on account of the 'normal' shaming processes in societies unequally divided by class, gender, ethnicity and the like, i.e. any contemporary society. In these cases, 'planned shaming efforts', as Van Stokkom concludes, 'seem to be abusive' (ibid: 354); and, we would add, potentially counter-productive.

The case material we introduce below illustrates how severe can be the defences mobilized among those whose lives are filled with shame. While it does not attend specifically to the case of an individual involved in a restorative-justice conference, it is illustrative because it attends to the role of shame in the life of someone who *had been both an offender and a victim of crime*. Even more importantly, the case is also illustrative of the way in which unacknowledged shame is quite commonly enmeshed in relationships of interdependency; perhaps the very kinds of communitarian relationships Braithwaite and others propose as critical to the reintegrative endeavour. As we will show, while shame can indeed bind people together, the interdependency it promotes can be at the expense of the psychological well-being of some of those exposed to it, a consequence that tends to play out in conjunction with the familiar social discriminators of ethnicity, class and gender. If this is how shame operates outside the context of crime and justice, it has therefore to be questioned whether embedding offenders in community-based networks of shame is necessarily, and predictably, a positive, fair and progressive development.

Ivy, agoraphobia and shame: a psychosocial case study

Ivy was a 70-year-old widow living alone on a 'rough' council estate in Northern England. Originally interviewed by Wendy Hollway, as were two of her children ('Tommy' and 'Kelly') as part of a project on fear of crime (Hollway and Jefferson, 2000), one of the themes that emerged was the role of shame in her life and its relationship with her long-term agoraphobia. As by now should not come as a surprise, the shame was completely unacknowledged by Ivy; if anything, she disavowed the idea. And echoing her disavowal of shame, her demeanour contradicted her feelings: seemingly 'tough' and somewhat cantankerous, successfully putting the experience of being burgled three times in one week behind her, she could not really explain why she had become so anxious that even accompanied visits to shops beyond her estate were liable to precipitate a panic attack. Why was this? Hidden shame, as we shall see, turned out to be the key.

Ivy had a troubled childhood and left home early – in her mid-teens – to escape. At the age of 18, she started seeing a much older, married man called Arthur and quickly became pregnant. Other children followed, eventually nine in total, most after she began living with Arthur. Arthur never divorced his first wife so Ivy and he never married. At some point, Ivy changed her surname to his, by deed poll, something she claimed not to be 'ashamed' of, but only admitted in the second interview, having referred to Arthur as her husband throughout the first interview. Only two of the children ever knew otherwise. Arthur worked long hours in a local factory and, according to Ivy, spent most of his free time drinking in local pubs. Ivy also went out, 'seven nights a week to Bingo', and drank a lot – 'I used to be drunk every night' – sometimes getting into fights. Physical discipline was commonplace for Ivy and Arthur's children: 'they've 'ad some 'ammer off me – them I've got', she said; and the privations were many, as their son Tommy remembered with more than a hint of nostalgic fondness: being 'skint'; the 'race 'ome' after school to try to get 'biggest plate'; sleeping two to a bed; freezing bedrooms; even his father's beltings (ibid: 55–8).

Perhaps predictably, given the size of their family and the hardships they endured, life was not always easy for Ivy's children. What interests us, and is useful for thinking about shame, is why it is that Ivy seemed to hold such radically different views with regard to her children's culpability. Her son Tommy had been in trouble with the law, as had several of his brothers, one seriously enough to be imprisoned. Yet, Ivy was resolutely positive about all of her sons: 'I 'ave got good lads', 'I've not had any trouble with those lads of mine'. Ivy's daughters were judged more individually, and not always in such glowing terms. Like her sons, one of her daughters had brushes with the law. This, however, was not the only reason why they were perceived as troublesome. Ivy's 'best lass', her eldest daughter Sally, got pregnant at 16 and later went on to marry the father of her child and move away. Fiona, who Ivy claimed never to have wanted (telling her she did not love her when she was a young child), was constantly in trouble, spent some time in prison (Ivy helping to 'put' her there on four occasions by reporting her to the police 'because she was always pinching and doing'), got pregnant aged 14, some six weeks after her sister. Fiona gave birth as an unmarried mum and, subsequently, had seven more children (to another man whom she never married). Deemed unfit to care for her child by social services, Ivy and Arthur 'adopted' Fiona's first son and brought him up as a younger sibling. Although she now lived in another city, Fiona spoke every week with Ivy on the phone, Fiona often crying on the phone 'love you. I miss you. I do miss you' with Ivy responding, 'well I love you and I miss you'. Finally, Ivy's youngest daughter, Kelly, whose job it was, effectively, to look after Fiona's child – a job she hated for robbing her of her childhood and teenage years – remained a virgin until marriage as her mother's constant reminders of how her two sisters had 'shamed 'er' had made Kelly petrified of following suit. However, three years and one daughter later, Kelly became 'besotted' with another man with whom she had two 'coloured' children, before he was eventually imprisoned for his domestic violence. Kelly then moved back to the street where she had been brought up, met someone else and moved to what she thought of as the 'better end' of the estate, just round the corner from Ivy. Although they saw each other regularly, Ivy spoke dismissively of Kelly, referring to her as 'er round t'corner', and her former husband as 'little black sambo'.

In many respects this is an everyday, general story of a big, 'rough', poor, working-class family growing up during the post-war years, struggling to make ends meet, using what would now be seen as harsh discipline to keep an ever-growing family in order, spending much leisure time drinking in the pub, and dealing as best they could with the various troubles constantly making an appearance courtesy of one or other of the many children. Not an easy family to parent or to grow up in. So far, so social. The same may also be said of Ivy's casual racism: she attributed the decline of her estate to the arrival of the 'coloureds', got alarmed when the neighbours had seen two black men entering Fiona's house, and was fearful when her sons went to confront Kelly's violent husband, forewarning them that 'black men 'ave all sorts, they can stab you'. Within this discourse all 'coloured' men, perhaps with the exception of her grandson, were the same: disreputable, potentially violent and sexually predatory. On the other hand, it is also a particular story of one unique family: an especially large family that is augmented at some point by Fiona's child; with parents who hid their unmarried status from most of their children; with children who got into serious trouble while others did not; with children whom Ivy found it easy to love and others whom she found it difficult to love; with no neat correspondence between how 'troublesome' the children were and how lovable Ivy thought they were. It is in tracking Ivy's unique biographical path through this general social context – her psychosocial route from unhappy child to a middle-aged agoraphobic – that we can discern the central role of shame dogging her life, eventually incapacitating her.

Let us start with Ivy leaving home, taking up with an older, married man and getting pregnant out of wedlock. Sennett and Cobb's (1973) interview-based study of white, working-class males noted the 'hidden injuries of class', the lack of respect felt by these men on account of their class background and the jobs they did. This link between class and (dis)respect has a long historical pedigree. Ever since the nineteenth-century division of the working class into 'roughs' and 'respectables', each generation of working-class men and women has been faced with the issue of avoiding the label 'rough'. Today's heightened demand for 'respect' by 'rough' working-class males confined to the margins of a world that has robbed them of their class heritage as well as their jobs bears ironic testimony to the continuing struggle. The often illicit entrepreneurialism of the white working-class can be seen in these terms (Hobbs, 1988), as can their tendency to blame successive generations of migrants for the consequences of de-industrialization and urban decay (Collins, 2004; Seabrook, 2003). More recently Scheff (2000: 90–1) has re-read Sennett and Cobb, concluding that the men's talk about lack of respect could be read in terms of shame, which is what lies behind the 'hidden injury of class'. For working-class women, sexual respectability lies at the heart of their attempt to achieve respect (Skeggs, 1997). Only by so doing can they hope to escape the label 'rough' ('slag'), and thus avoid shame. And for working-class women in the 1940s, the special conditions of wartime notwithstanding, sexual respectability entailed adhering (in public anyway) to chastity before marriage, monogamy after marriage and pregnancy within marriage. Having an affair with a married man was shameful enough; getting pregnant and having his baby (i.e. making it public) considerably compounded the 'offence'. Illegitimate children in the 1940s were still commonly referred to as 'bastards'. And if the man was 'black' the social ostracism could be harsher still, the shame associated with 'race-mixing' leading many 'mixed' couples to abandon their children to institutionalized care in the post-war period (Phoenix and Owen, 1996).

As Arthur was white, issues around race were probably not at stake for the teenage Ivy, even if they subsequently bothered her in relation to her daughters. But however personally happy the teenage Ivy might have been with Arthur, she could not have been unaffected by the social stigma surrounding her 'affair'. Her father had already thrown Ivy out of the family home at the age of 16, after assaulting her and her mother when they confronted him about having made another woman pregnant. This was probably a shameful event in itself insofar as it constituted a public demonstration of a failure to be the kind of family that manages to 'stay together'. The news of Ivy's pregnancy only worsened matters: Ivy's parents 'didn't like it' because of her unmarried status. That Ivy felt the need to change her name – to fake a marriage – is evidence of her desire to appear 'respectable' and avoid the shameful consequences of her actions. That she and Arthur managed to stay together and bring up a family no doubt helped Ivy to come to terms with her position – to exorcize her shame. Certainly, her revelation that 'I 'ad nine to 'im, didn't I?' and that Arthur had no children with his real wife seemed to imply that theirs was Arthur's 'proper' family. Likewise, Ivy's claim that she remained (sexually) faithful to Arthur during her 20-year widowhood (something she felt not many others could claim) would seem to be similarly revealing since a completely unnecessary revelation (from the interviewer's standpoint). These bits and pieces of information scattered about the various interviews conducted with Ivy and two members of her family, all seem to attest to her investment in respectability and, hence, her desire to avoid the shame of being seen as falling short – as mother, as wife, as woman.

But despite her attempts to have a 'proper' (respectable) family, things were never easy. They were hard up, they lived on a notoriously 'rough' estate (perhaps not at first, but it 'sank' fast) and they had a large family, many of whom got into trouble. Poverty, the linked question of where and amongst whom one lives, and having a large family, are all high-risk factors in the battle for respectability. Insufficient money makes keeping up the appropriate appearances of respectability harder, a 'sink' estate address ensures the stigma of greater police attention and greater difficulty in getting a job, and having a large family can, in itself, signify the fecklessness of siring more than one can afford to feed or control. Ivy's son Tommy's memories (even his idealized accounts) confirm that food, warmth and even affection were in short supply. It would have been hard for anyone to manage ('respectably') nine children on the resources that Ivy had available to her. But Ivy's relationships with her own parents suggest that, emotionally too, she was ill-equipped to do so. That is to say, her particular biography – unspeakably unhappy childhood ('nobody knows what life I 'ad when I were at 'ome'), early motherhood, the stigma surrounding the birth of her first child, for example – might be seen as both symptom and cause of emotional difficulties. Her extreme hostility to and neglect of her daughter Fiona, something she guiltily admitted, would seem to bear out this reading.

Predictably, things got harder as the children got older: trouble in school developed into trouble with the law; and the sexuality of her daughters produced, at very early ages, two unplanned, 'illegitimate' pregnancies. That some of her boys got into trouble was perhaps an example of the old adage 'boys will be boys': a useful discursive construction that enables 'respectable' working-class families to avoid being consigned to the category 'rough' simply on account of the temporarily unruly behaviour of their male members. But teenage girls getting into trouble with the law, as Fiona did constantly, apparently, is harder to shrug off: in the absence of a discursive defence, it is a much more potentially shaming experience. So, even before her first daughter's unwanted pregnancy, Ivy must have been struggling to avoid the shame accompanying the exploits of her second daughter (although her memory of these times was of brazen disregard, telling the police when they returned her errant daughter, to 'drop 'er in river').

The shame attaching to her oldest daughter becoming pregnant must surely have ignited Ivy's memories of her own traumatic experiences as a stigmatized teenage mother, even though Sally did go on to give birth within marriage. But then, almost immediately afterwards came the second pregnancy, to her 'bad' (and initially unloved) second teenage daughter, Fiona. Like Ivy, Fiona remained unmarried. The emotions accompanying this double whammy must have been complex. But, as with her eldest daughter's pregnancy, the social shame – which may have been weaker than in Ivy's teenage years – would have been compounded by her unique memories. Ivy's disclosures suggest this was indeed the case. At first, Ivy said that she would not go out, a response that Arthur dismissed; a reminder, should one be needed, of the specifically gendered nature of the issue of sexual respectability. However, when asked to clarify whether her not wanting to go out was because of what the neighbours might say, Ivy said she was unafraid. Moreover, in spite of this fear she could not keep away from the hospital and robustly stuck up for Fiona when the hospital's staff made slighting comments about her being unmarried, and used to 'show off if anybody said owt'.

Some might have disowned the errant daughter, especially given her history of getting into trouble and Ivy's apparently callous indifference. But Ivy's particular response, converting her shame into anger on behalf of her daughter, shows the importance once again of the psychic dimension. Ivy's conscious investment in standing up for her 'shamed' daughter, albeit in conflict with her desire to stay at home and avoid the embarrassment of facing the malicious gossip of her neighbours, becomes explicable in the light of her own biography: she had to stand up for Fiona – to identify with her – because, psychically speaking (through her identifications with Fiona), it was her own earlier self that was also being attacked. Then she had no-one to stand up for her, having left home at odds with her parents. Now at least she could do for her daughter what nobody did for her at a time when she was too young to defend herself. Several further factors reinforce this reading of Ivy's strong identification with Fiona: negatively, it is a form of recompense for her earlier hostility towards Fiona, something she clearly felt guilty about (and subsequently sought to rectify by somewhat anxious-sounding reassurances of love); positively, Ivy's own account of her past suggests she identified, no doubt ambivalently, with Fiona's waywardness; Fiona went on to have many children, like Ivy; and, finally, Ivy took Fiona's child into the family and raised him as one of her own – not an easy thing to do with an already large family, even though it helped to avoid the shame of illegitimacy.

Ivy's strong investment in sexual respectability gains further support from her contrasting statements about Kelly and Kelly's own accounts of her mother's preoccupation with unwanted pregnancies: of how her two sisters' unwanted pregnancies had 'let me Mum down and shamed 'er', and of how this tarnished Kelly's own relationship with her sexuality. Kelly's own story was littered with references to shame and embarrassment – about her family and the estate once she met her current partner; about her sexuality in having three children to two different men; about her disastrous relationship with the man who gave her two, illegitimate children. For her part, Ivy revealed that Kelly too had changed her own and her children's surnames to fit with that of her current partner, in much the same way, that she, Ivy, had done a generation earlier. This self-evidently was not enough to appease Ivy as she had told Kelly only 'the other day "you're not fit to wipe your shoes on"'. The shame of Kelly's 'coloured' children may have been one reason for this, perhaps explaining why Ivy had not found a common point of identification with Kelly despite their similar experiences of male violence and social stigmatization. Whatever the reasons, suffice to say there is ample evidence here of the unconscious inter-generational transmission of shame. It is this unconscious element that helps explain why Ivy's strong identification with Fiona's shame had devastating costs. Ivy's shame, evidenced by her not wanting to go out for fear of what the neighbours would say, may have been overridden by defensive anger; but it did not (and could not) disappear entirely.

It is a tenet of psychoanalysis that we forget nothing (Pontalis, 1993). It is also a psychoanalytic truism that whatever is too painful to bear will be repressed, or converted into a more bearable symptom. Ivy reported that her agoraphobia first developed around the traumatic period of her daughter's unwanted pregnancies. Ivy's agoraphobia, then, we suggest is a symptom of the unconscious dimension of the shame that, through her strong identification with her 'shameful' daughter (and, indirectly, her own, younger self) she consciously disavows. It constitutes, as we have argued it, the culmination of Ivy's lifelong struggle with class and gender norms of respectability, a struggle that she was ill-equipped to win, given her particular psychosocial starting point and unique biographical journey. Lewis might see it as an example of 'bypassed' shame; Scheff as 'unacknowledged' shame; and Sennett and Cobb as part of the 'hidden injuries of class'. In a social sense, it is all these things. But, what our psychosocial approach has been able to explain, albeit tentatively, in a way that none of the other approaches can manage, is why Ivy's shame is 'bypassed' in the particular way that it is, and why another mother's 'map of shame' would look different.

Conclusion

Some might want to argue that our use of the case of Ivy and her family is unfair because, although an example of shaming, it is not an example of reintegrative shaming. To that we can only reply that, however one approaches the notion of shame, whether psychologically or sociologically, the phrase 'reintegrative shaming' is an oxymoron. As we saw earlier, 'the core of shame', according to the psychologist Nathanson, 'is the feeling that we are both unloved and unlovable' (1992: 220). The 'large family of [shame] emotions', according to the sociologist Scheff, share 'the feeling of a threat to the social bond' (2000: 97). Either way, it is hard to see how invoking the disconnecting feelings of shame – feeling personally unloved or socially disconnected – can somehow be accomplished in a personally and socially accepting, or reintegrative, fashion.

Ivy, as we have shown, bypassed her shame in some of the ways corresponding to the psychologist Nathanson's compass of shame: changing her name by deed poll and taking in Fiona's child as her own could be perceived as a form of 'avoidance'; likewise, her continuing attacks on Kelly might be read as the 'rage of wounded pride'. Read more psychoanalytically, these responses resemble the defences of 'denial' and 'displacement', and are implicated in the different ways Ivy related to her children. Her relation to eldest daughter Sally and to her sons tended towards projective idealization, whereas Kelly, the denigrated one, was the recipient of Ivy's paranoid fantasies. Her belated identification with and recognition of Fiona showed signs of a transition that could be conceived of as a move towards the Kleinian 'depressive position'. Tellingly this achievement – what shame theorists conceive of as a transition from bypassed to acknowledged shame – did not come easily. It took Ivy most of her life, the infliction of more hurt in the form of the hospital workers' ostracism of Fiona, and Arthur's determined, perhaps paternal, insistence, that Ivy ignore what people were saying and concentrate on what ... she felt she ought to do for her daughter. Engineering such a transition – as we saw earlier in relation to some of our other cases – Jeffrey Dahmer, Stanley the Jack-roller and Greg the perpetrator of racial harassment – is never easy (nor necessarily permanent), not least because so many of the emotional dynamics entailed remain obscure and largely inaccessible to the people in question.

More generally, basing the case for reintegrative shaming purely on the beneficial low crime rates of Japan is possibly to ignore other, hidden costs. The idea that whole families and communities bear the shame of the offending of one of its members may be less progressive than it sounds. Remember Scheff's argument about the rise of Nazi Germany, where shared shame acted to increase its toxic effects rather than ameliorate them. Think of Ivy's shame and its reproduction, often in conjunction with the conventional discriminators of sex, race and class, in her daughters Fiona and Kelly. Think of some of the less desirable features that would seem also to be connected to Japan being a shame-based culture – the suicide missions of World War II kamikaze pilots or the suicide rates among the young who fail important exams. Think of contemporary honour killings and their relationship to the idea of family shame. If one is serious about adopting a shaming approach to punishment, its (hidden) psychic costs (and *their* social repercussions) as well as its apparent social benefits need addressing.

12

CONCLUSION

Throughout this book we have been making the case for a new approach to criminology, an approach we have defined as 'psychosocial'. Our promise was to show that by embracing a more complex notion of the subject than is usually presumed within the discipline, greater light is shed on the many puzzles and anomalies that empirical research has thrown up. Much of this work has involved attending to the individual offender, a notion that has become both deeply unpopular and associated with traditional, conservative approaches within criminology. Garland's choice of the term 'Lombrosian' to characterize all work of this kind tainted it thus, even before he added that such a project is 'deeply flawed'. But this is to confuse the object of enquiry (the offender) with the theory informing it ('a science of causes'). Our concern has not been to reinstate the Lombrosian project in its old form, or to suggest that work on the individual offender should be the prime concern of criminology. Rather, we have tried to show that as well as the many kinds of work subsumed under Garland's 'governmental' project, we also need work on crime and criminals, but suitably theoretically informed.

Jack Katz (1988) makes a similar plea in his phenomenological work on the foreground of crime (the under-theorized 'actual act'), in his case countering the limitations of criminology's focus on background causes. But, as we saw earlier, he does not go far enough. In not attending to inner world issues as well as situational contingencies, Katz is unable to explain why particular individuals become 'senseless' murderers: why it was Gary Gilmore, for example, who became the cold-blooded killer and Mikhail Gilmore who went on to become a journalist and to write a brave and exceptional book about his brother.

If there are still doubts about the need for such a project, perhaps the words of Roy Hattersley, formerly a senior Labour politician, now a broadsheet columnist, may help dispel them. Talking about a particularly vicious racial murder involving the abduction, stabbing and setting alight of a white youth by 'two apparently prosperous young men', Hattersley confessed to complete incomprehension about the causes of such behaviour, or 'sin': '"original" to some Christians, environmental to determinists, beyond understanding to most of us'. Conscious of the limits of his own understanding, Hattersley, resorted ultimately to the discourse of madness to explain the case, concluding 'only crazy people behave like that' (*Guardian*, 13 November, 2006: 27). In ending thus, he echoed the conclusions of the inquiry into another high-profile racially motivated killing about which criminologists have been deafeningly silent: the murder of Zahid Mubarek. Although the 691-page report produced by the inquiry team listed a litany of professional failings that contributed to Mubarek's death, it shied away from explaining why the murderer, Robert Stewart, did what he did. Like Hattersley, Mr Justice Keith, the inquiry's chair, ultimately surrendered to the discourse of madness.

> [Stewart, the killer's] lack of concern for other people or for the consequences of his actions meant that he was not constrained by the things that would restrain *a normal person*. At his trial, he said he just felt like attacking Zahid. Perhaps it was *as simple as that*.
>
> (Keith, 2006: 641, our emphases)

Throughout this book we have stressed that matters are rarely, if ever, '*as simple as that*'. We hope, at least, to have revealed the kind of theoretical tools that are necessary to make sense of such 'crazy' departures from the norm, and to have disturbed the criminological complacency that results in such cases routinely being left to the journalists, moralists and politicians to explain.

Our argument, then, commencing in Chapter 1, was that the history of criminological enquiry, shaped as it has been by the twists and turns of Lombrosian and governmental projects, has inhibited a proper consideration of what it is offenders share with non-offenders, and, at the same time, how it is that psychosocial differences, in terms of personality and social circumstance, nonetheless *make a difference* to involvement in crime. Following Stephen Frosh, we argued that what is needed is a new approach to criminology that is:

- sensitive to the anxious, desiring and contradictory qualities of human subjectivity;
- able to theorize the relationships between individuals and language, both the meaning-making dimension and the aspects of power that are always imbricated therein; and
- open, methodologically and theoretically, to the connections among uniquely biographical experiences, the social patterning of inequalities, and the discursive realm.

The new psychosocial criminology we proffer is, admittedly, an ambitious project, but it is not an isolated one if considered in the broader field of the social sciences. Lynne Layton, for example, makes a similar case for what she calls 'psychoanalytic social theory': 'The task for psychoanalytic social theory is', according to Layton, 'to uncover the mediating links between social norms, family dynamics, and psychic life' (2004: 48). It is, however, a project that clearly exceeds the intellectual parameters of the old, eclectic psychosocial approaches that were pivotal to criminology's development, at least in Britain. What we have salvaged from this older psychosocial criminology is the importance of the psychosocial, but now thoroughly theorized and empirically investigated. From traditional Freudian approaches we have retained an attention to the detail of complex case studies, together with a receptiveness to the idea that action is shaped by unconscious as well as conscious processes. Although the importance we attach to the role of the unconscious echoes the psychoanalytic case study, we hope also to have retained the attention to social detail characteristic of the sociological case study produced largely by the ethnographic work influenced by symbolic interactionism and phenomenology. What we bring to this sociological work is the idea that the subjects of criminological research are better perceived as the purveyors of motivated accounts that protect them from confronting uncomfortable home truths than the chroniclers of untainted self-knowledge.

Bringing these insights together, our new psychosocial approach makes at least two things necessary. First, a social and political awareness of the predominant discourses through which everyday experience is organized. Second, an interpretative approach that is sensitive to the inconsistencies in the way people behave towards others and talk about themselves. Thus armed, we can begin to appreciate how pervasive social discourses not only legitimize the social inequalities of gender, 'race' and class, for example, but also function to protect people against uncomfortable feelings of vulnerability. In other words, the subject positions offered up by discourses enable individuals to construct their own experiences in ways that make them feel in some sense empowered, or superior, in relation to others. In this way, we think we have managed to hang on to the social and psychic dimensions of experience: embracing both, privileging neither.

It is because we believe that it is necessary to attempt to theorize the unconscious attractions of discourse that we have looked towards recent developments in psychoanalytic theorizing for inspiration. As we argued in Chapter 4, Klein's critical insight that people move between paranoid-schizoid and depressive ways of thinking has enormously enriched psychoanalytic thinking on the question of unconscious conflict and intersubjectivity. Subsequent developments within the object relations approach have expanded our understanding of the importance of ideas like 'identification', 'recognition' and 'containment'. This new theoretical complexity, facilitated by the move from a drive-based to a relational psychoanalysis, makes it possible to attend much more thoroughly to questions of motive in relation to crime and social reactions to it, and hence to explain why it is that some people commit crime more frequently than others, as well as why some persistent offenders, including those seemingly driven by deep-rooted psychological or sexual needs, ultimately desist. This, we believe, is an obvious advance on the constructionist and structuralist perspectives sociology has brought to criminology; but it is also a delivery on the failed promises of symbolic interactionism, *The New Criminology* and its influential Left Realist successor.

We have shown the utility of our new psychosocial approach in relation to a number of criminological debates. Some – like those relating to rape – are hotly contested; others – like those pertaining to the fear of crime and domestic violence – are imbued with many taken-for-granted, overly rationalistic assumptions; and still others – like the perpetration of racially motivated crime – are addressed most commonly through typological approaches, or alternatively a form of cultural determinism that reduces offending to an intensified manifestation of mainstream attitudes or prejudices. We have also strayed into what some might perceive as academic extravagances: reinterpreting what the protagonists in a rape trial had to say about themselves; demonstrating the paucity of understanding in relation to Clifford Shaw's most celebrated case study, Stanley the jack-roller; and offering a tentative explanation for the bizarrely gruesome behaviour of one of the US's most infamous serial killers, Jeffrey Dahmer. We hope, however, to have shown that attending to the detail of such cases illuminates the shortcomings of more conventional approaches to explaining crime and reminds students of what is more generally at stake, theoretically speaking, in each of these cases.

One of the threads which unites our analyses of our case studies has been the argument that displays of excessive force, whether through robbery, murder, sexual or domestic violence, often conceal the protagonist's unacknowledged/unacknowledgeable sense of weakness. This is an important corrective both to those who mistake appearance for reality: who read the overt act only through its most obvious manifestation; what it reveals but not what it conceals. The idea of masculinity seen only as a manifestation of power but not also a defence against feeling powerless was one such shortcoming we sought to counter. Likewise, in the literatures on reintegrative shaming and restorative justice we discovered that, not only is the concept of shame under-theorized, but also that the field is largely disinterested in the working of intersubjective dynamics, especially their unconscious dimension. The same is true in the literature on cognitive behavioural work with offenders. By way of a contrast, what our use of case-study materials highlights is the powerful effect that unconscious patterns of identification and disidentification have in the production of stigma. In other words, the psychosocial theorization of shame underpinning our analysis enabled us to see how powerful and uncontrollable is the emotion of shame; far more so than survey measures of victim- and offender-satisfaction are able to convey. Using the example of an elderly woman we referred to as Ivy, we showed how intersubjective processes colluded to ensure the unconscious reproduction of shame across generational lines, together with the very damaging, sometimes stultifying, consequences to which this can give rise.

In relation to the case of Ivy we were also able to highlight the importance of containment, showing how the troubled and the traumatized, like all of us, need to be free enough of anxiety not to have to function *over* defensively; a point we made in relation to 'Hassan' in Chapter 5, but also in relation to Jeffrey Dahmer (Chapter 7), Greg (Chapter 8) and Stanley (Chapter 9). At the social level, these cases suggest to us that the 'cultures' of which criminologists speak – whether these be punitive cultures of control, the habits and mores of contemporary youth, or the patriarchal customs reproduced in nuclear families – can appear monolithic, not because they are without contradiction, but because, at the psychic level, people are heavily, if variably, invested in them. Although these kinds of cultural responses – or 'adaptations' as Mertonians might call them – are invested in defensively, to ward off unspeakable anxieties and desires, they are liable to oscillate because they are always socially situated and situations are always more or less containing, more or less anxiety-provoking. It is this feature of social situations that can help us make sense of why people are rarely unmovably punitive, violent, racist, or fearful. Or, why we are so apparently inconsistent: why, for example, abusers are abusive to their partners one minute yet, in situations where they feel less under attack (or more contained), are deeply ashamed of their actions the next; or, why some people want to send all asylum seekers back home but are willing, in situations where their anxieties have been sufficiently assuaged (or contained), to make many exceptions for the 'genuine' refugees.

Working out how to deal with such fluidity for the common good is no easy task. It is certainly part of the explanation as to why it is almost impossible to differentiate offenders from non-offenders in terms of their attitudes, and, notwithstanding criminological psychology's enduring quest to identify predictive risk factors, why there is so little that criminologists can say at a general level about the causes of crime. Not all men rape; not all victims of child abuse reproduce 'the cycle'; not all poor people steal; and not all the disadvantaged blame those who are different for their plight. The position we have argued in this book, however, is that when it comes to the capacity to act callously, much often hinges on whether or not the individual in question is willing and able to identify with the suffering of others. It is this that makes 'fantasy' such a critical concept, since it is through fantasy and the internalized object world that we perceive others: harbouring grudges; idolizing those we barely know; discovering the menace of persecution in our friends' and acquaintances' throw-away comments; or otherwise enviously eyeing those we perceive as the beneficiaries of goods or qualities we sense we lack. Exploring what it is that makes these normal psychic reactions the trigger for hateful actions in the case of some individuals but not others is a critical step on the way to answering the crucial criminological question 'why do they do it?'

It is through attending to this question that the new psychosocial criminology may take its most political turn, since by enabling people to understand a little more and condemn a little less it will moderate the demonizing discourses that the vast majority of criminologists perceive as part of the problem of crime. Talking more generally of the political role of psychoanalysis, Malone and Kelly make a similar point when they argue that 'psychoanalysis can do much to counter the tendency to invent interventions that suit the fantasy of the greater good' (2004: 26). What the new psychosocial criminology requires of the discipline in return, especially its more critical contributors, is a willingness to move beyond the rhetoric of folk devils and moral panics, to concede that while much political capital is made out of the sensationalizing of crime and the mythologizing of offenders – whether they be 'hooded youths', 'black muggers', 'hate crime' perpetrators, 'predatory paedophiles' or 'Islamic terrorists' – there is a need to address the question of who these folk devils really are, what they have done and why, and to try to make sense of their motives in a form that does not necessarily involve pathologizing. To dismiss such a project as hopelessly Lombrosian, or to focus instead on the greater menace posed by more everyday phenomena, is to leave a large (offending) elephant in the room, conveniently pushed beyond the conscious awareness of the criminological imagination.

We hope this book renders this kind of academic defensiveness easier to overcome. We also hope it redirects criminological attention towards a neglected component of the agency/structure dualism, namely the realm of intersubjectivity. What we have shown in relation to our various case studies is that it is through an engagement with the subjectivity of others that people are confronted by the force of their own projections. This is an important insight for criminologists to take on board. In the first place, it is important because offenders' identities, as we have seen throughout this book, are often overly reliant on the defence mechanisms of splitting and projection. However, it is also important because conventional responses to crime tend to minimize the opportunities for face-to-face confrontations to take place. This is most evidently so in the machinations of criminal-justice agencies which, despite their ultimate dependence on force to control offenders, handle them at an emotional distance, as subsets of the population to be processed according to type, levels of riskiness, and/or the resources available to the system. This is true of many progressive approaches to penality as well as the discourses of punitiveness and deterrence. The formation of multi-agency partnerships, for example – a development that was widely heralded as a progressive response to dealing with the problems confronting troubled young people – in practice tends to divide up the job of working with law breakers into one of managing so many component parts of the individuals in question. The result is that no one criminal-justice worker has to get to know, properly, any one single offender or victim; no-one has to establish the trust, compassion, and depth of understanding that is often needed to help client groups face up to painful or guilty self-knowledge; and hence no-one need establish the sense of shared identification that people undergoing change often need in order to value the containment of those who are trying to both help and control them (Gadd, 2003; Maruna, 2001).

The difficult ethical question raised by this argument is: who should be expected to engage with the subjectivities of the most troubled subsections of the population who commit the most callous crimes? Should we, as restorative-justice interventions tend to assume, expect victims – whether they be of property crimes, violent assaults or sexual abuse – to be willing and able to discover points of identification between themselves and those who have victimized them? And if so, how can we equip them for the emotional labour this kind of identificatory work might entail? Is this challenge more properly the responsibility of criminal-justice agents, other public-sector workers, or the 'state'? Put more conventionally, the questions we are raising are about the timeless issue of forgiveness: what it means and who has the capacity and right to confer it. But explored psychosocially such questions are also about the possibilities of emotional containment and recognition, entailing the struggle to identify adequately with the needs of the other, often in the face of hostility, and with no guarantee of reciprocity. The modes of psychoanalytic thinking we have drawn on in this book suggest that realizing these possibilities rarely come easily, not least because they almost always involve the working through of defensive patterns of idealization and denigration.

Inevitably, still other questions remain. Principally, for us, these questions involve how to think psychosocially at the level of the group and, beyond that, the level of society. We are not the first to raise such questions; and there is no shortage of attempted answers. The literature on racial hatred, for example, is peppered with such efforts: from the early classic work of Fromm ([1942] 2001) and Adorno et al. (1950) on the links between socio-economic conditions, the authoritarian personality and the rise of European fascism, to Dalal's (2002) recent attempt to link the idea of the 'social unconscious' with Elias' notion of the civilizing process. Here is not the place to offer a proper evaluation of this literature. However, what can be said is that the work on prejudice, which was originally open to the idea of psychoanalysis (see Allport, 1954), became narrowly cognitivist and thus seriously compromised in its efforts to understand the discriminatory behaviour of groups (for examples, see Tajfel, 1969; Tajfel and Turner, 1979). And even that work which remained receptive to theorizing the racist subject with all his or her irrational hostilities by-and-large failed to explain the exceptions to the rule: those who, within the prevailing socio-economic conditions and prevailing family structure, did not develop authoritarian personalities.

A similar problematic has recently emerged within the criminology of penal sensibilities. As Matravers and Maruna (2004) point out, David Garland's (2001) highly influential text *The Culture of Control* is replete with psychoanalytic metaphors. His argument that populist displays of punitiveness *act out* the state's *denial* of its own impotence with regard to crime control is self-evidently inspired by Freudian thinking. Matravers and Maruna illuminate the many different ways in which the state's acting out resonates with the miscellany of defensive reactions that can be detected among the general public, explaining the seemingly relentless thirst for 'get tough' crime policies. The question Matravers and Maruna's critique raises, however, is whether it is appropriate to move directly between clinically based concepts and cultural analysis, from individuals to the state, without showing how it is that person-centred concepts such as anxiety, guilt and envy can meaningfully (rather than metaphorically) function at other levels.

Jessica Evans (2003) attends, in part, to this question in her analysis of the Residents Against Paedophiles group that established itself in Portsmouth after the murder of Sarah Payne. After the *News of the World* launched its 'naming and shaming' campaign for the importation of Megan's Law, protestors on the Paulsgrove Estate marched, waved banners, torched cars and firebombed flats where suspected paedophiles lived. Some innocent members of the community had their property damaged, were physically assaulted and were forced to move. Evans asks how the protestors came to enter this 'vigilante state of mind'. Her answer is that a slippage between 'vigilance' and 'vigilantism' became possible because of the blurring of the two terms in the discourse of 'active citizenship'. The kind of 'responsibilization strategies' to which community partnerships were exposed created a 'fundamental ambivalence' about who was responsible for dealing with sex offenders (ibid: 171). This uncertainty agitated the anxieties of some of the women on the Paulsgrove Estate, some of whom identified themselves as victims of sexual abuse, and many of whom perceived their adequacy as parents to have been called into question by a political establishment content to blame single mothers for the problems of miscreant youth. More interestingly, however, Evans concludes that the vigilante attacks might not have happened had the government taken more responsibility for containing and modifying the 'disowned, unwanted and often persecutory feeling states' of some of its most 'distressed citizens' (ibid: 183). For Evans, a more containing response would have entailed less, rather than more, governance at a distance: a recognition that sharing information with those who do not know how to deal with it often increases anxiety. Ostensibly democratic approaches to information sharing, Evans observes, can evoke in some people the kinds of paranoid feelings that inhibit their capacities to identify with the greater needs of the more vulnerable members of their communities. Conversely, better-managed information sharing can help people come to terms with their fears about dependency, and hence, reduce their reliance on the fantastical belief that they can purge themselves of danger by forcibly banishing offenders beyond the boundaries of 'their' communities.

In the context of the new wave of uncertainties of the post-9/11 era, especially around terrorism and international migration and the warfare-like responses ('for us or against us') from politicians – sometimes reproduced at the community level by seemingly ordinary people who take out grievances on those they perceive, often erroneously, to be sympathetic to the terrorists' plight – it seems to us that Evans' prognosis has much wider application. Her approach makes us wonder, for example, what the long-term effects will be if some of the West's most beleaguered minority ethnic groups continue to be told it is primarily their responsibility to weed out the fundamentalists in *their* communities. It also makes us wonder whether a responsible 'containing' approach to governance necessarily entails revealing just how many 'terror plots' have been foiled to date, and by inference the unknown quantity of undiscovered plots out there waiting to happen. To what extent does the shame of dependency make immigrant communities less rather than more able to deal with the challenges of resettlement in new and unfamiliar places, and hence less able to deal with the problems of crime and victimization that people so readily associate with their presence? And could some attention to the biographical detail of the lives of those who plot atrocities reveal the finer gradations of difference that make acts of terror thinkable for some, but 'unthinkable' for many others members of the same demographic groups?

The tendency for psychoanalytic concepts to turn seemingly simple solutions into complex problems will undoubtedly make many wary of adopting the kind of psychosocial approach we would like to see applied to these questions. But, in a world beset by new forms of fundamentalism, religious and racial intolerance, genocidal violence, state-sanctioned torture, widening inequalities, ever-expanding risks and new sources of anxiety, 'psychoanalytic self-awareness' can also be part of the solution. As Karl Figlio astutely puts it:

> [P]sychoanalysis occupies a unique position … because it applies its naturalistic attitude and methods to itself, and develops concepts and practices based on

itself in action ... it resists idealization and ... projective communication ... It avoids abstraction and immerses itself in the process of making things better, of reparation.

(2004: 100)

And this in turn is what makes a psychoanalytically informed psychosocial approach invaluable for thinking about the kinds of crime control that might actually be beneficial in times of 'crisis'. If governments were to take psychoanalytic insights more seriously they would focus their efforts on protecting their citizens from the 'spiralling mutual aggression' (ibid: 94) projective processes engender; think very carefully about the long-term effects of agitating anxieties for political advantage; and avoid, wherever possible, deflecting responsibility for difficult, almost irresolvable, problems onto those communities least able to cope with them.

REFERENCES

Adorno, T. W., Frenkel-Brunswik, E., Levinson, D. J. and Sanford, R. N. (1950) *The Authoritarian Personality*. New York: Harper and Row.

Agnew, R. (1992) 'Foundation for a general strain theory of crime and delinquency', *Criminology*, 30(1): 47–87.

Allport, G. W. (1954) *The Nature of Prejudice*. Reading, MA: Addison Wesley.

Anderson, N. (1923) *The Hobo*. Chicago, IL: University of Chicago Press.

Back, L. and Keith, M. (1999) '"Rights and wrongs": youth community and narratives of racial violence', in P. Cohen (ed.), *New Ethnicities, Old Racisms*. London: Zed Books. pp. 131–53.

Barnish, M. (2004) *Domestic Violence: A Literature Review*. London: HM Inspectorate of Probation, Home Office.

Barrett, M. (1991) *The Politics of Truth*. Cambridge: Polity.

Bauman, Z. (2000) 'Social issues of law and order', *British Journal of Criminology*, 40(2): 205–21.

BBC (2003) 'Hitting home: domestic violence survey part II', 14 February 2003. http://news.bbc.co.uk/1/hi/uk/2753917.stm

Becker, H. S. (1953) 'Becoming a marijuana user', *The American Journal of Sociology*, 59(3): 235–42.

Becker, H. S. (1960) 'Notes on the concept of commitment', *American Journal of Sociology*, 66(1): 32–40.

Becker, H. S. (1963) *Outsiders*. New York: Free Press.

Bell, C. (2000) 'Men and violence', *Working with Men*, 1: 12–13.

Beneke, T. (1982) *Men on Rape*. New York: St. Martin's Press.

Benjamin, J. (1995) 'Sameness and difference: toward an "over-inclusive" theory of gender development', in A. Elliott and S. Frosh (eds), *Psychoanalysis in Contexts*. London: Routledge. pp. 106–22.

Benjamin, J. (1998) *Shadow of the Other*. London: Routledge.

Bilby, C. and Hatcher, R. (2004) *Early Stages in the Development of the Integrated Domestic Abuse Programme (IDAP)*. London: Home Office.

Bion, W. [1959] (1984) 'Attacks on linking', in W. R. Bion, *Second Thoughts*. London: Maresfield. pp. 93–109.

Björgo, T. (1997) *Racist and Right-Wing Violence in Scandinavia*. Tano: Ashehougs Fonteneserie.

Blacklock, N. (1999) 'Lessons learnt', *Working with Men*, 2: 15–17.

Bollas, C. (1992) *Being a Character*. London: Routledge.

Bowlby, J. (1946) *Forty-Four Juvenile Thieves*. London: Balliére, Tindall and Cox.

Bowlby, J. (1980) *Attachment and Loss, volume III*. London: Hogarth Press.

Bowlby, J. (1990) *Charles Darwin*. London: Hutchinson.

Bowling, B. and Phillips, C. (2002) *Racism, Crime and Justice*. Harlow: Longman.

Box, S. (1983) *Power, Crime, and Mystification*. London: Tavistock.

Braithwaite, J. (1989) *Crime, Shame and Reintegration*. Cambridge: Cambridge University Press.

Braithwaite, J. (2002) *Restorative Justice and Responsive Regulation*. Oxford: Oxford University Press.

Braithwaite, J. and Mugford, S. (1994) 'Conditions of successful reintegration ceremonies', *British Journal of Criminology*, 34(2): 139–71.

Brown, A. P. (2003) 'From individual to social defences in psycho-social criminology', *Theoretical Criminology*, 7(4): 421–37.

Brownmiller, S. [1975] (1976) *Against Our Will*. Harmondsworth: Penguin.

Burgess, E. W. (1930) 'Discussion', in C. Shaw (ed.), *The Jack-Roller*. Chicago, IL: University of Chicago Press. pp. 184–97.

Burn, G. (1984) *Somebody's Husband, Somebody's Son: The Story of Peter Sutcliffe*. London: Heinemann.

Burn, G. (1998) *Happy Like Murderers*. London: Faber & Faber.

Burt, C. (1925) *The Young Delinquent*. London: University of London Press.

Burton, S., Regan, L. and Kelly, L. (1998) *Supporting Women and Challenging Men*. Bristol: Policy Press.

Cameron, D. and Frazer, E. (1987) *The Lust to Kill*. Cambridge: Polity.

Caputi, J. (1988) *The Age of Sex Crime*. London: The Women's Press.

Carrigan, T., Connell, R. and Lee, J. (1985) 'Towards a new sociology of masculinity', *Theory & Society*, 14(5): 551–604.

Cartwright, D. (2002) *Psychoanalysis, Violence, and Rage-Type Murder*. Hove: Bruner-Routledge.

Cavanagh, K. and Lewis, R. (1996) 'Interviewing violent men', in K. Cavanagh and V. Cree (eds), *Working with Men*. London: Routledge. pp. 87–112.

Cayouette, S. (1999) 'Safety issues for women co-facilitating groups for violent men', in J. Wild (ed.), *Working with Men for Change*. London: UCL Press. pp. 153–68.

Chodorow, N. J. (1978) *The Reproduction of Mothering*. Berkeley, CA: University of California Press.

Chodorow, N. J. (1994) *Femininities, Masculinities, Sexualities*. Lexington, KY: University Press of Kentucky.

Cloward, R. and Ohlin, L. (1960) *Delinquency and Opportunity*. New York: Free Press.

Cohen, A. (1955) *Delinquent Boys*. Glencoe, IL: Free Press.

Cohen, S. (1972) *Folk Devils and Moral Panics*. London: MacGibbon & Kee.

Cohen, S. (1981) 'Footprints in the sand', in M. Fitzgerald, G. McLennan and J. Pawson (eds), *Crime and Society*. London: Routledge. pp. 220–47.

Cohen, S. (2001) *States of Denial*. Cambridge: Polity.

Coleman, C. and Norris, C. (2000) *Introducing Criminology*. Cullompton: Willan.

Collins, M. (2004) *The Likes of Us*. London: Granta.

Connell, R. W. (1987) *Gender and Power*. Cambridge: Polity.

Connell, R. W. (1995) *Masculinities*. Cambridge: Polity.

Connell, R. W. (2000) *The Men and the Boys*. Cambridge: Polity.

Cooley, C. H. (1922) *Human Nature and the Social Order*, revised edition. New York: Charles Schribner.

Cornish, D. and Clarke, R. V. (1986) *The Reasoning Criminal*. New York: Springer.

Craib, I. (1987) 'Masculinity and male dominance', *Sociological Review*, 34(4): 721–43.

Cronbach, L. J. (1975) 'Beyond the two disciplines of scientific psychology', *American Psychologist*, 30(2): 116–27.

Dahmer, L. (1994) *A Father's Story*. London: Little Brown and Company.

Dalal, F. (2002) *Race, Colour and the Processes of Racialization*. Hove: Brunner-Routledge.

Daly, K. (2002) 'Restorative justice: the real story', *Punishment & Society*, 4(1): 55–79.

Ditton, J. (2000) 'Inaugural lecture' presented 16 February 2000 at Sheffield University. Unpublished manuscript.

Ditton, J., Bannister, J., Gilchrist, E. and Farrall, S. (1999) 'Afraid or angry? Recalibrating the "fear" of crime', *International Review of Victimology*, 6(2): 83–99.

Ditton, J. and Farrall, S. (2000) 'Introduction', in J. Ditton and S. Farrall (eds), *The Fear of Crime*. Aldershot: Ashgate. pp. xv–xxiii.

Dixon, L. (1998) 'Rethinking domestic violence: which way now?', *Probation Journal*, 45(2): 92–7.

Dobash, R. E., Dobash, R. P., Cavanagh, K. and Lewis, R. (1996) 'Re-education programmes for violent men – an evaluation', *Research Findings No. 46*. London: Home Office.

Dobash, R. E., Dobash, R. P., Cavanagh, K. and Lewis, R. (2000) *Changing Violent Men*. London: Sage.

Downes, D. and Rock, P. (1998) *Understanding Deviance*, third edition. Oxford: Oxford University Press.

Dworkin, A. (1988) *Letters from a War Zone*. New York: E. P. Dutton.

Eadie, T. and Knight, C. (2002) 'Domestic violence programmes', *The Howard Journal of Criminal Justice*, 41(2): 167–81.

East, W. N. and Hubert, W. H. de B. (1939) *Report on the Psychological Treatment of Crime*. London: HMSO.

Elias, N. (1978) *The History of Manners*. New York: Vintage.

Ellis, L. (1989) *Theories of Rape*. London: Taylor and Francis.

Evans, J. (2003) 'Victims and vigilantes: thinking psychoanalytically about anti-paedophile action', *Theoretical Criminology*, 7(2): 163–89.

Eysenck, H. J. (1964) *Crime and Personality*. London: Routledge and Kegan Paul.

Eysenck, H. J. [1987] (2003) 'Personality theory and the problem of criminality', in E. McLaughlin, J. Muncie and G. Hughes (eds), *Criminological Perspectives*, second edition. London: Sage. pp. 91–109.

Faludi, S. (1999) *Stiffed*. London: Chatto & Windus.

Fanon, F. (1968) *Black Skins, White Masks*. London: MacGibbon & Kee.

Farrington, D. (2002) 'Developmental criminology and risk-focused prevention', in M. Maguire, R. Morgan, and R. Reiner (eds), *The Oxford Handbook of Criminology*, third edition. Oxford: Oxford University Press. pp. 657–701.

Fast, I. (1984) *Gender Identity*. Hillsdale, NJ: The Analytic Press.

Fast, I. (1990) 'Aspects of early gender development', *Psychoanalytic Psychology*, 7(supplement): 105–18.

Fekete, L. (2004) 'Anti-Muslim racism and the European security state', *Race & Class*, 46(1): 3–29.

Ferraro, K. F. and LaGrange, R. (1987) 'The measurement of fear of crime', *Sociological Inquiry*, 57(1): 70–101.

Figlio, K. (2004) 'Psychoanalysis, politics and the self-awareness of society', *Psychoanalysis, Culture & Society*, (9)1: 87–104.

Finney, A. (2006) *Domestic Violence, Sexual Assault and Stalking: Findings from the 2004/05 British Crime Survey*. London: Home Office.

Flick, U. (1998) *An Introduction to Qualitative Research*. London: Sage.

Fonagy, P., Moran, G. and Target, M. (1993) 'Aggression and the psychological self', *International Journal of Psycho-analysis*, 74(3): 471–86.

Foucault, M. (1972) *The Archaeology of Knowledge*. London: Tavistock.

Foucault, M. (1977) *Discipline and Punish*. London: Tavistock.

Fox, K. (1999) 'Changing violent minds', *Social Problems*, 46(1): 88–103.

Freud, S. [1905] (1977) 'Three essays on the theory of sexuality', in S. Freud, *The Pelican Freud Library, volume 7: On Sexuality*. Harmondsworth: Penguin. pp. 31–169.

Freud, S. [1923] (1984) 'The ego and the id', in S. Freud, *The Pelican Freud Library, volume 11: On Metapsychology: The Theory of Psychoanalysis*. Harmondsworth: Penguin. pp. 339–407.

Freud, S. [1924] (1977) 'The dissolution of the Oedipus Complex,' in S. Freud, *The Pelican Freud Library, volume 7: On Sexuality*. Harmondsworth: Penguin. pp. 313–22.

Freud, S. [1925] (1977) 'Some psychical consequences of the anatomical distinction between the sexes', in S. Freud, *The Pelican Freud Library, volume 7: On Sexuality*. Harmondsworth: Penguin. pp. 323–43.

Fromm, E. (1941) *Escape from Freedom*. New York: Henry Holt.

Fromm, E. [1942] (2001) *Fear of Freedom*. London: Routledge and Kegan Paul.

Frosh, S. (2003) 'Psychosocial studies and psychology: is a critical approach emerging?', *Human Relations*, 56(12): 1545–67.

Furstenberg Jr, F. F. (1971) 'Public reaction to crime in the streets', *The American Scholar*, 40(4): 601–10.

Gadd, D. (2000) 'Masculinities, violence and defended psychosocial subjects', *Theoretical Criminology*, 4(4): 429–49.

Gadd, D. (2002) 'Masculinities and violence against female partners', *Social & Legal Studies*, 11(1): 61–80.

Gadd, D. (2003) 'Making criminology good: a response to Shadd Maruna', *The Howard Journal of Criminal Justice*, 42(3): 316–22.

Gadd, D. (2004a) 'Making sense of interviewee–interviewer dynamics in narratives about violence in intimate relationships', *International Journal of Social Research Methodology*, 7(5): 383–401.

Gadd, D. (2004b) 'Evidence-led policy or policy-led evidence? Cognitive behavioural programmes for men who are violent towards women', *Criminal Justice*, 4(2): 173–97.

Gadd, D. (2006) 'The role of recognition in the desistance process: a case study of a far-right activist', *Theoretical Criminology*, 10(2): 179–202.

Gadd, D., Dixon, B. and Jefferson, T. (2005) *Why Do They Do It? Racial Harassment in North Staffordshire*. Staffordshire: Keele University.

Gadd, D., Farrall, S., Dallimore, D. and Lombard, N. (2003) 'Equal victims or the usual suspects? Making sense of domestic abuse against men', *International Review of Victimology*, 10(2): 95–116.

Garland, D. (2000) 'The culture of high crime societies', *British Journal of Criminology*, 40(1): 347–75.

Garland, D. (2002) 'Of crimes and criminals', in M. Maguire, R. Morgan and R. Reiner. (eds), *The Oxford Handbook of Criminology*, third edition. Oxford: Oxford University Press. pp. 7–50.

Geertz, C. (1973) *The Interpretation of Culture*. London: Hutchinson.

Geis, G. (1982) 'The jack-roller: the appeal, the person, and the impact', in J. Snodgrass (ed.), *The Jack-Roller at Seventy*. Lexington, MA: D. C. Heath and Company. pp. 121–34.

Gelsthorpe, L. (1997) 'Feminism and criminology', in M. Maguire, R. Morgan and R. Reiner. (eds), *The Oxford Handbook of Criminology*, second edition. Oxford: Clarendon. pp. 511–34.

Gibbens, T. C. N. (1971) 'Foreword to the British edition', in H. Toch, *Violent Men*. Harmondsworth: Pelican. pp. 10–13.

Giddens, A. (1984) *The Constitution of Society*. Cambridge: Polity.

Giddens, A. (1991) *Modernity and Self-Identity*. Cambridge: Polity.

Gilchrist, E., Bannister, J., Ditton, J. and Farrell, S. (1998) 'Women and the "fear of crime"', *British Journal of Criminology*, 38(2): 283–98.

Gilchrist, E., Johnson, R., Takriti, R. and Weston, S. (2003) *Domestic Violence Offenders*. Briefing 217. London: Home Office.

Gilmore, D. D. (1990) *Manhood in the Making*. New Haven, CT: Yale University Press.

Gilmore, M. (1994) *Shot in the Heart*. Harmondsworth: Penguin.

Glover, E. (1954) 'Team-research on delinquency: a psychoanalytical commentary', *British Journal of Delinquency*, 4(3): 173–88.

Glover, E. (1960) *The Roots of Crime*. London: Imago.

Gluckman, M. (ed.) (1964) *Closed Systems and Open Minds*. London: Oliver & Boyd.

Glueck, S. and Glueck, E. (1950) *Unravelling Juvenile Delinquency*. New York: Commonwealth Fund.

Godenzi, A. (1994) 'What's the big deal? We are men and they are women', in T. Newburn and E. A. Stanko (eds), *Just Boys Doing Business?* London: Routledge. pp. 135–52.

Gomm, R., Hammersley, M. and Foster, P. (eds) (2000) *Case Study Method*. London: Sage.

Goring, C. (1913) *The English Convict*. London: HMSO.

Gottfredson, M. and Hirschi, T. (1990) *A General Theory of Crime*. Stanford, CA: Stanford University Press.

Griffin, S. (1971) 'Rape: the all American crime', *Ramparts*, (September): 26–35.

Hale, C. (1996) 'Fear of crime: a review of the literature', *International Review of Victimology*, 4(2): 79–150.

Hall, S. (1992) 'The west and the rest', in S. Hall and B. Gieben (eds), *Formations of Modernity*. Cambridge: Polity/The Open University.

Hall, S. (2001) 'Foucault: power, knowledge and discourse', in M. Wetherell, S. Taylor and S. J. Yates (eds), *Discourse, Theory and Practice*. London: Sage. pp. 72–81.

Hall, S., Critcher, C., Jefferson, T., Clarke, J. and Roberts, B. (1978) *Policing the Crisis*. London: Macmillan.

Hammersley, M. and Gomm, R. (2000) 'Introduction', in R. Gomm, M. Hammersley and P. Foster (eds) *Case Study Method*. London: Sage. pp. 2–16.

Harris, N. (2001) 'Shaming and shame: regulating drink-driving', in E. Ahmed, N. Harris, J. Braithwaite and V. Braithwaite (eds), *Shame Management through Reintegration*. Cambridge: Cambridge University Press. pp. 73–207.

Harris, R. (1969) *The Fear of Crime*. New York: Praeger.

Hattersley, R. (2006) 'It takes a madman', *Guardian*, Comment section. Reproduced online at www.guardian.co.uk/Columnists/Column/0,,1946285,00.html

Healey, K., Smith, C. and O'Sullivan, C. (1998) *Batterer Intervention*. Washington DC: National Institute of Justice.

Hearn, J. (1998) *The Violences of Men*. London: Sage.

Heidensohn, F. (1997) 'Gender and crime', in M. Maguire, R. Morgan and R. Reiner (eds), *The Oxford Handbook of Criminology*, second edition. Oxford: Clarendon. pp. 761–800.

Henriques, J., Hollway, W., Urwin, C., Venn, C. and Walkerdine, W. [1984] (1999) *Changing the Subject*, second edition. London: Routledge.

Hester, M. A., Kelly, L. and Radford, J. (1995) *Women, Violence and Male Power*. Buckingham: Oxford University Press.

Hewitt, R. (1996) *Routes of Racism*. Stoke-on-Trent: Trentham.

Hinshelwood, R. D. (1991) *A Dictionary of Kleinian Thought*. London: Free Association Books.

Hinshelwood, R. D. (1994) *Clinical Klein*. London: Free Association Books.

Hirschi, T. (1969) *Causes of Delinquency*. Berkeley, CA: University of California Press.

Hobbs, D. (1988) *Doing the Business*. Oxford: Clarendon Press.

Hollin, C. (2002) 'Criminological psychology', in M. Maguire, R. Morgan and R. Reiner (eds), *The Oxford Handbook of Criminology*, third edition. Oxford: Oxford University Press. pp. 144–74.

Hollin, C., McGuire, J., Palmer, E., Bilby, C., Hatcher, R. and Holmes, A. (2002) *Introducing Pathfinder Programmes into the Probation Service*. London: Home Office.

Hollway, W. (1989) *Subjectivity and Method in Psychology*. London: Sage.

Hollway, W. (2001) 'Gender difference and the production of productivity', in M. Wetherell, S. Taylor and S. J. Yates (eds), *Discourse, Theory and Practice*. London: Sage. pp. 272–83.

Hollway, W. and Jefferson, T. (1996) 'PC or not PC: sexual harassment and the question of ambivalence', *Human Relations*, 49(3): 373–93.

Hollway, W. and Jefferson, T. (1997) 'The risk society in an age of anxiety: situating fear of crime', *British Journal of Sociology*, 48(2): 255–66.

Hollway, W. and Jefferson, T. (1998) '"A kiss is just a kiss": date rape, gender and subjectivity', *Sexualities*, 1(4): 405–23.

Hollway, W. and Jefferson, T. (2000) *Doing Qualitative Research Differently*. London: Sage.

Holmes, J. (1993) *John Bowlby and Attachment Theory*. London: Routledge.

Holmes, R. M. and De Burger, J. (1988) *Serial Murder*. London: Sage.

Holmes, R. M. and Holmes, S. T. (1998) *Serial Murder*, second edition. London: Sage.

Home Office (1959) *Penal Practice in a Changing Society*. Cmnd 645. London: HMSO.

Home Office (2000) *Break the Chain: Multi Agency Guidance for Addressing Domestic Violence*. London: HMSO.

Hood-Williams, J. (2001) 'Gender, masculinities and crime: from structures to psyches', *Theoretical Criminology*, 5(1): 37–60.

Horney, K. (1937) *The Neurotic Personality of Our Time*. New York: Routledge and Kegan Paul.

Hough, M. and Mayhew, P. (1983) *The British Crime Survey: First Report*. London: HMSO.

Hyatt-Williams, A. (1998) *Violence, Cruelty and Murder*. London: Karnac.

Ignatieff, M. (1978) *A Just Measure of Pain*. New York: Pantheon.

Jefferson, T. (1994) 'Theorising masculine subjectivity', in T. Newburn, and E. A. Stanko (eds), *Just Boys Doing Business?* London: Routledge. pp. 10–31.

Jefferson, T. (1997a) 'Masculinities and crimes', in M. Maguire, R. Morgan, and R. Reiner (eds), *The Oxford Handbook of Criminology*, second edition. Oxford: Clarendon. pp. 535–58.

Jefferson, T. (1997b) 'The Tyson rape trial', *Social & Legal Studies*, 6(2): 281–301.

Jefferson, T. (2002) 'Subordinating hegemonic masculinity', *Theoretical Criminology*, 6(1): 63–88.

Jones, H. (1956) *Crime and the Penal System*. London: University Tutorial Press.

Jones, S. A., D'Agostino, R., Gondolf, E. and Heckert, A. (2004) 'Assessing the effect of batterer program completion on reassault using propensity scores', *Journal of Interpersonal Violence*, 19(9): 1002–20.

Josselson, R. (1995) 'Imagining the real: empathy, narrative and the dialogic self', in R. Josselson and A. Lieblich (eds), *The Narrative Study of Lives, volume 3*. London: Sage. pp. 27–44.

Junger, M. (1987) 'Women's experience of sexual harassment', *British Journal of Criminology*, 27(4): 358–83.

Karstedt, S. (1999) 'Early nazis 1923–1933 – neo-nazis 1980–1995', in P. Cohen, C. Slomkowski and L. N. Robins (eds), *Historical and Geographical Influences on Psychopathology*. London: Lawrence Erlbaum Associates. pp. 85–114.

Katz, J. (1988) *Seductions of Crime*. New York: Basic Books.

Katz, J. (1999) *How Emotions Work*. Chicago, IL: University of Chicago Press.

Kearon, T. and Leach, R. (2000) 'Invasion of the "body snatchers": burglary reconsidered', *Theoretical Criminology*, 4(4): 451–72.

Keith, B. (2006) *Report of the Zahid Mubarek Inquiry*. London: The Stationery Office.

Kelly, L. (1988) *Surviving Sexual Violence*. Cambridge: Polity Press.

Kerr, J. (1994) *A Most Dangerous Method*. London: Sinclair-Stevenson.

Kitzinger, C. and Frith, H. (2001) 'Just say no? The use of conversation analysis in developing a feminist perspective on sexual refusal', M. Wetherell, S. Taylor and S. J. Yates (eds), *Discourse, Theory and Practice*. London: Sage. pp. 72–81.

Klein, M. (1988a) *Love, Guilt and Reparation and Other Works, 1921–1945*. London: Virago.

Klein, M. (1988b) *Envy and Gratitude and Other Works, 1946–1963*. London: Virago.

Kobrin, S. (1982) 'The uses of the life-history document for the development of delinquency theory', in J. Snodgrass (ed.), *The Jack-Roller at Seventy*. Lexington, MA: D. C. Heath and Company. pp. 153–65.

Laub, J. H. and Sampson, R. J. (2001) 'Understanding desistance from crime', *Crime and Justice: A Review of Research*, 28: 1–69.

Laub, J. H. and Sampson, R. J. (2006) *Shared Beginnings, Divergent Lives*. London: Harvard University Press.

Layton, L. (2004) 'A fork in the royal road: on "defining" the unconscious and its stakes for social theory', *Psychoanalysis, Culture & Society*, (9)1: 33–51.

Lea, J. and Young, J. (1984) *What is to be Done about Law and Order?* Harmondsworth: Penguin.

Lee, M. (2001) 'The genesis of "fear of crime"', *Theoretical Criminology*, 5(4): 467–85.

Lees, S. (1996) *Carnal Knowledge: Rape on Trial*. London: Hamish Hamilton.

Lees, S. (1997) *Ruling Passions: Sexual Violence, Reputation and the Law*. Buckingham: Open University Press.

Lemert, E. (1964) 'Social structure, social control and deviation', in M. Clinard (ed.), *Anomie and Deviant Behaviour*. New York: Free Press. pp. 57–97.

Lester, D. (1995) *Serial Killers*. Philadelphia, PA.: The Charles Press.

Levin, J. and Fox, J. A. (1985) *Mass Murder*. New York: Plenum.

Levin, J. and McDevitt, J. (1993) *Hate Crimes*. New York: Plenum.

Levin, J. and McDevitt, J. (2002) *Hate Crimes Revisited*. Cambridge, MA: Westview.

Levine, S. and Koenig, J. (1983) *Why Men Rape*. London: Star.

Lewes, K. (1989) *The Psychoanalytic Theory of Male Homosexuality*. London: Quartet.

Lewis, H. (1971) *Shame and Guilt in Neurosis*. New York: International Universities Press.

Lilly, R. J., Cullen, F. and Ball, R. A. (2002) *Criminological Theory*. London: Sage.

Lincoln, Y. S. and Guba, E. (2000) 'The only generalization is: there is no generalization', in R. Gomm, M. Hammersley and P. Foster (eds), *Case Study Method*. London: Sage. pp. 27–44.

MacKinnon, C. A. (1987) *Feminism Unmodified*. Cambridge, MA: Harvard University Press.

MacRae, R. and Andrew, M. (2000) 'The use of personal construct theory in work with men who abuse women partners', *Probation Journal*, 47(1): 30–8.

Mailer, N. (1979) *The Executioner's Song*. New York: Warner.

Malone, K. R. and Kelly, S. D. (2004) 'The transfer from the clinical to the social and back', *Psychoanalysis, Culture & Society*, (9)1: 23–32.

Maruna, S. (2001) *Making Good.* Washington, DC: APA Press.

Maruna, S., Matravers, A. and King, A. (2004) 'Disowning our shadow: a psychoanalytic approach to understanding punitive public attitudes', *Deviant Behavior*, 25(3): 277–99.

Masters, B. (1985) *Killing for Company.* New York: Stein and Day.

Masters, B. (1993) *The Shrine of Jeffrey Dahmer.* London: Coronet.

Matravers, A. and Maruna, S. (2004) 'Contemporary penality and psychoanalysis', *Critical Review of International Social and Political Philosophy*, 7(2): 118–44.

Maxwell, G. and Morris, A. (2002) 'The role of shame, guilt and remorse in restorative justice processes for young people', in E. G. M. Weitekemp and H.-J. Kerner (eds), *Restorative Justice.* Cullompton: Willan. pp. 267–84.

Maynard, M. and Purvis, J. (eds) (1994) *Researching Women's Lives from a Feminist Perspective.* London: Taylor and Francis.

McDevitt, J., Levin, J. and Bennett, S. (2002) 'Hate crime offenders', *Journal of Social Issues*, 58(2): 303–18.

McGuire, J. (2004) *Understanding Psychology and Crime.* Maidenhead: Open University Press.

McLaughlin, E., Fergusson, R., Hughes, G. and Westmarland, L. (2003) 'Introduction', in E. McLaughlin, R. Fergusson, G. Hughes and L. Westmarland (eds), *Restorative Justice.* London: Sage. pp. 1–18.

Mead, G. H. [1934] (1967) *Mind, Self and Society.* Chicago, IL: University of Chicago Press.

Merton, R. K. (1938) 'Social structure and anomie', *American Sociological Review*, 3(5): 672–82.

Merton, R. K. (1958) *Social Theory and Social Structure.* Toronto: Collier Macmillan.

Messerschmidt, J. W. (1993) *Masculinities and Crime.* Lanham, MD: Rowman & Littlefield.

Messerschmidt, J. W. (1994) 'Schooling, masculinities and youth crime by white boys', in T. Newburn and E. A. Stanko (eds), *Just Boys Doing Business?* London: Routledge. pp. 81–99.

Messerschmidt, J. W. (1997) *Crime as Structured Action.* London: Sage.

Messerschmidt, J. W. (2000) *Nine Lives.* Boulder, CO: Westview Press.

Messner, D., McHugh, S. and Felson, B. (2004) 'Distinctive characteristics of assaults motivated by bias', *Criminology*, 42(3): 585–618.

Miller, D. L. (1973) *George Herbert Mead: Self, Language, and the World.* Austin, TX: University of Texas Press.

Milner, J. (2004) 'From "disappearing" to "demonised": the effects on men and women of professional interventions based on challenging men who are violent', *Critical Social Policy*, 24(1): 79–101.

Milner, J. and Jessop, D. (2003) 'Domestic violence', *Probation Journal*, 50(2): 127–41.

Minsky, R. (1998) *Psychoanalysis and Culture.* Cambridge: Polity.

Mirrlees-Black, C. (1999) *Domestic Violence: Findings from a New British Crime Survey Self-Completion Questionnaire.* London: Home Office.

Mishler, E. G. (1986) *Research Interviewing.* Cambridge, MA: Harvard University Press.

Mitchell, J. (1975) *Psychoanalysis and Feminism.* Harmondsworth: Penguin.

Mitchell, J. C. (2000) 'Case and situation analysis', in R. Gomm, P. Hammersley and P. Foster (eds), *Case Study Method.* London: Sage. pp. 165–86.

Modell, A. H. (1999) 'The dead mother syndrome and the reconstruction of trauma', in G. Kohon (ed.), *The Dead Mother.* London: Routledge. pp. 76–86.

Mollon, P. (2000) *Freud and False Memory.* Cambridge: Icon.

Morgan, R. (1982) 'Theory and practice: pornography and rape', in L. Lederer (ed.), *Take Back the Night.* London: Bantam. pp. 125–40.

Morran, D. (1996) 'Working in the CHANGE Programme', in T. Newburn and G. Mair (eds), *Working with Men.* Lyme Regis: Russell House. pp. 108–22.

Morran, D. (1999) 'Violent men: terrifying others, scared of themselves?', *Working with Men*, 2: 3–5.

Morran, D. and Wilson, M. (1999) 'Working with men who are violent to partners – striving for good practice', in H. Kemshall and J. Pritchard (eds), *Good Practice in Working with Violence.* Good Practice Series 6. London: Jessica Kingsley. pp. 74–90.

Morris, C. W. [1934] (1967) 'Introduction', in G. H. Mead, *Mind, Self and Society.* Chicago, IL: University of Chicago Press. pp. ix–xxxv.

Morrison, B. (1998) *As If*. London: Granta.

Mullender, A. (1998) *Rethinking Domestic Violence*. London: Routledge.

Mullender, A. (2000) 'Reducing domestic violence ... what works?', *Policing and Reducing Crime Briefing Note*. London: Home Office.

Murphy, G. and Kovach, J. K. (1972) *Historical Introduction to Modern Psychology*, sixth edition. London: Routledge and Kegan Paul.

Nathanson, D. L. (1992) *Shame and Pride*. New York: W. W. Norton.

Norris, J. (1989) *Serial Killers*. New York: Anchor.

Oevermann, U., Allert, T., Konau, E. and Krambeck, J. (1987) 'Structures of meaning and objective hermeneutics', in V. Meja (ed.), *Modern German Sociology*. New York: Columbia Press. pp. 436–48.

Office for Criminal Justice Reform (2006) *Convicting Rapists and Protecting Victims – Justice for Victims of Rape*. London: Home Office.

Paglia, C. (1992) *Sex, Art, and American Culture*. New York: Vintage.

Pearson, G. (1983) *Hooligan: A History of Respectable Fears*. London: Macmillan.

Pearson, G. and Twohig, J. [1976] (2006) 'Ethnography through the looking glass: the case of Howard Becker', in S. Hall and T. Jefferson (eds), *Resistance Through Rituals*, second edition. London: Routledge. pp. 100–5.

Perry, B. (2002) *In the Name of Hate*. London: Routledge.

Phillips, L. M. (2000) *Flirting with Danger: Young Women's Reflections on Sexuality and Domination*. New York: New York University Press.

Phoenix, A. and Owen, C. (1996) 'From miscegenation to hybridity: mixed relationships and mixed-parentage in profile', in B. Bernstein and J. Brannen (ed.), *Children, Research and Policy*. London: Taylor and Francis. pp. 111–35.

Pizzey, E. (1974) *Scream Quietly or the Neighbours Will Hear*. Harmondsworth: Penguin.

Pontalis, J.-B. (1993) *Love of Beginnings*. London: Free Association.

Potts, D. (1996) *Why Do Men Commit Most Crime?* Wakefield: West Yorkshire Probation/HM Prison Service.

Povey, D. (2004) *Crime in England and Wales 2002/2003, supplementary volume 1: Homicide and Gun Crime*. London: Home Office.

Prins, H. (1973) *Criminal Behaviour*. New York: Pitman.

Radzinowicz, L. (1961) *In Search of Criminology*. London: Heinemann.

Radzinowicz, L. and King, J. (1977) *The Growth of Crime*. London: Hamish Hamilton.

Ray, L. and Smith, D. (2001) 'Racist offenders and the politics of "hate crime"', *Law & Critique*, 12(3): 203–21.

Ray, L. and Smith, D. (2004) 'Racist offending, policing and community conflict', *Sociology*, 38(4): 681–99.

Ray, L., Smith, D. and Wastell, L. (2003) 'Racist violence from a probation service perspective', in R. M. Lee and E. A. Stanko (eds), *Researching Violence*. London: Routledge. pp. 217–31.

Ray, L., Smith, D. and Wastell, L. (2004) 'Shame, rage and racist violence', *British Journal of Criminology*, 44(3): 350–68.

Raynor, P. (2004) 'The probation "pathfinders": finding the path and losing the way?', *Criminal Justice*, 4(3): 309–25.

Retzinger, S. M. and Scheff, T. J. (1996) 'Strategy for community conferences: emotions and social bonds', in B. Galaway and J. Hudson (eds), *Restorative Justice*. Monsey, NY: Criminal Justice Press. pp. 315–36.

Riger, S., Gordon, M. and Bailley, R. (1978) 'Women's fear of crime', *Victimology*, 3: 274–84.

Riley, D. (1983) *War in the Nursery*. London: Virago.

Roberts, C. (1989) *Women and Rape*. London: Harvester Wheatsheaf.

Roiphe, K. (1994) *The Morning After: Sex, Fear and Feminism on Campus*. New York: Little Brown & Co.

Rosenthal, G. (1990) 'The structure and "gestalt" of autobiographies and its methodological consequences'. Unpublished paper presented to the 12th World Congress of Sociology, Madrid.

Rosenthal, G. (1993) 'Reconstruction of life stories', in R. Josselson and A. Lieblich (eds), *The Narrative Study of Lives, volume 1*. London: Sage. pp. 59–91.

Rosenthal, G. and Bar-On, D. (1992) 'A biographical case study of a victimizer's daughter's strategy: pseudo-identification with victims of the Holocaust', *Journal of Narrative and Life History*, 2(2): 105–27.

Roth, A. and Fonagy, P. (1996) *What Works for Whom? A Critical Review of Psychotherapy Research.* New York: Guilford.

Rutter, M. (1981) *Maternal Deprivation Reassessed*, second edition. Harmondsworth: Penguin.

Rutter, M. and Giller, H. (1983) *Juvenile Delinquency*. Harmondsworth: Penguin.

Sampson, R. J. and Laub, J. H. (1993) *Crime in the Making*. Boston, MA: Harvard University Press.

Sampson, R. J. and Laub, J. H. (2003) 'Life-course desisters? Trajectories of crime among delinquent boys followed to age 70', *Criminology*, 41(3): 301–339.

Scheff, T. (2000) 'Shame and the social bond', *Sociological Theory*, 18(1): 84–99.

Scheff, T. J. (1994) *Bloody Revenge*. Boulder, CO: Westview Press.

Schuetz, A. (1944) 'The stranger', *The American Journal of Sociology*, 49(6): 499–507.

Schumacher, J. A. Smith, A. and Heyman, R. (2001) 'Risk factors for male-to-female partner psychological abuse', *Aggression and Violent Behavior*, 6(2): 255–68.

Schutze, F. (1992) 'Pressure and guilt: the experience of a young German soldier in World War Two and its biographical consequences', *International Sociology*, 7(2): 187–208; (3): 347–67.

Schwartz, P. and Ogilvy, J. (1979) *The Emergent Paradigm*. Analytical report 7, Values and Lifestyle Program. Menlo Park, CA: SRI International.

Scourfield, J. B. and Dobash, R. P. (1999) 'Programmes for violent men', *Howard Journal of Criminal Justice*, 38(2): 128–43.

Scully, D. (1990) *Understanding Sexual Violence*. Boston, MA: Unwin Hyman.

Seabrook, J. (2003) *A World Growing Old*. London: Pluto Press.

Segal, H. [1975] (1981) 'A psycho-analytic approach to the treatment of schizophrenia', in H. Segal, *The Work of Hanna Segal*. New York: Jason Aronson. pp. 131–6.

Segal, J. (2000) *Phantasy*. London: Icon.

Sekoff, J. (1999) 'The undead: necromancy and the inner world', in G. Kohon (ed.), *The Dead Mother*. London: Routledge. pp. 109–27.

Sennett, R. and Cobb, J. (1973) *The Hidden Injuries of Class*. New York: Vintage.

Sereny, G. (1995) *The Case of Mary Bell*. London: Pimlico.

Sereny, G. (1999) *Cries Unheard*. London: Papermac.

Shaw, C. R. (1930) *The Jack-Roller*. Chicago, IL: University of Chicago Press.

Short Jr, J. F. (1982) 'Life history, autobiography, and the life cycle', in J. Snodgrass (ed.), *The Jack-Roller at Seventy*. Lexington, MA: D. C. Heath and Company. pp. 135–52.

Sibbitt, R. (1997) *The Perpetrators of Racial Harassment and Racial Violence*. London: Home Office.

Skeggs, B. (1997) *Formations of Class and Gender*. London: Sage.

Smith, D. J. (1995) *The Sleep of Reason*. London: Arrow.

Smith, H. M. [1922] (1933) *The Psychology of the Criminal*, second edition. London: Methuen.

Smith, J. (1993) 'There's only one Yorkshire ripper', in J. Smith, *Misogynies*. London: Faber. pp. 163–205.

Snodgrass, J. (ed.) (1982a) *The Jack-Roller at Seventy*. Lexington, MA: D. C. Heath and Company.

Snodgrass, J. (1982b) 'A note on Stanley's psychology', in J. Snodgrass (ed.), *The Jack-Roller at Seventy*. Lexington, MA: D. C. Heath and Company. pp. 167–72.

Stanko, E. A. (1990) *Everyday Violence*. London: Pandora.

Stake, R. (2000) 'The case study method in social inquiry', in R. Gomm, M. Hammersley and P. Foster (eds), *Case Study Method*. London: Sage. pp. 19–26.

Tajfel, H. (1969) 'Cognitive aspects of prejudice', *Journal of Social Issues*, 25(4): 79–96.

Tajfel, H. and Turner, J. C. (1979) 'An integrative theory of intergroup conflict', in W. G. Austin and S. Worchel (eds), *The Social Psychology of Intergroup Relations*. Monterey, CA: Brooks/Cole. pp. 33–47.

Taylor, G. (1985) *Pride, Shame and Guilt*. Oxford: Clarendon.

Taylor, G. (1996) 'Guilt and remorse', in R. Harré and W. Gerrod Parrott (eds), *The Emotions*. London: Sage. pp. 57–73.

Taylor, I., Walton, P. and Young, J. (1973) *The New Criminology*. London: Routledge & Kegan Paul.

Tjaden, P. and Thoennes, T. (2006) *Extent, Nature, and Consequences of Rape Victimization: Findings from the National Violence Against Women Survey*. Washington, DC: National Institute of Justice.

Toch, H. (1961) 'Introduction to criminal psychology', in H. Toch (ed.), *Legal and Criminal Psychology*. London: Holt, Rinehart and Winston.

Toch, H. (1972) *Violent Men*. Harmondsworth: Pelican.

Tomkins, S. (1963) *Affect/Imagery/Consciousness, volume 2*. New York: Springer.

Van Stokkom, B. (2002) 'Moral emotions in restorative justice conferences', *Theoretical Criminology*, 6(3): 339–60.

Walby, S. and Allen, J. (2004) *Domestic Violence, Sexual Assault and Stalking: Findings from the British Crime Survey*. Home Office research study 276. London: Home Office.

Ward, C. (1995) *Attitudes Toward Rape*. London: Sage.

Webster, C. (2003) 'Race, space and fear', *Capital & Class*, 80: 95–122.

Wengraf, T. (2001) *Qualitative Research Interviewing*. London: Sage.

Young, J. [1986] (2003) 'The need for a radical realism', in E. McLaughlin, J. Muncie and G. Hughes (eds), *Criminological Perspectives*, second edition. London: Sage. pp. 316–27.

Young, J. (1997) 'Left realist criminology', in M. Maguire, R. Morgan and R. Reiner (eds), *The Oxford Handbook of Criminology*, second edition. Oxford: Clarendon. pp. 473–98.

INDEX